MW01491635

"J. D. Lyonhart's *The Journey of Gi* place in it. Written with a playful, insight and curiosity, J. D. retells the entire biblical story with fresh insight, cinematic expression, and a plea to behold the beauty embedded in the broken, the dignity shrouded by despair, and the hope beheld by God 'in the beginning' that guides us to his end. *The Journey of God* is a powerful and provocative read for the seeker and the saved alike."

Shane J. Wood, professor at Ozark Christian College and author of *Thinning the Veil*

"J. D. Lyonhart continues to bring his wit, vulnerability, and sharp theological mind to his latest book, *The Journey of God*. This journey is an invitation to enter a story, a story of being lost and finding home in the Christian story. Dialogue partners from all disciplines abound (e.g., philosophy, science, theology, and modern film) to instruct and inspire you. Prepare to be captivated, encouraged, and to laugh out loud!"

Jennifer M. Matheny, associate professor of Christian scriptures at the George W. Truett Theological Seminary at Baylor University

"Oh, my stars, what a find! J. D. Lyonhart tells the story of the Bible like an art film mash-up of *Barbie* and Aristotle . . . and so faithful to Scripture. I have been searching for a book to give my friends in our post-Christian city—something intelligent, human, convincing, and quirky, all at once. Now, here it is. I'm buying multiple copies. My fourteen-year-old daughter has put her hand up for one."

Mark Glanville, director of the Centre for Missional Leadership at St. Andrew's Hall and author of *Preaching in a New Key* and *Improvising Church*

THE JOURNEY OF GOD

Christianity in Six Movements

J.D. Lyonhart

IVP Academic

An imprint of InterVarsity Press
Downers Grove, Illinois

InterVarsity Press
P.O. Box 1400 | Downers Grove, IL 60515-1426
ivpress.com | email@ivpress.com

InterVarsity Press® is the publishing division of InterVarsity Christian Fellowship/USA®. For more information, visit
intervarsity.org.

While any stories in this book are true, some names and identifying information may have been changed to protect
the privacy of individuals.

The publisher cannot verify the accuracy or functionality of website URLs used in this book beyond the date
of publication.

Cover design: Faceout Studio, Tim Green
Interior design: Daniel van Loon

ISBN 978-1-5140-0924-6 (print) | ISBN 978-1-5140-0925-3 (digital)

Printed in the United States of America ∞

Library of Congress Cataloging-in-Publication Data
A catalog record for this book is available from the Library of Congress.

31   30   29   28   27   26   25 | 13   12   11   10   9   8   7   6   5   4   3   2   1

To Art, Nathan, Christian, and Stephanie.

Thanks for being patient with me all those years ago.

I'd also like to thank my mom for combing through the manuscript

countless times, and to acknowledge **Seth, Sy, Cody, Atlas, and my**

wonderful wife, Madison, *for their edits, insights, and support.*

CREATION

Creation Begins ●

Creation Is Not God ●

Creation Is Good ●

FALL

Humanity in God's Image ●

Humanity Gone Wild ●

NATION

Abraham Finds Faith ● 2000 BC

Moses Meets I Aᴍ ● 1400–1200ish BC

Goodness Is Commanded ●

Beauty in the Promised Land ●

King David and His Boy ● 1000ish BC

Justice Exiles the Nation ● 586 BC

REDEMPTION

Jesus Is Born ● AD 0

Jesus Is Walking Around Saying Stuff ● AD 30

Jesus Is Dying to Meet You ● AD 33

CHURCH 🏠

The Spirit Arrives ● AD 33

The Church Begins ● AD 33

The Apostle Paul Converts ● AD 35ish

The Church Expands ● AD 300ish

The Church Today ● The Present

END ✳

The End of the World as We Know It ●

Highway to Hell or Stairway to Heaven? ●

Contents

Introduction

I REMEMBER THE FIRST TIME I saw the Lord of the Rings as a kid. I apparently sleepwalked into my parents' room later that night, where I stood over their bed calmly informing them I was an elf and that doom was upon us all.

I remember rising early one morning before anyone else and catching *Ghoulies II* on TV. A ghoul monster tunneled through the pipes and came out of an in-use toilet. Subsequently, I only squatted over—never fully sat down on—a toilet seat again until well into high school. Aerial precision was difficult from such heights, spawning a mythology at my local summer camp, where the staff often whispered about an unidentified youth known only as the "mad crapper." The case remains unsolved to this day.

I remember the first time I saw the movie *The Matrix*, about how our material reality is a dream. I was walking home afterward and looked up at the sky, wailing through my outstretched throat, "I want to be woken up! Somebody help me! *Please!* I wanna wake up!"

In hindsight, I was a boy in desperate search of a story. Not merely to lose myself in entertainment but to find myself in a narrative. I think I was trying to glimpse a bigger journey in which to locate myself, my character arc, and what I was or was not scripted for. And while a thousand years ago I may have struggled to fit into the prevailing story stained in glass at the local cathedral, my much more contemporary problem was the exact opposite: there were a thousand stories coming all at once, in ever-multiplying mediums and screens, often with inconsistent visions, morals, aesthetics, and philosophies. Some of those stories even claimed that there was no story, no script, no plot, no higher meaning binding together each act in a grand play of existence; that life was a tale told by no one, signifying nothing.

I was not born into the Christian story, which might help explain why I was always searching for something in its place. I was raised in downtown Vancouver, Canada, where people are statistically more likely to meditate before meals than to pray. Vancouver has the lowest number of people going to church weekly (3 percent) in North America.[1] And the household I was born into was not, at least originally, part of that 3 percent. Even when Christianity became a bigger part of my life, it initially did so as just one option amid a smorgasbord of other stories, religions, and philosophies to choose from, with seemingly nothing unique to make it stand out from the crowd. God was getting out-told by beat poets, songwriters, comics, playwrights, philosophers, scientists, and Quentin Tarantino. In comparison, I'd just never heard the Christian story told well enough. In fact, I hadn't really heard it *told* at all—Christianity only ever seemed to sputter out in fragmented pieces, cherry-picked to preach such and such a point, tied together more by appeals to faith than by any narrative logic, beauty, or moral power. If Jesus were still dead, he'd be turning in his grave.

My wife likes to joke that I became a preacher because I couldn't stand to listen to anyone else talk. My goal as a pastor and now as a professor has always been to say things my younger Vancouver self might actually have bothered to listen to—to present the Christian story in a way that is deep with philosophy, science, or history yet also widens eyes with drama, play, and wit. I've tried to do the same thing with this book. I didn't write it for you; I wrote it for my younger self. But you are more than welcome to listen in.

The original title of this book was *A Sexy, Dramatic, Philosophical Introduction to Christianity*. I wanted to combine big ideas with big tales told provocatively, wedding my love of storytelling with my academic training as a professor of philosophy and religion. The stories would make the book engaging and exhilarating enough for a wider audience—regardless of one's age, education, background, beliefs, or (non)religious upbringing—while the philosophy would make it deep enough to challenge even the most seasoned Christian to see things in a new way. The closest parallel might be C. S. Lewis's book *Mere Christianity*, which used to be *that one book* you could hand almost anyone at any stage of faith, nonfaith, or vehement antifaith and still cause to them think. Yet that book was written nearly a century ago for a different time and culture, and no longer fills that hole in our contemporary marketplace (no matter how hard we try to make it fit). We desperately need more contemporary introductions to Christianity that are also sexy, dramatic, and philosophical. However, my publisher hurriedly informed me that philosophy was not sexy enough to sell books and that Christians would not buy a book with *sexy* in the title. So instead, you got *The Journey of God: Christianity in Six Movements*.

However, I've slowly warmed to this new title, for the beauty of a journey is that it doesn't need to be just one thing but can be many things spread out over time and over the many legs of the adventure. A fight scene with knives and lovemaking can be followed up by a philosophical interlude over a pint. As such, I've allowed each chapter in the book to feel a little different from the last. I've tried to dance between philosophy, science, poetry, romance, violence, history, historical fiction, comedy, drama, dialogue, and death, weaving them through various genres and styles into one mostly coherent, occasionally bonkers journey—less Sunday school, more *Pulp Fiction*. And while we toyed with the language of six *acts* rather than six *movements*, we ended up going with the latter. For while *acts* suggest closed segments—with one act ending for the next to begin—the language of *movements* is more fluid, brash, and overlapping, like waves in a wartime sea. The Christian story may have already played out with robed people in a bygone past, but I believe it also continues to *move*, roll on, slosh, and rise in me each morning and moon. *The Journey of God* is my own, a movement I not only assent to but am swept up by. It is the story I never saw coming but to which in desperation I came. And in which I now find and lose myself.

This book is the whole Christian story in six movements: *creation, fall, nation, redemption, church, end*. God creates the world, humans ruin it, God works through the Jewish nation to fix things, bringing about redemption through the Jewish Messiah (*cough* Jesus), leading to a community of supposedly redeemed people who like to call themselves the church, and then the whole thing ends with an apocalypse and dragons. I think it's a good story, a story worth telling even if it's not true. The crazy thing, though, is that I think it just might be. And so do billions of other people, too. So if you're not going to read this book to understand God, the universe, or yourself, then perhaps you might read it simply to understand the rest of us and why we still believe in Bronze Age myths in an age of iPhones, nuclear warfare, gene editing, online dating, AI, VR, and 3D-printed cupcakes.

MOVEMENT 1
Creation

AS A LITTLE BOY, I would sometimes sneak past the foot of my parents' bed (this was before their divorce, when there were seemingly no snakes in our garden) and creep out onto their balcony and up to the roof, where I'd fall asleep under the stars. I did this so often that we eventually set up a tent out there. Sometimes, I'd awake in the morning staring directly up at a sky of blue filled bright with sun, and there would be a brief moment where I didn't know where I was, experiencing the sights and sounds of creation as if for the first time. Morning rising, moon receding, trees twitching with the wind, birds joining the chorus, everything good and glorious and unspoiled. It was like being born and surprised by everything. But then I'd shake awake, brush my teeth, catch the bus, and move on with my day, forgetting that first moment when I didn't take the universe and existence itself for granted.

What is this world into which we are thrown? What is nature, and how did it and the universe and all of us get here? Why is there something rather than nothing? These questions are so basic we sometimes forget to ask them at all. It's with these questions that we start our story in the first movement: creation. When God supposedly *created* everything. It's the first moment, the first set piece, the first act in the cosmic drama, when everything is newborn, surprising, unfamiliar, and unassumed. And so fittingly, the very first line of the Bible goes, "In the beginning God created the heavens and the earth" (Genesis 1:1).

CREATION

Creation Begins

Creation Is Not God

Creation Is Good

FALL

Humanity in God's Image

Humanity Gone Wild

NATION

Abraham Finds Faith ● 2000 BC

Moses Meets I AM ● 1400–1200ish BC

Goodness Is Commanded ●

Beauty in the Promised Land ●

King David and His Boy ● 1000ish BC

Justice Exiles the Nation ● 586 BC

REDEMPTION

Jesus Is Born ● AD 0

Jesus Is Walking Around Saying Stuff ● AD 30

Jesus Is Dying to Meet You ● AD 33

CHURCH

The Spirit Arrives ● AD 33

The Church Begins ● AD 33

The Apostle Paul Converts ● AD 35ish

The Church Expands ● AD 300ish

The Church Today ● The Present

END

The End of the World as We Know It ●

Highway to Hell or Stairway to Heaven? ●

ONE

Creation Begins

"In the beginning . . ."

(GENESIS 1:1)

WITH THESE FIRST THREE WORDS, the Bible already puts its foot in it.[1] For the Greek philosopher Aristotle had argued that the universe never began to exist but stretched back and back into infinity, without any first moment or beginning. And since Aristotle was a big deal, it seemed for a while like all the smart folks thought the Bible was wrong from the get-go. There was no *in the beginning*—the universe had always existed. And if the universe has always existed, then why, you might wonder, would we need a God to bring it into existence? If there is no first moment of creation, what need have we of a Creator?[2]

Fast-forward to 1929. American Astronomer Edwin Hubble has made some fascinating observations about the universe. Hubble expected all the galaxies to be unmoving and fixed in space. He anticipated that one galaxy would be a set distance from another galaxy and that the distance between them wouldn't change over time, any more than the distance between Paris and Berlin changes over time. Yet when Hubble actually looked through his telescope, it was as if every galaxy was moving away from every other galaxy. No matter what angle Hubble looked at it from, everything seemed to be shooting away from everything else. The universe was like a polka-dot balloon being blown up, with every dot expanding away from every other dot.

But then something even more radical happened. Astronomer and Catholic priest George Lemaître (you don't need to remember all these names) asked: What would happen if we reversed the expansion? What if we played the tape backward and watched the cosmic balloon shrink instead of expand? The universe would shrink and shrink until it was nothing but a one-dimensional dot, which could shrink no further. If going forward in time blows the cosmos up, going back in time shrivels it back to barely anything at all. (When I give this talk, I usually blow up an actual balloon, and at this point I'd slowly let the air flatulate out to illustrate the reversal.)

Lemaître realized that if we imagined going back in time—if we played the expansion of the universe in reverse—eventually there would have been a first moment of creation, when the entire universe ballooned into being. And so the universe *must* have a beginning. Picture a grenade exploding in a war movie, all the fragments blowing up in every direction, expanding outward in a great circle. But then play it in reverse and see all the fragments coming back together until they meet again in the middle, at the first instant of the explosion. At the first instant of the Big Bang.

Usually when we speak of something beginning to exist, we mean the beginning of a particular thing within time and space: The beginning of spring. The beginning of puberty. The beginning of a weeklong vacation. *The beginning of some event within time.* But the Big Bang is not the expansion of matter outward into space and time. Rather, the Big Bang is the expansion of space and time *itself.* The Big Bang is not just the beginning of our universe within time; no, it is the beginning of time itself. It is the beginning of spacetime, the beginning of there being beginnings, the very first beginning. Ours is a tale *older* than time. The universe may end with a whimper but it began—like all of us—with a bang.

Now, a young-earth creationist might be tempted to put the book down at this point (though there are creationists who believe in the Big Bang; they just think it happened more recently than mainstream science does). However, I'm not talking about the Big Bang to try to get you to believe in it. Rather, I'm trying to help you enter a conversation—one that has been going on for thousands of years. Since at least Aristotle in the fourth century BC, many of the brightest minds assumed that the universe was not created but had always existed from infinity past. But in the early twentieth century, mainstream science began embracing the Big Bang, and suddenly everyone was saying what Jews and Christians had said all along: that the universe had a beginning. It has not always existed but was created at some point in the past. And if it was created, then what created it? Who is the cosmic balloon artist?*

〈 ▮ ▮ 〉

"In the beginning *God created . . .*" (Genesis 1:1).

So after the Big Bang, mainstream science says the universe burst outward, like a grenade exploding. Yet if everything is flying away from everything else, how did enough pieces come together to form stars and galaxies? How can you stop the force of the grenade and bring some of the fragments back together again? What force brought together enough exploding chunks of the universe so that there was sufficient matter clumped together to create stars, galaxies, planets, humans, and Mark Zuckerberg?

Gravity, that's what. The pull of gravity was just enough that some of the exploding chunks of the universe began to draw close to one another again, like gravity drawing our feet back down to earth. Gravity means that mass draws mass to it; that's why we stand on the earth's surface instead of bouncing about like moonwalking Teletubbies. The Big Bang explodes the fragments of the universe away from each other, but then gravity draws some of them near again. These clumps of matter are gravitationally drawn to one another, snowballing until they become big enough to form stars, galaxies, and planets, which eventually allow for intelligent life.

But for this to happen, the force of gravity had to be just right. If it were even slightly *weaker*, the outward push from the Big Bang would have been

---

*Considering that two of the earliest atomic building blocks of the universe are hydrogen and helium—both of which have been used to fill balloons (google "Hindenburg")—I think a real case can be made that referring to God as a balloon artist is more accurate than calling him Father, Jehovah, or G-d. This started as a joke, but I think I've almost convinced myself.

too strong for gravity to counteract it, and everything would have kept flying away from everything else forever. But if the force of gravity were slightly *stronger*, then it would have been too powerful, and all the bits of the universe would have slammed back together again with a giant crunch, like the Hulk crushing someone's skull in his fist. And so, again, no stars, galaxies, or planets could have formed. Thus, the force of gravity had to be just right. In fact, if it had deviated in just one part out of 10^{59}, then we wouldn't exist at all. When I give this talk, I usually make the audience watch while I write out fifty-nine zeros on the board. It takes a bit, and I have to switch writing hands halfway through. Thankfully, I now have a computer (and an overindulgent editor):

1 out of 100000000000000000000000000000000000000000000000000000000000

That's how big an improbability—how perfectly precise—the gravitational rate is. And gravity is merely one of dozens of such perfect conditions that had to be just right. The expansion rate of the universe could not have deviated one part in 10^{55} or else we wouldn't exist. The proportion of energy released when helium is created had to be exactly 0.007—if it were even 0.006 or 0.008, we wouldn't exist. The ratio of electrons to protons couldn't have deviated one part in 10^{37} or else—you guessed it—*we wouldn't exist.* Sir Martin Rees, a professor at Cambridge and the former president of the Royal Society, lists six such factors that had to be *just right* in the early universe for us to exist.[3]

Recognizing such statistics, Sir Roger Penrose, a Nobel Prize–winning mathematician and physicist at the University of Oxford, calculated that the odds of our universe randomly bringing together all these factors in just the right way are one out of $10^{10(123)}$. I would have typed that number out for kicks as well, but if I typed at a rate of one digit per second I'd still be typing when our galaxy crashes into the Andromeda galaxy five billion years from now. There are more zeros in that number than there are atoms in the universe, so even if we had forever to write it, there wouldn't be enough ink or paper to write it upon. That's how precisely tuned the universe is for life.

Now, I don't think that this magically *proves* God exists. In fact, it's probably better that you don't suddenly change your whole belief system just because I threw some random statistics at you. Especially because there are many different ways to try and make sense of those statistics. For example, Rees, the guy who came up with those six numbers above, is actually an atheist. Rees admits that the scientific evidence makes it look like the universe is perfectly designed; he just disagrees on how to interpret that evidence. Rees takes a multiverse approach, according to which there are potentially an infinite numbers of universes, and so one (or more) would eventually get it right by chance, no matter how insane the odds. We just so happen to be that lucky one. If you have an infinite number of lottery tickets, you will strike it rich eventually.

Perhaps Rees's thesis is right. Probability is an odd and wonderful thing—you're only here because you were the one blessed spermatozoa out of one hundred million who won the lottery. Crazy stuff happens; maybe our universe just got lucky. Or maybe, just maybe, it wasn't sheer dumb luck. Perhaps the initial conditions of the universe seem perfectly crafted precisely because there was a perfect craftsman. Perhaps, even if the odds of there being a God are only one in twenty, that's still preferable to the one in a trillion million billion Brazilian reptilian odds that we just got lucky. Perhaps, "In the beginning, God created . . ."

(P.S. You might have wanted a stronger start to the book and to the universe than just "perhaps." But I think that uncertainty and open-mindedness are actually the perfect place for faith to begin. God cannot enter a closed mind.)

◀ ▬ ▬ ▶

"In the beginning God created *the heavens and the earth*" (Genesis 1:1).

The Bible rounds out its opening statement by specifying that what God created was *the heavens and the earth*. The heavens up there and the earth down here, the skies and the ground, space and matter. So, you know, pretty much *everything*—the entire universe that stretches from down here out unto the heavens in every direction.

And isn't it staggeringly insane that any of it exists at all? It didn't have to. It might not have been this way; there just as easily could have been no universe. Indeed, a famous philosopher once said that the greatest mystery of all is, "Why is there something rather than nothing?"[4] Yet we take mere existence for granted, as if this were just obviously how things had to be. We've become so used to our daily lives, so accustomed to sleeping, waking up, driving to and from work, that we've forgotten how bizarre it all is, how strange that anything exists at all! How strange that we reside on a bluish-green marble, hanging midair, suspended by nothing, frolicking around a great big ball of fire.

None of this is normal. The gift of life is not a given. Even the most assumed aspects of our existence might have been radically different. As Martin Heidegger wrote, "To philosophize means to be constantly perplexed by what common sense considers self-evident and unquestionable."[5] But Heidegger was a Nazi, so let's appeal to a different source: "Unless you change and become like little children, you will never enter the kingdom of heaven" (Matthew 18:3). For Jesus, heaven is beheld by wee eyes—little children who haven't had their senses sanded down by the dull repetitions of adulthood, glimpsing each wonder and thingamabob as if for the very first time. As children, we used to hungrily squeal, "Why?! Why?! Why?!" about every little thing, until we learned to be quiet and just pass the dang salt. We've grown up and come to take for granted that which is most mysterious. We're like fish who've forgotten water. Like rich people who don't remember how privileged they are. Like readers who take for granted how much time authors spend searching for the perfect analogy.

We've grown up and forgotten how shocking it all once seemed, forgotten how different it all might have been. There could just as easily have been *no heavens and no earth*. The laws of the universe might never have been or might have been totally different. Gravity might not have existed, and so matter would never have pulled itself together to form galaxies, stars, or planets. Perhaps we could have been created in a universe where light and sound waves didn't exist or where our five senses were different. Perhaps we'd get around by following our noses, or evolve to use telepathy, or communicate through farts like herrings do (this is true).[6] Perhaps, instead of three or four dimensions, we could have been created in just two dimensions, like stick people. Or seventeen dimensions, or 525,600 dimensions. Perhaps, instead of a logical, mathematical universe, we just as easily could have been born into a crazy, illogical, *Alice in Wonderland* universe.

The fabric of space and time itself might not have been. According to mainstream science, spacetime only comes into existence at the Big Bang, and so might not have been. We can't even take space and time for granted! Perhaps, instead of space spreading things out into distinct regions, there might have been no space at all, and so all things would have been stuffed into one tiny, unextended dot · Perhaps, instead of time existing and allowing movement and change and growth, we all might have been frozen in place like unmoving, timeless statues in a cosmic Medusa's garden.

Nothing about the way our world works is obvious or how things had to be or just the way things *are*. Because once, *they weren't*. Once there was no heavens or earth. Once there was no universe. Once upon a time, before the beginning of all things, there was nothing. And then suddenly, mysteriously, wondrously—and with a great Big Bang—there was something.

TWO

Creation Is Not God

"MOM, IS GOD REAL?" the little girl asked, looking down with grim concern. They'd had the Santa talk a few years earlier, and I suppose she was worried that yet another brick from her childhood was about to come crashing down.

Mother didn't answer that day. Instead, later that week, she took her young daughter on a hike up the local mountainside. After marching upward in sweat and sun, they finally turned around at the tippy-top to behold the beautiful valley below. Glacier mountains stretched from the right side all the way down to the Pacific Ocean, where Bowen Island poked up and out of the choppy, sun-gleamed surf. Greeting the waters at the shoreline were endless pines standing at attention, swayed by the back-and-forth breath of ocean breeze. Enthralled, the mother pointed out at the natural world in front of them, proclaiming with breathless praise, "*This is God*."

I learned about this encounter years later from the daughter, and it deeply resonated with me at the time. This romantic merging of God and nature is one of the few ways faith can still seem relevant today. A bearded father figure in the clouds feels distant, dull, and outdated. But a cosmic Mother Nature still tickles our spiritual itch, as shown by these quotes from popular thought leaders:

> Oprah Winfrey: "I think if you believe in the awe and the wonder and the mystery [of the universe], then that is what God is. That is what God is, not the bearded guy in the sky."[1]

Lee Bladon: "God/Life/Universe is everything and everyone. . . . Life becomes so simple when we remember that everyone is an aspect of God."[2]

Neale Donald Walsch: "There is no separation between me and God, nor is their [sic] any difference. . . . God and I are one."[3]

John Lennon: "I believe that what people call God is something in all of us."[4]

Millions of people today believe that the difference between us and God is an illusion. *God* is the birds, trees, dogs, and bees, and everything in between, including us (because we're part of nature too). *I* am God. *You* are God. *We* are God. *I am he . . . as you are me . . . as we are we . . .* (and we are legally restricted from quoting more than three lines of a Beatles song in print). Creator and creature are one. And if I am one with God, and God is one with you, then, logically, we are one with each other. Hi, me! I am one with you, and you are one with the ocean, and the ocean is one with the sky. We are in a dream state on earth, and when we wake up we realize there are no real distinctions between things. There is only God.

And we can really see this seeping into our cultural conversation. By which, of course, I mean Disney movies. In *Avatar*, the goddess Eywa is made up of all living things, connecting the entire forest and the natives into one united consciousness. In *Moana*, the sea and the islands are depicted as gods, with nature alive and full of divinity. In *The Lion King*, Mufasa says, "Simmm-ba, we are all one." (Five bucks says you read that in a James Earl Jones voice.)[5]

Now, in the first chapter, we tried to go back to the beginning and experience the universe as if for the first time, recapturing the beauty, intelligence, and awe of creation. And as soon as we do that—as soon as we appreciate how awesome the universe is—it makes sense that our next response might be almost worship-like. Many of our ancestors bowed down and prayed to nature itself, and as someone who used to sneak out and sleep under the stars, I very much understand that impulse. Leave me alone in the woods too long, and I'll be tempted to worship a goat's head and make sacrifices to a tree (just kidding, mostly).

However, the first chapter of our story also made something else clear: God is not the universe but exists *before* the universe. The Creator and creation cannot be the same thing, because one made the other: "In the beginning God *created* the heavens and the earth." That's precisely why Christians will often refer to the universe as *creation*—because God *created* it. God is the artist; we are the art. We exist within time and space; God created time and space. God is the Creator; we are the creatures. We are *not God*, and God is *not us*.

This is known as the Creator-creature distinction, which is an obnoxious mouthful of a way to say, "You're not God, Melissa!" In the Christian story, there is a difference, a divide, a distinction between God up there and us down here. The Creator is not part of creation but exists before and beyond creation. The Bible takes this distinction very seriously, warning us not to worship creation as if it were the Creator and declaring such worship to be idolatry.

But who cares? What's the big deal? Why does the Creator-creature distinction really matter?

〈 ▪ ▪ 〉

Well, first of all, if my friend's mom was right and I really am one with God, then where does God end and I begin? If all the things that make me distinct from God are an illusion, then what's left of me? What's left of you? You and I would not be different people with unique personalities. No, we would just be one divine hive mind. The differences and distinctions between us would be an illusion of the body. Your unique personality, choices, dreams, heartaches, and idiosyncrasies would be deceptions to be shed. All the things that make you *you* wouldn't be real. The only thing that would be real would be God. Which is actually what millions of people believe:

> What is truly "me" is no other than what is truly "you" and what is truly all. By losing self you find [the universal God].—Adyashanti, *The Direct Way*[6]

> The tangerine I am eating is me. The mustard greens I am planting are me. —Thich Nhat Hahn, *The Miracle of Mindfulness*[7]

I am the tablet, I am the stylus. I am Abraham, Moses, Jesus. I am Gabriel, Michael, Israfil. Whoever comes into true being is dissolved in God, is God.
—Bayezid Bistami[8]

You are but a drop in a divine ocean, dissolving into God. The droplet gains the ocean but loses itself. Once you blur the line between Creator and creature, it can become hard to tell where God ends and we begin in the homogenous God-blob. *The creature is lost in the Creator.*

Another thing that can happen is that the *creature begins to be worshiped like the Creator.* For if we are one with God, then yes, that might mean we lose some of our individuality. But it also means we're gods. You have an inner god-self, which has helped advance a culture that absolutizes the self as the only God worth serving: Be true to yourself. Get in touch with your inner goddess.

In fact, there is a recent religious movement built around chanting the words "I am."[9] Ancient Jews reserved the words "I am" to describe God alone, but this group takes this divine title and applies it to themselves, affirming their own divinity. They wake up and start the day by chanting "I am!" then combine it with other phrases: "I am all things. I am the captain of my own soul. I am perfect. I am absolute. I am the creator of my world. I am all-powerful."[10] And these aren't exaggerations. A lot of popular spirituality books say that when you get in touch with your inner god-self, you acquire the powers of a god. You develop telepathic, telekinetic control over nature.

You might be familiar with the bestselling, Oprah-featured book *The Secret,* by Rhonda Byrne. It claims you can alter the world around you through your mind. Negative thoughts can cause disease, natural disasters, car crashes, or even bad weather. Positive thoughts can heal cancer and bring wealth, good luck, and, of course, good weather. More extreme versions claim you can fly, predict the future, or move objects with your mind. Like a god.

So once you merge Creator and creature, perhaps it's inevitable that creatures will start to worship themselves and believe that if only they'd figure out the secret, they too could have the powers of a god. And even if creatures don't worship themselves, we may often worship other parts of creation like a god. I know how quick I am to worship money, houses, and shiny things. How quick I am to worship coffee, narcotics, or food. Fishline a pork chop in front of me, and I'll run on water like a cartoon.

❰ ❱ ❰ ❱

So the Bible says it's wrong to worship ourselves and other created things. Yet once you break down the Creator-creature distinction, it's hard to believe anything can be *wrong* at all. There can't be any moral standard that is higher than me because there is nothing outside or beyond me—I am everything! There can be no evil or sin or fall away from God, because I am God, and God is perfect. This is why popular channeler Paul Selig writes, "It was always illusion that you were separate from God. . . . It was always illusion that there was war . . . always illusion that you were not loved by your fellow man. . . . You are all perfect."[11] So if the Creator-creature distinction is removed, then nothing can truly be wrong. *Everything is awesome.*

In which case, the goal is no longer to shape up or face our flaws. No, the goal is to awaken from the illusion and realize that we already are perfectly divine and divinely perfect. There is no immaturity, no cruelty, no abuse, no poverty, and no need for us to do anything about it.*As Shakti Gawain states, "There is no separation between us and God. . . . There can be no real lack or scarcity; there is nothing we have to try to achieve."[12] Everything is bright and bubbly; you are a perfect ray of sunshine who doesn't need to change a thing.

❰ ❱ ❰ ❱

What is more, if there is no Creator-creature distinction, then God is one with not only the good parts of creation but the evil parts as well. If God is

---

*They might retort that we really do *feel* suffering, but only because we have bought into the illusion that something is wrong. Once we see through the illusion and accept that things are actually perfect, then the pain goes away as well. The illusion was the source of suffering, not reality itself. However, if nothing is wrong, how could we be deceived by an illusion to begin with? Wouldn't us buying into the illusion itself be something that's gone wrong? Now, some might retort that we willingly chose to fall into the illusion in order to learn some kind of lesson on earth. Yet wouldn't that suggest that the god-self was previously lacking some kind of wisdom or understanding, and so wouldn't have truly been God/omniscient to begin with?

one with all of creation, then God is as much one with Joseph Stalin as with Mother Teresa. The difference between loving someone and hating them is an illusion, for all things are one in God. If goodness is one with God and God is one with evil, then goodness is one with evil. If A = B and B = C, then A = C.

You see this in Star Wars, where the force is one with all things. If you pay attention to the script, the light side of the force is not morally superior to the dark. The goal isn't to bring more light to the universe; no, it's to bring balance to the force, to bring light and dark, good and evil, into harmony, and to hold both together equally as *one* in the force. That's why it's said that Anakin brought balance to the force even though he killed the young-lings and became Darth Vader. We root for the light side when we watch the movies, but according to its own logic, there's no reason we should. The force is one with all things, and so the dark side and the light side are equally one with the force and each other. And if the Creator is one with good and evil—and good and evil are one in the Creator—then morality is an illusion. Sorry, younglings.[†]

So if the Creator is one with creation, then yes, God is the rosebushes, mountains, and sunsets. But God is also disease. God is the tumor in your mother's flesh. God is the bullet of the oppressor, the fist of the abuser, the walls and pipes of the gas chamber. And this would not just lower God in moral terms but would also lower God in dignity: God is the leftover pizza. God is your nail clippings. God is the fungus on your left foot. God is para-sites, feces, and Justin Bieber. Once the distinction is gone, *the Creator is lowered to the level of creation.*

❮ ▬ ▬ ❯

So those are some of the potential pitfalls of breaking down the Creator-creature distinction. Yet some of the authors who talk about oneness with

---

[†]One might perhaps avoid this issue by saying evil isn't real, in the same way darkness isn't real but is just the absence of light. All is one, yes, but there is no evil in that "all," for evil isn't real. However, a lot of contemporary spiritual authors don't take advantage of this option, instead maintaining that good and evil are equal and opposites sides of a coin in a "yin and yang" (or at least a Western misappropriation of those terms) sort of way.

God and the universe mean something more along the lines of connect-edness, not literal one-to-one sameness. For them, oneness is used in the sense that I am one with my spouse rather than in the sense that the Rock and Dwayne Johnson are one and the same person. They mean a oneness of intimacy, not identity. They want unity, yes, but a unity amid diversity, with at least some of the differences and distinctions between things re-maining intact. In this way, some of them may avoid the pitfalls we've explored above.

Yet note that in order to do so, they inevitably have to reassert some Creator-creature distinctions somewhere in their belief system. And that's the point. I'm not trying to argue that everything these thinkers say is stupid (in fact, I quite like the idea of the mystical interconnectedness of all things). I'm just trying to show that the Creator-creature distinction is important, and that's why even those who may seem to reject it in one place often end up reaffirming it in another. We may be *connected* to God, but that doesn't mean we *are* God. An artwork may reflect its artist, and yet da Vinci himself is not hanging in the Louvre. How terrifying it would be if he were.

❮■■❯

My wife and I have twin toddlers named Søren and Augustine. Which tells you two things: first, that I clearly won the battle over who got to name the kids, and second, that I am a twin parent. *Double trouble.*

With twins, it can be hard for them to figure out who each of them is as an individual. They're always together. They look the same. They get treated the same. So something I used to do at night, right after bath time, is take them one at a time on their own and hold them up to a mirror. I'd point at myself in the mirror and say, "Da-da." Then I'd point at each one of them and say their name. I'd do that over and over, trying to get them to see themselves, to help them understand they exist on their own, as an indi-vidual. And when I'd point and say their name and they'd realize it was them in the reflection, their eyes would light up and they'd lose it with this joyful, ridiculous laughter.

As my boys grow up, I want to do everything I possibly can to preserve that original joy they have in realizing that *they exist*. I want them to believe the words of Dr. Seuss, "Today you are you! This is truer than true! There is no one alive who is you-er than you!"[13] I want them to know that they were created as distinct individuals and they don't have to dissolve who they are to be close to their Creator. *I want to affirm who they are.*

But at the same time, I also want them to know they're *not* the center of the universe. They are not God. They are creatures—fallible, finite, flawed creatures. They will make mistakes and need forgiveness.

I want them to grow up in the real world—to know that people really are struggling, starving, and hurting each other, to know that it's not all an illusion. I want them to grow up to see the world as it really is and to try with everything they have to make it better. And then, at the end of their lives, when they haven't managed to fix everything, I want them to still be able to rest in the grace of God, to accept that they're not perfect, that they can't carry the weight of the whole world.

Because they're not God. Only God is God.

THREE

Creation Is Good

FOR ONE OF MY FAVORITE TALKS I GIVE, I stay outside the room and wait until it's a minute or two past starting time, right to the point where everyone's wondering where I am. Then I stride into class and calmly write on the board, *Is sex good?*

I stand there waiting and enjoying the awkwardness of our small-town, traditional, polite, Christian university class as their conversational hubbub slowly turns to stunned silence. Some of them glance wide-eyed at each other, as if to say, *Isn't this supposed to be a Bible class?* I force my lips to suppress a smile, overly amused with myself.

Eventually, one brave soul ventures an answer. "I'd say no. Sex just makes things more difficult. Like, how many families and marriages are ruined because someone can't keep it in their pants?" A nod of agreement circles the room. Another student chimes in, "Yeah, totally. God wants us to focus on spiritual stuff, not sex and body stuff. Earth isn't our true home; heaven is. We aren't physical beings. We are *spiritual* beings who happen to be having a *physical* experience."

A kid in the back snorts, and I, being the cruel master that I am, call on him to share his thoughts. "Well," he retorts, "At first, I was gonna say it's not good, cause I thought that's what you'd want us to say. But . . . God made the body, right? God made sex. So it can't be all bad, can it?"

A few heads in the room nod, seemingly won over by his reasoning. So I decide to complicate things a bit with not just one but ten more questions.*

---

*Mwahahaha.

I erase the word *sex* from the board, and insert a new word, entailing a whole new provocation: Is *alcohol* good?

Some students respond with examples (often personal) about how horrible it is to grow up with an alcoholic parent. Others retort that God made the grapes of the field and that Jesus turned water into wine. Not wanting to argue with Jesus, most of the class ends up on the yes side, admitting that alcohol is good in and of itself when used appropriately.

With consensus nearing, I decide to further gum up the conversation by once again replacing the central word and forging an entirely new question: Is *marijuana* good?

Groans reverberate through the room. Many are realizing the tension between their knee-jerk dismissal of weed and the logic they just proposed regarding alcohol. If alcohol is inherently good because God made it, then is weed inherently good because God made it?

I then take this opportunity to verbally reiterate to the class that I am not advocating for drugs (you know, because I like having a job) but am just pushing them to think through their beliefs and make them consistent. It's better for students to wrestle with these things now in the safety of my pedagogical man-bosom rather than out there in the real world.

With that job-saving, legal fine print in place, I then write out the next question on the board: *Is eating a spiritual act?*

The gut reaction of most of the students is no. They argue that food is not *inherently* spiritual, even though you can incorporate spiritual things into it. You can pray before eating, or have a dinner conversation about God, or feed a poor person a meal. Food can be put toward a good and holy cause, but it's not holy in and of itself. Spiritually, they are empty calories. Or as one student put it, "There is nothing holy about a meatball sub."

Next question: *My soul is what makes me* me. *Yes or no?*

Almost the whole class goes to the yes side now. I ask why, and someone invariably responds, "Well, when you die, your soul goes to heaven, right?

So your body is gone, but you are still around and still you. So, you are your soul. It's what makes you *you*."

This line of thought tends to go on for a while, and I usually throw a wrench in there halfway through to see what happens. I walk over to the board and scrawl this question below the previous one:

Can souls see, hear, touch, taste, or smell?

If the students weren't annoyed already, this Catch-22 of a question usually gets them there. On the one hand, they don't want to say no and have their souls be eternally blind and deaf in some tasteless, smell-less, dull, dark, sensory abyss for the entire afterlife. On the other hand, if they say yes—souls *can* see, hear, touch, taste, and smell—then the body becomes entirely redundant, and there is no reason God should have made it to begin with. Why do we need a body if the soul can already do everything it does and more?

Next question: *Is science good?*

I observe that most students don't know what this question has to do with anything, and I hypothesize that they're kind of just ready for the discussion to be over by this point.

Final question: *Should Christians be pro-environmentalism?*

Some of the class grew up watching polar bear puppies die in Disney documentaries and are vehemently pro-environment and anti–whoever isn't. Other students think global warming is a hoax concocted by satanic reptiles to fund their anarchist bowling league. Most of the class is somewhere in the middle, with a general sense that we shouldn't be unnecessarily wasteful but that the environment is still not a huge priority for Christians. After all, God is going to rapture us to heaven and destroy the earth, right?

I then erase this question and replace it once again. It may seem like I'm smuggling in yet another final question, but this one doesn't count, because it's just meant for rhetorical effect to drive home the overall theme: *Does God create bad things?*

I then dramatically pull a Bible out from under my arm, and—wielding it like a mace—open it to page one, reading from Genesis 1:

> In the beginning God created the heavens and the earth. . . . And God saw that
> it was *good*. . . . The land produced vegetation. . . . And God saw that it was *good*.
> God set [the stars] in the vault of the sky. . . . And God saw that it was *good*. God
> created the great creatures of the sea and every living thing. . . . And God saw
> that it was *good*. God made the wild animals. . . . And God saw that it was
> *good*. . . . God created mankind in his own image; in the image of God he created
> them; male and female God created them. . . . God saw all that he had made, and
> it was very *good*. (Genesis 1:1, 10, 12, 17-18, 21, 25, 27, 31)

I then close the Bible slowly for effect and say, "Nature and the physical
universe are so good that the very first chapter of the Bible says *it was good*
seven times in a row. Let's go back through our questions with that goodness
in mind. . . ."

❮ ❚❚ ❚❚ ❭

Is sex good?

God could have created us as asexual, annelid worms that can reproduce
without a partner. But instead God gave us bits and bobs and made them
feel good when they bashed together. And it was *good*. The Bible does not
seem to be even one bit ashamed about this, as seen from even a cursory
reading of Song of Solomon, which is just eight solid chapters of erotic love
poetry. It's so raunchy that it's often joked that Jewish children weren't allowed to read that part of the Bible until they were thirty.

Spirituality and sexuality are not inherently opposed. Which is perhaps
why the Bible also uses lots of romantic metaphors for God's relationship
with us: We are the bride of Christ (Revelation 19). God is a jealous lover
(Exodus 34). Indeed, there's a reason why "knowing" someone is often followed up with "in the biblical sense."

Around this point, some students are usually confused and (God bless
them) concerned for my soul. Inevitably, one of them can't contain it any
longer and says, "But, but . . . are you telling us all to just go and have lots
of sex?!?"

"No," I emphasize. "I'm *not* saying that. What I'm saying is that the
problem is never *sex itself*. It's what you do with it. The problem is never with

the *body itself*. It's what you do with it. The problem is never with *physical matter* itself. It's what you . . . ? It's what you . . . ? It's what you . . . ?" I keep repeating myself and glaring at them until they fill in the blanks.

"It's what you do with it," they finally mumble. (Yay! Class participation!)

The Bible recognizes this distinction between *use* and *abuse*, which is why it has two different Greek words to distinguish the body (*sōma*) from our sinful abuses of it (*sarx*).[1] But we so easily forget that. We do bad things with the body (*sarx*) and forget that it is not the body itself (*sōma*) that is bad. We've thrown the baby out with the bathwater, along with the tub, the house, the planet, and every other physical thing as well. Spirituality can so quickly slip into pitting the soul against the body and heaven against earth.

So is sex good? Yes. God made the body, designed it for sex, and called it *good*. And when it is going as it was intended to go, with lip-locked lovers trading the same breath back and forth, how could it not be? Just because good things can be used for bad doesn't make them bad in themselves. Just because love broke your heart once doesn't mean love itself is bad. Just because sex came too early or at the wrong stage of life or with the wrong person at the wrong time doesn't necessarily mean there won't be a right place and a right person and a right time.[†]

❮ ▬ ▬ ❯

Is alcohol good?

Similar to sex, there's a use/abuse distinction here. Something can be good, but that doesn't mean everything we do with it is. Likewise, God made dirt, and dirt don't hurt—unless you bury someone alive in it.

❮ ▬ ▬ ❯

Is eating a spiritual act?[‡]

[†]Not to imply that singleness is somehow lesser (1 Corinthians 7 is pretty clear it's not). In the same way, admitting that food is good does not negate the spiritual discipline of fasting but is precisely what makes that discipline a spiritually rewarding sacrifice.

[‡]Yes, of course I skipped the weed question. You didn't really think I was going to answer it, did you? I work at a Christian university. What are you, high?

My gut says yes. There must be a reason why so many Bible stories involve food, or miraculously making food appear, or table fellowship with lepers, prostitutes, and tax collectors. Food brings people together and reminds us that despite our differences, we are all earthly creatures of flesh, blood, dirt, appetite, longing, and thirst.

There must be a reason why, when Elijah was about to give up in despair, God gave him some cake (1 Kings 19). Because as much as we might want to think we're above it, half of the time our existential and spiritual crises could be alleviated if we just ate a snack, took a nap, went for a walk, and re-engaged our senses in creation.[§] Our physical states are never as isolated from our spiritual states as we imagine them to be. We are embodied creatures and should access the divine not only by closing our eyes in prayer but by opening them wide in creation, experiencing God through every last one of our bodily senses, including taste.

God could have just populated the planet with bland energy packets that we collected to regain power and stay alive (like in a video game). Instead, God gave us strawberries, blackberries, grapes, wine, cheese, grain for pasta, warm bread, rice, salmon, salt, corn on the cob, coffee beans, and bacon. I've heard people say their eyes can see the beauty of God in a shimmering horizon or that their ears can almost *hear* the moon in Beethoven's *Midnight Sonata*. So why can't our taste buds be aroused to the presence of God through burnt crunches, soft cream, whipped taters, melted brie, paired wine, salted caramel, or even through a perfectly timed, humble, greasy, salt-of-the-earth cheeseburger? As a wise man once said, "This is God, speaking to us, through food."[2] Indeed, what are Communion and the Eucharist if not a recognition that the bodily act of eating and drinking can have spiritual weight?

◖ ▬ ▬ ◗

[§] I once knew a psychologist whose favorite prescription for sex and food addiction was to take a daily, hourlong walk in the woods, dragging your fingers against tree bark, feeling the moss sink and the twigs snap beneath your feet, taking the air deep into your lungs. He claimed that half of our issues and addictions stem from a deprivation of sensory and embodied experiences in our modern, housed-in, screen-distracted world, and the subsequent attempts to refind those lost sensory experiences in all the wrong places.

My soul is what makes me me. *Yes or no? / Can souls see, hear, touch, taste, or smell?*

When I think of who I am and what defines me, I tend to recall bodily sensations, sights, and sounds. I replay words of affirmation or insult that came to define me. Or recall the warmth of my wife in winter. Or the smell of my children's hair after a bath. Or the first time alcoholic wine burned my breath in Communion and I knew I was a man.

When I think of God, I recollect songs my ears once heard that lifted me to eternity (Cohen's "Hallelujah" or Sufjan Stevens's "Chicago" get me there every time). Or I recall the taste of salty waters rushing round me during my baptism in the Pacific Ocean. Or the smell of incense in a passing church in Cambridge. Or the spirals of light I saw when a dentist put me on laughing gas and I started mumbling prayers out loud to God mid-surgery like a freakin' lunatic.

I couldn't lose these things without losing part of myself. Indeed, what would be left of my identity if every bodily sensation, sight, sound, flavor, scent, and bodily experience I've ever had were removed? What is left of us if, as George Harrison is often thought to have said, "We are not these bodies, but just souls having a bodily experience"?[3] This is why it is so crucial that the Bible does not say that when we die our souls float up to heaven, but rather that we will receive resurrected, renewed, physical bodies, just like how Jesus did not resurrect as an ethereal ball of light but with an actual physical body (which one of his more skeptical disciples poked to make sure was really there). The Bible does not depict the body as disposable but as an essential part of who we are.[5]

Now, I don't believe human identity is solely reducible to physical matter and atoms bouncing around. However, while reality may mean *more* than matter, it certainly doesn't mean *less*. The physical body is not everything, but it's not nothing, either. God incarnated in it, for Christ's sake.

[ ]( )( )( )

---

[5]The soul may still *survive* the body, but that doesn't mean we are fully ourselves or fully human until we bodily resurrect later on.

Is science good?

If you were to judge based on the loudest voices on social media, you might assume science and Christianity were at war. But did you know that some scholars—such as Oxford's Michael Foster or Templeton Prize–winner T. F. Torrance—argue that it was Christianity's emphasis on the goodness of matter that explains why science arose in the Christian West instead of somewhere else?[4]

Their argument goes something like this: Many cultures and religions have seen matter as unreal, dirty, or evil. And if matter is unreal or inherently evil, why study it? Why plumb the depths of a delusion? In contrast, because Christians believed creation was good, we assumed it was worth studying, worth knowing, worth exploring to uncover the intricacies of God's handiwork (as Johannes Kepler allegedly wrote, science is "thinking God's thoughts after him").[5] So even when Christians occasionally disagreed with particular conclusions from the sciences, they still tended to assume the goodness of the endeavor itself.

We know science is worth doing because we have the hindsight of seeing how it turned out. But before all the tech and medicine and so on, science was actually a hard sell. You had to have just the right balance of philosophical, religious, and cultural assumptions to get it off the ground. The goodness of creation may have been a prerequisite.

Should Christians be pro-environmentalism?

In the United States in 2022, 72 percent of the general population said that climate change was an extremely serious problem. But among highly religious respondents, that number plummeted to 42 percent.[6] While there may be multiple reasons for this, a good deal of the blame is likely due to an overemphasis on heaven at the expense of earth.

Yet the most famous prayer in the Bible (and perhaps in history) goes, "Your kingdom come, your will be done, *on earth* as it is in heaven" (Matthew 6:10). So the point is not to ditch earth for heaven but to bring heaven down to earth—to manifest the light of eternity here and now. Which is why the Bible talks about heaven not as some place up in the clouds but as the new earth (Isaiah 65:17; Revelation 21:1). Contrary to how some Christians talk about it, the earth is not going to be destroyed forever in the end but rather reforged, resurrected, and made anew as the eternal home for our physical, resurrected bodies. Ours is an earthly faith of dirt, sweat, and soil.

Which means that Christians—if they understand their own story—should be the ones leading the charge for environmentalism. And some Christians have been, even if others haven't always followed suit. Christians such as John Muir, father of the national parks. Christians such as Jane Goodall, famed pioneer of animal welfare and environmental conservation. Christians such as Katharine Hayhoe, a climate scientist recently named one of *Time* magazine's one hundred most influential people.

Does God create bad things?

Broadly, there have been three types of answers given to this question throughout history. Nature is either (1) God, (2) garbage, or (3) good. Most of us assume an answer to this question, often without realizing it. We might assume one answer while advertising a shampoo's *natural* ingredients, another when talking about *natural* disasters, another when doing *natural* science, another when giving thanks to Mother Earth, another when raping her for resources.

In the previous chapter we saw the consequences of turning nature into (1) God. In this chapter we've seen what happens when we overcorrect and go to the opposite extreme, seeing nature as gross, evil (2) garbage. Thankfully, we've also uncovered a third, ancient option, where we heed the words of Genesis 1, "In the beginning, God created the havens and the earth. . . . *And it was good.*" Creation may not be God, but we can see God's goodness radiating through it. It is not God, nor garbage, but it is (3) good. And we should treat it as such.

At this point in the lecture, all the students erupted into spontaneous applause and stood on their desks chanting, "O captain, my captain." They left that day forever changed, and never again littered, denigrated science, abused alcohol or their bodies, nor had any more confusion about this issue whatsoever.**

**True story.

fall MOVEMENT II

As a young child, I was initially excited about encountering the universe for the first time. But then I hit the teen years and started to think mostly about *myself.* Yes, the universe exists, but what are we humans within it? Who am I? What does it mean to be Jonathan? I was beginning to notice I was good at some things: talking in class, performing in plays, making others laugh. Yet I often used those gifts to wound, mock, dismiss, and one-up others. I was a tender and sweet kid, but I would often find myself weaponizing even those aspects of myself, for I understood how to get someone where it really hurt and how to do it with a smile. I encountered within myself much that was good, yet always shrouded by a murky cloud of ulterior motives. It was as if there was a higher nature within me that had somehow *fallen.*

I remember a debate in one of my high school classes about whether human nature was basically good or evil. Most of my fellow teens took one side or the other, but I stood in between, wanting to say human nature was somehow both. Then the teacher told me the middle ground was for "sissies," and that, more than anything, convinced me human nature was evil. It wasn't the content of his words but their cruelty that convinced me. Yet the empathetic looks of some of my classmates when he said it reminded me that even falling people can reach for one another midair. Humans are complicated.

These questions around good and evil and human identity are what is at stake in the second movement of our story: fall. After creating the heavens and the earth, God got around to us. God made humans in God's own image and likeness, and God called us *good*. We have something good and divine and beautiful within us, for we are made in the image of God.

Yet because we are made in God's image, we are not robots or computers but real, personal entities with freedom and autonomy. With that freedom, we chose to begin messing up everything that God once called good. So we are not just good or just evil, not just one or the other. Rather, we are goodness gone bad, the divine image twisted and contorted, paradise lost and overgrown, the height of creation that has somehow fallen.

 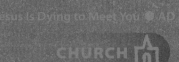

FOUR

Humanity in God's Image

DOES GOD HAVE A PENIS?

Hold on to that idea for a second, and we will come back to it after we've read the Bible first: "In the beginning God created the heavens and the earth. . . . And God saw that it was good. . . . Then God said, 'Let us make human beings in our image, to be like us. . . .' So God created human beings in his own image. In the image of God he created them; male and female he created them" (Genesis 1:1, 10, 26-27 NLT).

I am made in God's image. So . . . does that mean God is one handsome devil? Does that mean God looks and sounds like me? Does God have a great big bushy beard? Does God get back pain? Does God get crow's feet and hippos' gut? Does God have a body or bodily functions? *Does God have a penis?* (See, I wasn't just being provocative before.) If we are made in God's image, does that mean God has genitalia, or is that logic fallacious?

On the one hand, when someone says you're just like your mother or father, that could mean you physically look the same as your parents. It could mean you have a similar nose, equally long legs, or comparably hairy arms. Or it could mean there is a deeper, almost spiritual likeness—something about your way, your essence, your unspoken mannerisms, your sense of humor, your wandering spirit, that is just so *like* your parents at that age. It is in this deeper sense that we are supposedly made in the image of God.

But what is this deeper image? If the image of God is not a literal, physical image but more of a vague, subtle, spiritual likeness, what then is that vague, subtle, spiritual likeness?

Now, theologians sometimes focus quite narrowly on what Genesis 1:27 means by *image*. However, for this chapter, I'm going to sidestep that more narrow, controversial, textual conversation and use the language of *image* more philosophically to explore a broader array of proposed ways humans might be *like* God in general.

CREATIVITY

God loves to *create*: God sketched the shoreline, dotted the starry night, spun the spider's web, and brushed the wind into being. If God is real, then God is the greatest, most creative artist of all time, and human artists who draw the world are merely attempting to capture a dim reflection of that first painting—the world itself.

God is creative, and so are we. We build things, invent games, write songs, spin yarns, make crafts, craft jokes, draw doodles, pen poems, paint paintings, take risks and logical leaps, and mix and match and imagine connections where they didn't exist before (e.g., our eyes saw a horse and a rhino, but it was our creative imagination that combined them into a unicorn). Humans are creators, made in the image of the ultimate Creator.

So what if God's image is imagination itself? We can imagine other things because we first were imagined; we were once but an image in the mind of our maker. To *imagine* (from Latin *imago*) is literally to *image* something, to picture or conceive an image or representation of something in your mind. It is in this sense that God says, "Before I formed you in the womb I knew you" (Jeremiah 1:5), for you were on God's mind long before you were on this earth. We are the image of the divine imagination, made in the likeness of one who imagines marvels and then actually makes them. So we too conceive, craft, carve, weave, thread, forge, and hammer.

EMOTIONS

According to the Bible, we are made in the image of a feeling giant.[*] It describes God as feeling joy, love, anger, sorrow, and even grief. In which case, to suppress our emotions is to suppress part of what makes us like God. We are not to

---

[*] This is actually quite controversial. I address this more in my first book, explaining why temporal emotions don't undermine classical theism. See *MonoThreeism: An Absurdly Arrogant Attempt to Answer All the Problems of the Last 2000 Years in One Night at a Pub* (Eugene, OR: Cascade Books, 2021).

repress them, nor leave them wild and uncared for, but feel them, wrestle with them, harness them, be harnessed by them, and become emotionally mature. Only then will we be fully human, living up to the divine image within us all.

CONSCIOUSNESS

Humans don't just exist but are awake to our existence. We are not only conscious and aware but self-conscious and self-aware. Rocks do not reflect on their own death, nor wonder whether they were made for something more than the riverbed (if they do, I apologize).

Philosophers and neuroscientists still aren't totally sure how consciousness works. Some say it's just an illusion created by our physical brains. Others say that no amount of material neurons firing could create our experience of consciousness, and that robots and computers may mimic human actions on the outside but will never truly become conscious on the inside. These thinkers quickly find themselves going beyond neuroscience and into the realm of the soul. For if consciousness cannot be reduced to matter, nor replicated in a physical computer, then there must be something about consciousness that is not just physical but *metaphysical*, not just material but *spiritual*—as if it were a reflection of the divine image. Perhaps there was cosmic consciousness even before there was a cosmos, and we flicker with embers from its eternal flame. Perhaps we are conscious because the divine mind is conscious and we are its brainchild.

SEX

Many refer to God using masculine imagery (*Father, Son, he/him*, etc.). But notice what Genesis 1:27 says: "In the image of God he created them; male and female he created them." The very first elaboration on the divine image seems to imply that both men and women are reflections of it. Which means that human maleness is not more indicative of the divine than femaleness. Perhaps that's why the book of Job refers to the Creator using both male and female imagery in the same breath:

Does the rain have a father?
  Who fathers the drops of dew?

From whose *womb* comes the ice?

 Who gives *birth* to the frost from the heavens? (Job 38:28-29)

Now, it may not be surprising that the Bible *primarily* uses male images for God, as it was written in an ancient, male-dominated culture. What might shock us, though, is all the places where the Bible also uses feminine imagery for God, such as in Genesis 1, Hosea, Deuteronomy, Isaiah, Psalms, or here in Job.

So, does God have a penis? I think that might be taking things a bit too literally. But if God *were* to have a penis, then God would probably also have to have a vagina. And that imagery might sound a bit too provocative to some born-again Christians. But you do know what's implicit in the imagery of being born again, right?

INHERENT WORTH

A key argument on both sides of the slavery debate was whether Africans were made in the image of God. Because if Black people were equal participants in the divine image, then to abuse them was to violate divine goodness itself. Every person has a spark of the eternal flame within them, and woe to those who dare blow it out. If God is within us all, then to violate another image-bearer is like desecrating a temple or holy space. We are, all of us, cathedrals. As Martin Luther King Jr. wrote:

> Living with the system of slavery and then later rigid standards of segregation, many Negroes lost faith in themselves. Many came to feel that perhaps they were less than human. Nagging clouds of inferiority actually formed in their mental sky. Then something happened to the Negro. . . . The Negro came to feel that he was somebody. His religion revealed to him that God loves all of his children and that *all men are made in his image* and that the basic thing about a man is . . . his eternal dignity and worth.[1]

REASON

Isn't it odd that the world makes sense to us at all? Isn't it strange that the Pythagorean theorem—an abstract equation of symbols thought up in the mind of Pythagoras thousands of years ago—perfectly parallels the external world? Isn't it a tad suspicious that reality mostly functions in mathematical, consistent, logical ways that just so happen to align with human reason? I mean, shouldn't we have expected just the opposite—that there would be no scientific laws, natural order, or rational structure to reality? Isn't chaos far simpler? Shouldn't our default expectation have been lawless disorder?

As such, it's hard to know whether reality is rational or we are just filtering it through our rational lens, seeing what we want (and expect) to see. Does two plus two actually equal four, or is that just us shrinking infinity to fit into our finite skulls? Are time and space real, or does the human mind just think in spatial and temporal categories and impose that on reality? (Indeed, relativity and quantum mechanics have shown that the commonsense rationality of the human mind cannot be assumed to be true of the broader universe.) And there is no way out of this problem, because anything your mind comes up with to try to argue its way out already assumes your mind can be trusted to tell you the way things really are to begin with. Which is what you're supposed to be trying to prove.

Given that, belief in God ironically becomes a giant gamble wherein we actually place our chips on human reason. For to believe in God is to say that the human mind really reflects the nature of the divine mind at the heart of all things. What goes on in my head parallels what goes on out there, because I am made in the *image* of the mind that structured and shaped the whole universe. I can understand the design plan because I speak the same language as the designer. Reason is not just a social construct; it is the image of the one who is the rational foundation and architect of reality itself. Reality aligns with the human mind because reality is itself the product of a mind. Faith doesn't negate reason, it absolutizes it, seeing it everywhere and in everything.

Which is exactly what the Bible is getting at when it refers to God as the word or *logos*, through which all things were made (John 1). *Logos* is the Greek word here, and it's where we get the term *logic*. The divine mind is the *logos*; God is reason itself. Humans are rational because we are made in the image of the one who is reason itself and who designed our rational world. *Logos* is also the basis for the *-logy* at the end of the academic disciplines: sociology is the study of the logic—the *logos*—of the social world; zoology is the study of the logic—the *logos*—of the animal world. And this applies pretty much across the board: psychology, geology, archaeology, anthropology, proctology. The academic study of the world was built on the assumption that the human mind could actually understand reality, for our minds were made in the image of the divine mind who created, structured, and permeates reality. Sigmund Freud said we project our daddy issues onto the clouds and see a bearded father-God staring back; the same thing can be said of reason. To project our intelligence onto the universe means we will inevitably see a higher intelligence staring back at us. And if that means God is a delusion, then so is the rational enterprise itself.

Many assume that having faith means not having a brain, but I think it's just the opposite: I think when all of our humanity is firing at once—when we are creative, emotional, and rational—we are closer to our Creator and closer to ourselves. Any Christian who neglects the mind is neglecting part of their own humanity, part of the image of God implanted within them.

However, an interesting question here raises its head: When do you think Christians most emphasized that God's image was our reason? During the scientific Enlightenment, of course. *How convenient.* We'd previously said the image was reason, but not to the extent that we began to say and emphasize it during the Age of Reason. *A rational time sees a rational god.* Which raises the question: Did God create us in his image, or do we create God in our own image? If we were goats, would we think God was a goat? If we were cows, would we think God was a cow? As our heavenly heifer taught us, we are bold to say: This is my ground chuck, shed for you. Drink milk in remembrance of me.

I think this is a fair critique. Yes, God has to be somewhat similar to us or else we couldn't relate to God, know God, or say anything about God. But any God who just looks like you, talks like you, and thinks like you probably isn't God at all—it's just you, reflected off the clouds. As soon as we forget that, we turn God into ourselves, worshiping our own image instead of the one who drew it. Which is why I always add one final category, to remind myself of the tentativeness of this whole bloody exercise.

MYSTERY

God is ultimately a mystery. Yes, I think God is creative, emotional, and rational in a way that is somewhat analogous to human creativity, emotion, and reason. God is all those things, but God is also *more*; more than anything I could ever put in this book; more than all the libraries in all the world could ever contain; more than all the run-on sentences and excessive semicolons could allow. Which, on the one hand, seems to make God inhuman and unknowable. God is so mysterious, so beyond us, so different from us, so other from us, that God seems inhuman.

But that is also what makes God the most human. *For we too are mysteries.* Each person is made unique; no one fits perfectly into any category or preconception. Just when you think you've figured someone out, they surprise you. I've been married to my wife, Madison, for over a decade, and she's still surprising me all the time. Even old folks who've been married fifty years can still find themselves shocked when their partner's defibrillator goes off.

Others are truly *other*. As soon as you try to reduce another human to a mere extension of yourself and your own ways of seeing or thinking or feeling, you lose what makes them *them* and not *you*. To admit that God is mysterious takes no more faith than to accept your fellow humans on their own terms. The same fragile dance of a human reaching beyond themselves for another is mirrored in humanity reaching out for the holy. Ironically, it is when God is least human, least like us, least understandable, least knowable, least reducible to a manmade scalpel or sermon or textbook, that God is most human. For we are made in the image of a mysterious God. So we too are mysteries.

◄ ▧ ▧ ►

So God made us in the divine image, and *it was good*. However, because we are made in the image of God, we are not just impersonal robots. God gave us the same personal space and autonomy and dignity that God has—the space to decide for ourselves how we'll live and who we want to be. The freedom to choose to love, to nurture, to do good. Or the freedom to go ahead and do the exact opposite. . . .

CREATION

Creation Begins

Creation Is Not God

Creation Is Good

FALL

Humanity In God's Image

Humanity Gone Wild

NATION

Abraham Finds Faith ● 2000 BC

Moses Meets I Am ● 1400–1200ish BC

Goodness Is Commanded ●

Beauty in the Promised Land ●

King David and His Boy ● 1000ish BC

Justice Exiles the Nation ● 586 BC

REDEMPTION

Jesus Is Born ● AD 0

Jesus is Walking Around Saying Stuff ● AD 30

Jesus Is Dying to Meet You ● AD 33

CHURCH

The Spirit Arrives ● AD 33

The Church Begins ● AD 33

The Apostle Paul Converts ● AD 35ish

The Church Expands ● AD 300ish

The Church Today ● The Present

END

The End of the World as We Know It ●

Highway to Hell or Stairway to Heaven? ●

FIVE

Humanity Gone Wild

> In the beginning God made the heavens and the earth. . . . And . . . it was
> good. . . . God created [humankind] in his own image. . . . The LORD God took
> the man and put him in the Garden of Eden to work it and take care of it. And
> the LORD God commanded the man, "You are free to eat from any tree in the
> garden; but you must not eat from the tree of the knowledge of good and evil."
> (Genesis 1:1, 10, 27; 2:15-17)

God created the world, called it good, and then made humans in the
divine image. Now God puts the first choice before us, the first fork in the
road. As soon as God says not to eat from the tree, we have the *choice* of
whether to obey or disobey—whether to continue in the goodness of creation or birth evil into the world. God could have forced everyone to
always do the right thing and be morally perfect carbon copies of each
other. God could have created robots who followed their programming,
doing exactly as they were told and saying, "I love you," every time you
squeezed them.* But a forced love is no love at all. The love of a good robot
means little. Which is why God made us free to love, free to roam and run
and rejoice, free to do good. But with the freedom to do good there comes
the freedom *not* to do good:

> [Eve] took some [of the fruit] and ate it. She also gave some to her husband, who
> was with her, and he ate it. Then the eyes of both of them were opened, and they
> realized they were naked; so they sewed fig leaves together and made coverings
> for themselves. (Genesis 3:4-5)

---

*Although I do know some people who are exactly like that.

Adam and Eve took what did not belong to them, bringing *sin*—that bogey of a word—into the world. Our culture has some baggage with the term *sin*, associating it with guilt trips, hypocritical preachers, and an evil almost too comic to take seriously, involving horny teenagers, dancing, and cackling demons with pitchforks. If you would find it helpful, you could perhaps take the suggestion of one author, who always swaps *sin* out it in his head and replaces it with "the human propensity to f*** things up."[1] Yet I personally appreciate the Shakespearean epic-ness of the term *sin* and will spend the rest of this chapter attempting to better define it.

So, Adam and Eve sin. Yet the first thing that happens is not hellfire, wrath, or evil things going bump in the night. No, the first thing that comes with sin is insecurity. Adam and Eve become self-conscious, realizing they are naked and hurriedly covering themselves with fig leaves. Once sin enters, vulnerability becomes a weakness, something others can expose or use against us. We can hurt each other now. Others might laugh at our bodies, or leave us for someone better looking, or make fun of our lumps and scars. So now we look in the mirror and worry: *Does my stomach droop? Are my breasts too little? Is my penis too small? Am I too short?* If I handed you a fig leaf right now, what part of your body would you wish you could cover with it so that others could never see it again? I know exactly what I would cover.

I knew this one woman. When she was sixteen, she wore a dress on a date, and her boyfriend made a casual joke about her calves being a little chubby. And she hasn't worn a dress or shorts ever since. She's in her sixties now. For nearly half a century, she's been haunted by the memory of a cruel comment a teenage boy once made.

And as someone who spent the first twenty-five years of his life wearing a shirt in the swimming pool, I can sympathize. This is what happens to us when sin enters the equation. *This is not how it was supposed to be.*

◖▮◗▮◗

"And [God] said, . . . 'Have you eaten from the tree that I commanded you not to eat from?' The man said, 'The woman you put here with me—she gave me some fruit from the tree, and I ate it.' Then the LORD God said to the woman, 'What is this you have done?' The woman said, 'The serpent deceived me, and I ate'" (Genesis 3:9).

God asks Adam why he ate the fruit, and Adam blames his wife, Eve. Then God asks Eve why she ate the fruit, and she blames the serpent. Sin has entered the world, and with it comes guilt. We feel bad about ourselves for sinning. But we have no idea what to *do* with that guilt, no idea how to bear it. We are terrified of being wrong, terrified of admitting our failures, terrified of looking bad. So we pass the buck to everyone else: "It's not my fault; it's the woman's. It's not my fault; it's the snake's." We feel guilt when we sin, and we don't know where to put it. All we know is we can't bear it ourselves, so we pass the blame on to whoever's nearest. Husbands blaming wives, wives blaming their parents, parents blaming culture, culture blaming immigrants, and on and on it goes, an infinite chain of passing the buck.

This is not how it was supposed to be.

❰❱❰❱❱

In response to what they had done, God informs the woman that now "your desire will be for your husband, and he will rule over you" (Genesis 3:16). To the man, God informs him, "Cursed is the ground because of you; through painful toil you will eat food from it all the days of your life" (Genesis 3:17).

Throughout history, some have used this text to say men *should* dominate women. However, note that it's only after sin has entered the world that it says men will try to rule over women. This implies that things were not that way before in the perfect paradise of the garden. Male dominance is not the ideal way things *should* be—it is just how they actually *would be* as the tragic result of the fall.[†] God is not prescribing male dominance here but describing how it will infect everything once sin enters the picture. In

---

[†]While Adam previously recognized Eve as a human woman, he did not actually try to name her Eve (and thereby take ownership over her) until the verses immediately following the fall (Genesis 3:20). Phyllis Trible, *God and the Rhetoric of Sexuality* (Minneapolis: Fortress Press, 1986), chapter 4.

which case, the Bible is actually exposing that male dominance is irrevocably bound up with evil, and misogyny will be the vomit our fallen world constantly returns to. *This is not how it was supposed to be.*

God also says to Adam that it's not only humanity that has been tainted by sin but the earth itself: "Cursed is *the ground* because of you; through painful toil you will eat food from it all the days of your life." Once humans begin our downward cycle, we draw all of creation into our falling vortex. We destroy ecosystems and rob the earth of her resources in order to erect soaring monstrosities such as the Tower of Babel. Communion with creation is replaced by tar, asphalt, plastic fields, manmade fog, black-bleeding oceans, playgrounds of garbage, and skyscrapers so tall and bright we can't see the stars anymore. We ruin the ground until it is almost impossible to farm or till anymore. *This is not how it was supposed to be.*

And while some think the first statement about women is prescribing what *should* happen, it is telling that no one interprets men's painful toil that way. No one says we ought to make the ground more cursed or more difficult to farm. No one thinks we ought to actively prescribe that men's work be more painful than it needs to be. Which means there are two similar and back-to-back statements in verse 16 and 17, which people choose to read in totally opposite ways—it's *prescribing* when it makes women's lives harder and it's *describing* when it makes men's lives easier. Humans often pick and choose the parts of religion we like and selectively interpret away the things we don't. This too is part of the fall.

◖ ▮ ▮ ◗

The Lᴏʀᴅ God banished [them] from the Garden of Eden. . . . Adam made love to his wife Eve, and she became pregnant and gave birth to Cain [and then Abel]. . . . In the course of time Cain brought some of the fruits of the soil as an offering to the Lᴏʀᴅ. And Abel also brought an offering—fat portions from some of the firstborn of his flock. The Lord looked with favor on Abel and his offering, but on Cain and his offering he did not look with favor. So Cain was very angry, and his face was downcast. . . . Now Cain said to his brother Abel, "Let's go out to the field." While they were in the field, Cain attacked his brother Abel and killed him. (Genesis 3:23; 4:1, 3-5, 8)

And so it begins. Humanity has fallen from its former state of goodness, as signified by being cast out of the spiritual ideal of the garden. This is what we call the fall, the second movement of the Christian story. *Fall* is the perfect word not only because it represents a past falling from a former height but because it's easy to visualize us still falling today, tumbling further and further down. Indeed, one sin in the garden snowballs bigger and bigger until the *invention* of murder. Cain kills Abel; blood is in the soil. The tapestry of creation that God called good has been splattered with red. And it just keeps trickling on down. Cain soon has children of his own, and those children have children. Generational sin is passed from parent to child, with each new generation struggling to break the cycle.

Dysfunctional families create children who get married and make their own dysfunctional families. Broken homes become the norm. Children with divorced parents are now twice as likely to drop out of high school and twice as likely to attempt suicide.[2] The vast majority of sexual abuse does not occur in back alleys or at random parties; no, statistically, most sexual abuse now occurs at home with a partner, parent, sibling, or family friend, in the place where we should have felt the most safe.[3] *This is not how it was supposed to be.*

◖▮▮◗

So broken individuals lead to broken families. Put a bunch of broken families together, and you get a broken village. Put some of those villages together, and you get broken cities, countries, empires—humanity multiplying, scattering, expanding across the earth. And, of course, the more humans there are, the scarcer resources and land become, leading to the invention of war. Now we have to fight for what we want. The victors of these conflicts then get to remake society in their own image, placing themselves and those like them at the top. Soon the Egyptians enslave the Jewish race. Egypt builds an entire economy, infrastructure, and social system on top of hunched Jewish backs. Human sin is no longer just *individual* but *social*—flawed human beings create flawed social hierarchies, governments, courts, schools, workplaces, and public services. With sin comes systemic injustice, injustice that isn't just perpetrated by individuals but by entire societies, economies, ideologies, and social systems.

Such as, for example, systemic racism. In, say, America, the average Black household makes $33,000 less per year than the average White household (some studies suggest this wage gap is the same as it was in the 1950s),[4] and have barely 10 percent of their median net worth.[5] One in four Black males will go to prison at some point in his life (some studies say one in three),[6] and receive around 20 percent longer sentences than White people do *for the same crime*.[7] And, insanely, Black people were 50 percent more likely to die of Covid than White people, due to the systemic racism baked into the medical and educational systems.[8] So I as an individual might not be racist. But the *social systems* I participate in, benefit from, and prop up are undeniably, ridiculously, almost comically racist.

This is not how it was supposed to be.

❮❰❰❱

Now, the primary point with all this hasn't really been the details of Adam and Eve and the snake. I mean, the serpent might as well have been a tiger, or a triceratops, or a she-bear, and the point of the story would still be the same (though much, much more awesome). God could have changed their names, and had them be Adam and Margaret or Bill and Betsy. Instead of a garden, God could have made Eden a palace or an island or a mountaintop. Because the details of the story, while they may be true, are not really the main point.

The real point is one that any honest person will recognize: something's off. Earth is cracked, paradise is lost, perfection has been postponed. The ideal and the real are not the same thing—there is a distinction between what *is* and what *ought* to be. The world that God called *good* has devolved into shame, insecurity, murder, abuse, social injustice, and suffering. The humans God made in the divine image have turned their creativity and reason against one another. The good life is something we can't quite reach, something too high for us to attain and from which we've fallen. So, contrary to some bad sermons you might have heard, not everything happens for a reason. The fall is precisely the moment when things stop happening for a reason and start happening because humans are unreasonable. The fall is the spiritual equivalent of the second law of thermodynamics.

The real point of Genesis 3 has to do with what it says about the human condition. We didn't just fall in the Garden of Eden; the Garden of Eden fell in us. For even if Adam and Eve had not fallen, each of us today would still be faced with that same choice they had to make. The fall isn't just something that allegedly happened in our prehistoric past but something that replays itself daily in our hearts. This is the dark truth lurking behind pleasant smiles, perfect-looking families on social media, and almost every book or movie or news story we encounter. As J. R. R. Tolkien said, "All stories are ultimately about the fall."[9] Atheists, priests, poets, politicians, philosophers, scientists, novelists, and environmentalists may all have competing narratives about how to make things right, but we all implicitly assume there's something wrong to begin with. *This is not how it was supposed to be.*

In short, we are *sinners*. There it is, I said it.[‡] You might not like the term, and that's okay; you can use a different one if you want. But I am not entirely sure how we could reject the underlying concept itself. For as soon as we say we're not supposed to use shameful terms such as *sin* anymore because they cause guilt, repression, and self-hatred, we've already granted that something is *not how it's supposed to be.* You can only say we *shouldn't* talk about sin if you've already assumed something isn't how it *should* be. And it is that *should*, that lack, that sense that reality somehow falls short of the ideal, that the Christian story tries to capture with the word *sin*. So perhaps in attempting to articulate the fallen nature of human sin, angry preachers have overdone it at times and only made the world worse. Indeed, Christian history is full of evil Christians doing evil deeds. But at least our story can help us make sense of why they are evil and why humans will

---

[‡]*Wrote it.

inevitably take even the best stories and weaponize them. Humanity is fallen.

Yet it's one thing to see that out there in the world and another thing entirely to see it in yourself. I don't know about you, but I am constantly amazed by all the creative new ways I manage to mess things up. I see my fallenness in my questions feigning concern for others but that are actually fueled by curiosity and gossip. I see it in the face of the older man I mocked last Sunday for not sharing my views. I see it in the girl I cruelly led on for years. I see it in the carefully curated words I spit at my spouse, which I know will hurt her in the moment but which are ambiguous enough for me to defend later on. I see it in the really messed-up deed I almost listed here, and in my chickening out and deleting it at the last moment out of shame.

Now, that doesn't mean I hate myself. I love the goodness and beauty I also see within—those traces of the divine image. I am fallen, yes, but fallen from such great heights. I am goodness tripped off its pedestal, the heights of Vesuvius cast down to the sea, the painted image of God melted and dripping down the cosmic canvas like tears. I am awesomeness gone astray. I am overcooked filet mignon, lobster bisque with too much salt, Michael Jordan playing baseball. Yet recognizing that misplaced awesomeness doesn't negate any of what I said before but only heightens the height from which I fall, while deepening the crater left in the communities I fall upon. In fact, the more good that is within me, the more ghastly it is when I turn it against others—Hitler without great passion and natural talent might have just been the weird conspiracy theorist down the street.

But it's not all bad news. For once we finally face the fallen reality of the human heart beating within, we can then get to the real question: What can be done about it?

MOVEMENT III
Nation

I WAS ENTERING SENIOR YEAR (GRADE TWELVE). Like many on the cusp of adulthood, when I became a man I began to take off my rose-colored glasses. I could see there was a problem in myself and in the world, but I wasn't sure what to do about it. (Though like many young adults, I had a whole lot of fun experimenting with different ways to make myself feel better. Some of them worked better than others, but none of them felt like permanent solutions.) I was learning a lot, trying to work on myself and improve and find the good life. But I kept tripping over my insecurities and proclivities, hurting myself and those I cared about. Everything felt like two steps forward, two steps back—the fall reached too deep within me to climb out. Nonetheless, despite my failings, I couldn't shake the sense that something was astir, as if some force was on the move, preparing me for something more.

A similar feeling hovers over the third movement of our story. From within fallen creation, God plucks out one faithful couple, Abraham and Sarah, and creates an entire Jewish nation out of their descendants. God works on this nation for millennia, instructing them, refining them, healing them of their sins, and raising up what had fallen. They learn and grow, developing bold ideas, laws, and practices that are still relevant today. Yet everything is two steps forward, two steps back, with the nation being faithful one day then committing adultery, murder, and sacrilege the next. We have the sense that something important is being slowly unveiled, and God is building to something—but to what?

CREATION

Creation Begins ●

Creation Is Not God ●

Creation Is Good ●

FALL

Humanity In God's Image ●

Humanity Gone Wild ●

NATION

Abraham Finds Faith ● 2000 BC

Moses Meets I Am ● 1400–1200ish BC

Goodness Is Commanded ●

Beauty in the Promised Land ●

King David and His Boy ● 1000ish BC

Justice Exiles the Nation ● 586 BC

REDEMPTION

Jesus Is Born ● AD 0

Jesus is Walking Around Saying Stuff ● AD 30

Jesus Is Dying to Meet You ● AD 33

CHURCH

The Spirit Arrives ● AD 33

The Church Begins ● AD 33

The Apostle Paul Converts ● AD 35ish

The Church Expands ● AD 300ish

The Church Today ● The Present

END

The End of the World as We Know It ●

Highway to Hell or Stairway to Heaven? ●

SIX

Abraham finds faith

"ABRAHAM!" A VOICE BOOMED IN THE BLACK, jolting old-man Abraham awake. He glanced every which way in the desert for the source of the sound, yet it seemed to come from everywhere.

"Abraham!" it tolled again. Abraham's heart now caught on faster than his head, transfixed by a speech more akin to song, which no mortal throat could utter or contain. Such notes could only roll off the tongue of the gods.

"Abraham!" the divine voice continued, trembling the desert floor like dust on a drum. "Abraham, I will make you into a great nation! All peoples on earth will be blessed through you. To your offspring I will give the Promised Land of Canaan. Your offspring will be as numerous as the sand on the seashore and the stars in the sky."

That night God promised Abraham a land of his own and that his descendants would become as numerous as the sand and the stars, with enough of them to create a whole nation to live in this Promised Land. There was just one problem. Abraham and his wife, Sarah, were nearly a hundred years old and didn't have any children.

When Sarah heard about Abraham's vision and that her ancient, barren womb would bear a whole nation, she laughed. Laughed because it was too good to be true; laughed, for she had longed for a child longer than many of us have been alive; laughed because there was so much pain and disappointment there that she couldn't let herself hope again; laughed because she didn't have faith that God could or would do it.

Yet soon she felt sickness as if at sea, and her stomach stretched like a sail in too much wind. Months of pregnancy and cramps followed, walking around in the desert heat, aching everywhere, sweat in crevices she didn't used to have. The wrinkles of her aged belly disappearing as it filled and stretched tight to the point of popping.

After months of cramps and aches and worry and prayer and blood and sweat and tears, finally—*finally!*—the day came. Everyone outside the tent was hugging and kissing and rejoicing. Sarah and Abraham just sat there, holding their little miracle, holding what they never thought they would hold. They named their son Isaac, which means "laughter." For while she once laughed in mockery, now Sarah smiled and laughed with joy, for God had come through faithfully with what was promised. She held baby Isaac for as long and as tight as she could. But you can't hold on to them forever. . . .

◄ ▬ ▬ ►

"Abraham, Abraham!" God thundered.

"Here I am, Lord!" Abraham stammered. It had been a decade or more since God last spoke to Abraham, but that booming intonation was hard to forget.

"Abraham!" God continued. "Take your son, your one and only son, whom you love, and go to the region of Moriah. Sacrifice him there on the mountain."

I doubt Abraham slept the rest of the night. That's the sort of night where you stare at the ceiling without even pretending to close your eyes. Where your mind plays out a million possibilities, as if retelling the coming tale would give you control over it. Where you get up and pace outside in desperate, pleading, inane agony. Where you knock yourself out so you don't have to be awake anymore. Where you come face to face with yourself and everything you've ever believed or thought you believed.

But whatever doubts or disgust he felt, come morning, Abraham got up, loaded his donkey, and made preparations for their journey to the mountain. Sarah probably came out and asked, "What's going on, Abraham?" The Bible doesn't say what Abraham told his wife, but I can't imagine him answering her honestly.

For three endless days and nights Abraham and Isaac journeyed to Moriah. Then up they went to the top of the mountain. With every step closer to the heavens, Abraham was sinking further into his own personal hell. His son Isaac was probably making small talk, wondering what was going on, why was his father acting so weird? Just imagine it:

"Nice night tonight, Father," Isaac might say.

"Yes," Abraham might reply, dead inside.

"Lots of stars out, Father."

"Yes."

"Want to count them with me?"

"No."

"As many as our offspring will be someday, according to God's promise."

Abraham just looked down in silence.

They finally reached the top of the mountain, where the damnable deed had to be done. Abraham reached his arthritic hand back into his robes, fumbling about, then twitching forth a knife. The morning continued on in the background, birds chirping, insects humming, bees buzzing, nature indifferent to the horror about to be unleashed in its presence. Abraham lifted up the blade, his breath drawing so deep into his belly he feared he'd never exhale again. Limbs quivering like palm trees in a hurricane, terrified of the moment the blade finally reached the highest threshold, ready to be brought crashing back down . . .

"Abraham!!!"

Just like all the other times, a voice from heaven shook the earth.

"H-h-here I am," Abraham sputtered through tears.

"Abraham!" God said. "Do not lay a hand on the boy. Do not do anything to him. Now I know you fear and faithfully trust God, because you have not withheld from me your son, your only son. Because you have done this, I will surely bless you and make your descendants as numerous as the stars in the sky and as the sand on the seashore. Your descendants will take possession of the Promised Land, and through your offspring all nations on earth will be blessed." And so, for his faith, Abraham became the father of the whole Jewish nation.

While our first few chapters were more topical, the rest of this book will be driven largely by the story of Abraham's descendants and the impact they would go on to have on the world. For from Abraham's offspring would come the entire bloodline of the Jewish people. His son Isaac would beget Jacob and Esau. Jacob would beget twelve sons. Those twelve sons would become the twelve tribes of Israel. Those tribes would move to Egypt, become enslaved, and then be freed by Moses, moving to Israel and becoming the Jewish nation of David, Solomon, and, eventually, a Jewish carpenter named Jesus. It is from this nation of Abraham's offspring that all Jews today claim to be descended. As the kids' song goes: "Father Abraham had many sons, and many sons had Father Abraham." Because he had faith, Abraham became the father of the whole Jewish nation and the father of the Jewish *faith*.

❮❯

Yet what is faith? Does it regularly require child sacrifice, or is that more of a once-a-year type of thing? How did Abraham's having faith make him worthy to be the father of the whole Jewish faith? I mean, if a father tries to kill their child, we don't generally promote them to father of the whole country.

Now, the stereotypical definition of faith has often been (1) blind faith.* On this view, Abraham's story was not rational. Abraham's story was not ethical. If it had been rational and ethical, then it would have made sense to Abraham, and it would not have been faith. Blind faith means that Abraham was trusting in God, not in his own understanding of what is good or what made sense. If faith hadn't required him to fundamentally go against his own rational and ethical understanding, then he'd just be doing what he already would have done on his own. He would have had respite in what made sense to him already and not have needed to go beyond himself to trust another.

---

*The term *blind faith* is a bit ableist. But I'll leave it to proponents of this position to better articulate themselves.

Not everything can fit inside the human mind. If God is supposed to be this infinite, eternal, transcendent, almighty being, then how could we ever expect to fully understand the divine plan? If God is more than a projection of ourselves, then of course God will say and do and request things that we would never expect or understand or do of our own accord. Of course, God will tell us to slaughter our kids once in a while on a Middle Eastern mountaintop then hilariously back out at the very last second for kicks.

On this view, true religion requires setting aside faith in your own basic understanding. And as a parent myself, I can tell you that there is nothing more basic to my mentality than protecting my kids. Nothing would test my faith more than getting a call saying my sons were missing. Nothing would shake my surety or dis-orbit my universe more. Nothing would bring me closer to burning down the whole world to try and find them. Nothing could be a deeper test of faith than that, for there is no deeper need or stability or comfort within me than the well-being of my kids. Faith requires us to go beyond ourselves, and there is nothing more basic to my very self than my desperate, obsessive, all-in, unrequited anxiety for my children.

Faith requires a leap, a transfer of personal momentum up and away from solid ground in order to ambiguously hover midair, not knowing whether safe landing or a plummeting pit awaits, trusting only in a voice from the other side telling you it is going to be okay. Abraham is the father of the Jewish faith because he went beyond himself and his own understanding and actually had faith in another.

Yet . . . if something has no evidence and makes no sense, why believe in it? Why not have faith in anything at that point? Why not believe in the flying spaghetti monster or trust in Charles Manson? Why not believe that vaccines gave your mom syphilis, or that Elvis is still alive, or that Elvis gave your mom syphilis? Once you go beyond your own rational and moral sense of the world, why not believe anything and anyone? And why would the divine *logos* give us reason if we weren't supposed to use it? Which is why many religious people reject blind faith, striving instead for (2) rational faith.

Some of the world's most brilliant thinkers, including Oxford professor of philosophy Richard Swinburne, have argued that a reasonable case can be made for the existence of God on the basis of evidence alone. For example, we talked earlier about the scientific evidence for the complexity of the universe, with the odds of its happening by chance being one part out of ten with a comically large army of zeros marching behind it.

Proponents of such a rational faith find themselves having to argue that Abraham's actions were not irrational. They claim these actions made sense (at least to Abraham) and so do not constitute blind faith. Here's how they might try to argue that.

First of all, the Bible says that Abraham believed God had the power to bring his son back to life (Hebrews 11:19). The same faith he had in *doing* the act made him believe God could *undo* it. Now, you might not like nor agree with that rationalization. But the fact that Abraham made it shows that Abraham's actions were not completely blind, at least from his perspective.

Second, the gods asking for a human sacrifice was fairly standard in the ancient world. Within Abraham's cultural expectations, this was not an unusual request out of nowhere. This was just what the gods did, and it would have seemed only logical to stay on the good side of the gods by submitting to their requests. While that might seem irrational from our modern perspective, back then it would have seemed par for the course. It would have culturally *made sense* to Abraham. Likewise, everyone at my American university would be appalled if I came to work naked, but it would make complete sense if I were a member of the Scottish Picts during the late Iron Age (who famously went naked into battle with the Romans; sadly, it was a flop).

In fact, the part of the story that would have made the *least sense* within its ancient context was when God stopped the sacrifice. For there are many ancient tales where the gods devour their sacrifices, but few if any tales where they cry out to prevent it. When this story was first told, the part that would have shocked the ancient audience was that God *didn't* go through with the sacrifice, not that Abraham almost did.

Likewise, imagine if a story were told in imperial China of a girl about to begin the painful foot-binding process but whose family intervened at the last second to stop it. Within our Western context today, we might be appalled that the family ever let it get that far. But within the story's original context—where feet were broken and bound every day—what would stand out about the story was that they *didn't* go through with it. It would be clear that this story was actually told as a rebuke to those who bound their children's feet. As such, the point of the story is not that Abraham's God is immoral or irrational but that he is actually far more moral and rational than these other gods who devour their unquestioning followers. It's important to understand what a story's trying to communicate within its original context before we try to figure out what it might have to say to us today. And within its original context, it would have made a lot of sense (and actually would have provided a strong critique of human sacrifice).

Once we do our homework and study how ancient people thought, Abraham's actions seem a bit more rational. Yet should faith really require cultural analysis and rationalizations and thinking things through to this insane degree? Is this really what faith means for little old church ladies, or for people with cancer who feel the presence of God comforting them in the x-ray machine? Indeed, for most people, faith is not blind, but neither is it the product of a deeply rational argument. For many, faith is (3) experiential.

As a young child, I did not understand why I shouldn't stick my finger in the electrical outlets. I did not have a reasoned-out, philosophical argument against it, nor a scientific grasp of electricity. What I did have was my mom's voice in the back of my head, saying, "Honey, stay away from there." What I had was a personal experience of my mother, which taught me that she wanted what was best for me. For when I hadn't listened to her in the past, my hand got burned on the stove and a cyclist ran over me when I was on the wrong side of the pathway. I had personal experience of my mother as trustworthy, and those experiences were the basis for my taking her word when it came to the electrical socket. So while I didn't have a fully articulated set of arguments against sticking my finger in the electrical socket, my faith in my mother was not entirely blind either. It was based on *personal experience.*

Likewise, Abraham might not have had rigorously rational arguments for God. But neither was his faith entirely blind. God had previously told

Abraham his wife would give birth even though she was well past the age of natural conception, and God had come through on that promise. So Abraham knew from personal experience that God was trustworthy. While he may not have rationally understood why he was taking Isaac up the mountain, he knew that God had promised that a great nation would be descended from Isaac, so he chose to trust that God would somehow come through in the end.

This kind of personal experience is not an absence of evidence. Rather, it is allowing for a different type of evidence, allowing for an expansion of what we mean by *evidence*. Even if you can't put God in a test tube or prove the existence of God using arguments, if God showed up one day, shook the ground, and spoke audibly too you, that would seem like a pretty good basis on which to believe. Many atheists would happily admit that if they had that kind of experience, then belief in God would be justified. They just haven't had that kind of experience. In fact, some atheists experience the world as actively *not* having a higher purpose, sensing that there is no one up there looking out for them. That personal experience doesn't disprove God's existence once and for all, but it certainly should (and does) make God less likely in their estimation. And the same is true in reverse. If I have a personal sense of God's presence, that might not prove once and for all that God is real, but it certainly makes it more likely than if I didn't have that experience.

Personal experience is what we actually base most of our life choices on. Most of us aren't consulting science textbooks or rigorous arguments or statistics for every decision we make as we go about our day. Yet neither are we totally blind in our decisions. We trust that our personal experience is accurate enough for us to get by most of the time. To throw out personal experience altogether would be to throw out your primary access to reality. If you couldn't trust your personal experience, you couldn't trust anything (including more traditional forms of evidence, because your knowledge of the facts is always mediated through your personal experience of it. You don't know what experts think; you only know what *you* think they think through *your* interpretation of what *you've* heard them say).

So even if you haven't had some miraculous encounter like Abraham did, your simple sense of God's presence might be a form of personal, experiential evidence. It might not be scientifically provable or an argument you could use with someone who hadn't had that same experience.[†] Yet, at least for you, it should still provide some form of experiential evidence that God is there. When Lucy returned from the wardrobe and the magical land of Narnia, it may not have been rational for her siblings to believe a word from her lips, but it was certainly rational for her to believe her own eyes. She knew what she'd seen, even if no one else did.

Indeed, many religious people have experienced a sense of something higher or divine. Perhaps it's a subtle, ineffable sense you've always had that you are not alone, that someone is watching out for you, that when you stare out at the starry heavens, some cosmic eye is twinkling back and you are not only seeing but seen. Perhaps it's strolling through the countryside feeling gratitude for the goodness of creation, then looking around for someone to thank. Perhaps it's something within you that still longs for God, like songbirds following their instincts home for winter. Perhaps it's looking in another's soulish eyes and seeing more than material flesh, meat, and bone—a glimmer of the divine image. Or perhaps God literally spoke to you, like God spoke to Abraham.

So blind faith is a leap in the dark, like breaking into a pool at night and jumping off the diving board before you've checked whether the water has been drained. Rational faith is jumping in the daylight after twice measuring the distance of the diving board to the pool below. Experiential faith is not being fully convinced you'll survive, yet jumping nonetheless because you trust your mother's voice down below, cheering, "It'll be fine, honey. You've got this!"

Faith need not be blind. Yet perhaps we should let blind faith get in one final word. I've argued that faith can be raised from the level of blindness

---

[†]Note that even science can only give you high probability, not certainty or proof. Even something as "certain" as Newtonian mechanics was later overturned by Einstein.

to the level of reason and experience. Yet there is another tack that can be taken here, which is to lower reason and experience to the level of blind faith. Let me explain what I mean with an old riddle I heard once.

Once upon a time, Baron Münchhausen got stuck in a swamp, reasoning to himself: "Anything I could grab hold of to pull myself out of this swamp would either be supported by something else, by itself, or by nothing.

"Now, if I grab onto a vine or branch that is supported by something else, then that something else would itself have to be supported by something else. And whatever supported that would also need to rest on something else, and so on into infinity, and I'll never actually hit rock bottom and find something solid by which to pull myself out of this swamp."

"But," Münchhausen exclaimed, "if I take option two, if I grab onto something that's supported by itself, that can't help me either, for it is circular, like trying to pull myself out of the swamp by my own hair. Like pulling myself up by my own bootstraps!"

"But," he said again, "if I grab onto something that is supported by nothing, then it will fall out from under me, and I'll get nowhere. So, neither anything supported by something else, nor anything supported by itself, nor anything supported by nothing can get me out of this swamp. I might as well settle down to die."

As a survival manual, Baron Münchhausen's story is not very helpful. But as a parable about the nature of faith and evidence, it is telling indeed. For, you see, any belief must also be justified based on (1) something else, based on (2) itself, or based on (3) nothing.

If a belief is justified based on the evidence of something else, then that something else must also be justified based on something else, and it just keeps going further back, without ever hitting rock bottom or finding a solid basis for one's belief. How do I know the baker murdered the carpenter? Because the farmer told me. How does the farmer know? Because the fisherman told her. How did the fisherman know? Because the sailor told him. But how did the sailor know? And it never ends. *This is true because this is true because this is true. . . .*

Yet if a belief is justified based on itself, then it is circular. Like saying the Bible is true because the Bible says so. Or Kim Jong Il is God because Kim Jong Il says so. Or J. D. Lyonhart is a handsome devil because everyone everywhere thinks so, and I know everyone everywhere thinks so because it says so in his book, *The Journey of God.*

However, if a belief is justified based on nothing at all, then there is no reason to believe in it. Why do I believe? Well, because *I just do.*

So how do we get out of the intellectual swamp, if every belief is either supported by something else, by itself, or by nothing? For every truth claim someone makes, you can always ask, "How do you know that?" Whatever they say, you can respond, "Well how do you know *that?*" And it can just keep going on and on, until they admit that they can't go any further, they have no more reasons, they believe it because *they just do.* This is one of the reasons the constant queries of little children can be so frustrating. For if one asks, "Why!? Why!? Why!?" long enough, eventually you will get to a point where you no longer can explain why you believe anything at all. It's not that children are too stupid to understand the answer; it's that adults are too stupid to keep asking questions.

Every worldview has to start from a set of assumptions that cannot be proven, because if they could be proven, whatever you used to prove it would itself be your starting assumption, and the problem would just be pushed further back. So there are a number of things that we cannot prove or even make probable but we just sort of accept.

For example, we cannot prove that the human mind is rational. Any argument we would make that we are rational already assumes we're rational enough to make the argument. And if we weren't rational, how would we know? Do insane people know they're insane?

We also can't prove the external world exists. Any physical evidence you'd use to prove the physical world exists already presupposes precisely what you are trying to prove. How do I know my hand is real? *Well, because it stings when I slap myself in the face.* But how do I know my face is real? I can also feel pain in a dream, but that doesn't mean the dream is real—what if all of life is a lullaby?

Many philosophers have also argued there's no way to prove cause and effect are real. Anything that would cause us to believe in cause and effect would already assume that cause and effect were real, such that they could *cause* us to believe in it. What is more, the sciences test what is repeatable, because they assume that what happens in the past will continue to happen in the future. But how do we know that what happens in the past will continue to happen in the future? Well, because *that's what's happened in the past*. How do we know the sun will rise tomorrow? Because that's what it's done in the past. But how do we know that what things do in the past is what they will do in the future? *Because that's what's happened in the past.* And so the scientific method itself is ultimately circular (and whatever you say in response, I'll just ask how you know that's true, and the problem will restart all over again).

Despite this, we still go on living and acting as if our beliefs are really true. Because at some point, you have to stop questioning and accept some things on faith. There are dozens of things we believe because *we just do*, and there's no deeper argument or evidence to support it; we just have this strong sense that that is simply how things are at the end of the day. It's this strong sense that's probably been making you annoyed with me as you've read along, because while you might not know how to reject my argument, deep down you *just know* that the physical world and human reason and causality are real and that I'm stupid for questioning them.

And if some things can be believed without evidence because we *just know* that's the way things are, why can't the divine be one of those starting things? Indeed, leading philosopher Alvin Plantinga at the University of Notre Dame argues that even if we could prove the existence of God, whatever we used to prove it would itself need to be proved, and then whatever we used to prove the proof would itself need to be proved, and so on and so forth, and it would never end.[1] So perhaps the spiritual outlook is not something that needs to be proven but is one of the assumptions you start with in order to then prove other things. The vast majority of humans throughout history have believed in some sort of spiritual beings or divine presence, so perhaps it's one of those starting assumptions that we as a species seem almost hardwired to embrace. Now, that spiritual sense might not get you all the way to a specific religion, but perhaps it can get you started with the general idea of God. For everyone, like Münchhausen, has to start somewhere.

So, a purely rational or evidential worldview is not even possible, because whatever you use to argue for something would itself need to be argued for, and you'd end up back in the swamp. As such, our worldviews are never just one of the options, never just blind or just rational or just experiential. People aren't compartmentalized that cleanly. We all mix and match and combine elements of all three options in our daily lives.

Spirituality is not much different. Some days I'm rationally convinced that God probably exists; other days I am racked with doubt. Some days my experience of God is strong. Other days I have no sense of God's presence, and it feels odd and insane and ridiculous that other people think they do. Some days my reason and experience are fired up at the same time, with God meeting and overflowing the measures of both my mind and my heart. Other days, neither the confidence of reason nor the comfort of experience is present, and I leap into an existential void with nothing to cling to, choosing to faithfully continue in prayer and service and hope, despite everything. I imagine Abraham would sympathize.

SEVEN

Moses Meets I Am

ABRAHAM SIRED ISAAC and then casually tried to murder him. Isaac couldn't wait to have that same father-son dynamic with his own kids, begetting Jacob and Esau. Jacob went on to beget twelve sons during a time of great famine, moving away from the Promised Land of Abraham to seek refuge in the fruitful abundance of the Nile River in Egypt.

Their descendants lived in Egypt for hundreds of years, multiplying and becoming as numerous as the sand on the seashore, just like God had promised their forefather Abraham. Yet as Abraham's descendants (called Hebrews at the time, though to make it easy on you I'll use the more recent term, *Jews*) became more numerous, the local Egyptians began to feel threatened by them. Their numbers were making them a rival nation within the nation, who might one day challenge Pharoah for power. So Pharoah got proactive, enslaving them all to work on his pyramids and building projects. Jewish blood oiled the levers and pullies that raised Egyptian stone to the sky.

Despite their chains, Abraham's descendants multiplied all the more, having children in slave camps throughout the land. And to the reigning Pharoah, the pitter-patter of little Jewish feet sounded a lot like the marching of future revolutionaries. So he murdered them. Pharoah ordered all newborn Jewish boys be thrown into the Nile River.

In desperation, one Jewish mother fled to the last place anyone would expect to find her. The gates were blocked and the streets full of soldiers, making the Nile the only escape from the city as well as the very thing she was trying to escape from. The river mouth swelled with the mucus of death, yet she chose to flow with the coming tide rather than against it. She placed her baby boy in a basket and released him into the surf to seek harbor somewhere, *anywhere*, else.

This little bundle rose and dipped through swells and rapids, perhaps even escaping the odd crocodile mouth. He stared up in wonder at over-hanging statues of river gods Hapi and Khnum and drifted by riverside tributes to the crocodile god Sobek and to Osiris, god of floods. Whatever his journey, the little lad eventually found himself lazing right into the royal palace, scooped up by Pharoah's own daughter as she bathed in the river. She took pity on the weeping bundle, adopting him as her own and naming him Moses (for he moseyed into her arms).[*]

Growing up in the royal Egyptian household, little Moses had every-thing. It would have been easy to forget all about his origins, and even easier to forget the ongoing plight of his fellow Jews. But you can't run from who you are forever. . . .

◄ ■ ■ ►

Decades later, a now fully grown Moses was surveying Pharoah's latest building project when he saw a guard lashing a Jewish slave. The guard was pounding this poor old Jew to bits. Skin and cloth peeled off his hunched back like old paint. Moses lunged forward, striking the guard over and over. Before he even fully realized what he was doing, the guard lay silent in the sand. Blood dripped down his hands and legs, settling between his toes.

I imagine you might also be willing to kill for your people. And in doing this, Moses was indeed admitting they were *his people*. Through royal powder and an Egyptian wig peered eyes like father Abraham's. Decades of palace lessons and the lore of Osiris had not drowned out the memory of his mother singing him slave songs and Jewish lullabies.

Word spread quickly of what Moses had done, and so he fled into the desert, glancing back to look at his former home in the distance, watching

---

[*] I really want this to be the actual etymology of the name and so have decided to be the change I want to see in the world.

as the pyramids dipped beneath the horizon like voyaging masts. Weeks of hardened sun and sand awaited him as he moseyed toward the faraway land of Midian, a safe enough distance from the arm of Egypt and the eye of Pharoah.

In Midian, Moses took a wife, raised a family, and started shepherding sheep to support them. His days were filled with fields, wool, and wolves, while nights belonged to shrieking, singing, boisterous children and the mother who bore them. For forty years, that was Moses' life. For forty years, no one would have known whom he once was, nor whom he'd soon become.

❮ ▬ ▬ ❯

One day, Moses was out leading his flock on the far side of Mount Horeb when he nearly stumbled into a fire. Usually he would have seen billows of smoke or sniffed burning wood at a distance, yet this flame snuck up on him. Somehow it burned without consuming the bush, like an eternal flame.

"Mooosssses! Moosssses!" a voice suddenly bellowed with the wind, or perhaps gave shape to the wind itself.

Moses trembled backward in surprise before managing to stutter, "H-here I am!"

"Mosessss! I am the God of your ancestors, the God of Abraham," the voice bellowed. Moses buried his face in the dirt, somewhat in submission but mostly in terror. The celestial speech thundered on: "I have come to rescue my people and bring them up into the Promised Land flowing with milk and honey. I am sending you! Go to Pharoah and free my people."

Despite how terrified Moses was, perhaps some part of him was still used to how things worked in Egypt. The Egyptians had many gods to choose from, such as Horus, Osiris, Isis, Anubis, Set, Ra, Amun, and Amun-Ra, to name a few. And so, in confusion, Moses dared respond: "What if I go to them and say God has sent me, and they ask: 'Which one? What is his name?' What shall I tell them your name is?"

To this, the voice roared, "I am."

❮ ▬ ▬ ❯

"I am"? What in God's name does that mean? Scholars disagree. Is it just God's way of saying, "Hey, I exist. I am real. *Notice me!*" Is it God's way of saying I am present, near, and close to you? Or is it God's way of avoiding the question altogether?

Notice, though, that Moses' question already assumed something. Moses asked, Who *is* it? What *is* your name? But that already assumes one knows what the meaning of *is* is. But what is *is-ness*? What does it mean *to exist*— to be something that *is* rather than *isn't*?

What is the capital-B source of *Being* from which all lowercase beings derive their existence? If the gods are just other beings that exist, then they must derive their existence from something else, and that source would be the true God, wouldn't it? Think about Zeus. Zeus is supposed to be the mightiest of the Greek gods. And yet, there was a time when even he didn't exist, a time before he was created. Zeus was the child of Cronus, and Cronus was the son of Uranus, and Uranus emerged from chaos. Zeus is not the source of all Being; no, he is just another particular being like you and me, only stronger. Zeus is a creature—a created being. Zeus is only a god to us, in the same way that a human might seem like a god to an ant. Zeus is merely the strongest being among other beings. But he is not Being itself.

Or consider the Egyptian god Ra (or Amun-Ra). In some accounts, Ra created heaven, earth, and the underworld. And yet Ra himself was the child of his mother, Neith. Ra is not the source of all Being; no, he is just another particular being like you and me (only way stronger and with a falcon's head). Or think about the Norse gods. Loki killed Heimdall. All-seeing Odin was devoured by a giant wolf. Even mighty Thor eventually succumbed to snake poison. All of them were created, and all of them perished. Being was lent to them for a time, then relinquished at Ragnarök.

But the Jewish God is not like that. That day in the desert with the eternal flame, Moses dared to ask God which *being* God was, and God replied that he was *Being itself*. God replied that he was not just another being that happens to exist; no, *he was existence itself*. Who God is, is the one *who is*. God is the one from whom all other beings derive their Being. A particular being may or may not exist—may be born one day and die the next—but Being itself is ever present. Who are you, Lord? "I am."

Other religions debate whose tribal God killed whose tribal God in some ancient, mythical war of heaven. Yet the true God cannot be born or killed. The true God is not another being coming in and out of existence but the source of all Being, from whom other flickering things first derived their existence. The true God is not another powerful being within nature but the supernatural source of nature itself. What other religions worship as gods would only be angels or demons in the Jewish worldview—powerful yet ultimately *created* beings (and so they cannot be the Creator itself).

Many religions debate whether God reigns from Mount Olympus, or from the underworld, or from Asgard, or from a temple throne. But if God exists, he is not *a being* on top of a mountain but must be Being itself, the one who sustains the very existence of the mountain, along with the valley below, the earth beside, and the abyss beyond.

Other religions debate whether the God of thunder or the God of the river is stronger, whether God has a sword or a bow, whether God was born from fire or from the sea. *But those questions aren't that interesting!* For even if one of those gods did happen to exist, that would be neat, but it wouldn't tell us much more about the universe than the discovery of a new species would tell us. Because that's all these gods would be—a powerful new species. A created class of super creatures, but *creatures* nonetheless. It would be like discovering dragons or Bigfoot or fairies; super cool, but not metaphysically significant. It would be somewhat similar to when we first discovered dinosaurs or the megalodon shark. Even the god's superpowers wouldn't shock us once we got used to them—just like when we discovered that bats use sonar, tardigrades can survive in space, turtles live for hundreds of years, dogs know when you have cancer, elephants know when something bad is about to happen, and a mother's adrenaline can lift a car.

Many religions debate which of the gods is top dog.[†] But God is not simply the strongest creature among other creatures. God cannot just be

---

[†]There are significant and fascinating exceptions to this, such as some Hindu conceptions of Brahman.

one step higher than the next most powerful being on the food chain; no, the true God must be the one who created the chain and sustains the existence of every one of its links. The true God is not just Hulk in comparison to Hawkeye, not just Zeus in comparison to Apollo, not just Michael Jordan in comparison to Larry Bird, not just ten power points stronger than the next strongest contender. The true God is not at the upper end of a continuum with other created beings; no, the true God made the continuum and everything in it. The true God is eternity when everything else is in time. The true God is infinity when everything else is finite. The true God is the Creator while everything else is its creation. The true God is not the highest link in the food chain; no, the true God is off the frickin' chain. God existed before the chain, shook the chain into being, and rattled its highest members into existence when they were but wee babes terrified by the clatter.

God is not the highest being amongst other beings but is Being itself. God is not just the most powerful creature among other creatures but is the ultimate Creator, here before the land and sky and stars, before even time itself. Moses asked, "Who are you?" And God boomed back, "I am."

〈 ▣ ▣ 〉

And so Moses went back to Egypt and told the Jews that "I am" had sent him, demanding Pharoah let his people go. And of course, Pharoah said no. Which is when things got really interesting.

I am brought a plague on the Egyptians; God turned the Nile into blood. It was like liquid rust, with fish suffocating on the thickened fluid and rendering the air rancid with death. Yet this plague wasn't just to be cool and show off God's power. No, this was judgment on Hapi, the Egyptian god of the Nile. This plague showed that I am was stronger than the random gods who may or may not exist—stronger than the river gods.

But Pharoah still refused to let the Jews go, and so came a second plague of frogs. You couldn't step anywhere without cracking frog legs or hear anything over the constant, infernal ribbiting. This was judgment on the Egyptian goddess Heket, who had the head of a frog. Then a third plague came, and the dust was turned into lice, in judgment of Geb, the Egyptian god over the dust of the earth. Lice wriggled between people's toes and blew through their hair and made the sand dunes in every direction seem alive and teeming. Then came a fourth plague of flies, in judgment of the fly god, Khepri. And at least those flies ate up the dead frogs.

Then a fifth plague came, killing all the livestock. This was judgment over Hathor, who had the head of a cow. Overnight the means of production had been turned upside down, and the slave without a goat suddenly found himself the equal of the rich man who formerly had hundreds. Then a sixth plague of boils and sores arrived, in judgment of Isis, the god of medicine. A seventh and an eighth plague soon came, of fiery hail and locusts from above, in judgment of Nut and Seth, gods of the sky. Then came the plagues of darkness and against the male heir, the former in judgment of the sun god, Ra.[‡]

Each plague was a judgment over one of the Egyptians gods. These gods were but particular beings, ruling over one particular thing or another. One being ruled over the Nile, another being ruled over the frogs. But the Jewish God is Being itself, and so his domain is over all things that *are*.

The Egyptians had many gods, as did most nations on earth. There were as many gods as there were rivers, activities, animals, towns, and temples. And it's not like all the other gods were wrong, and ours just happens to be right. No, it's that their claims weren't even really about God to begin with. They kept talking about creatures—powerful creatures but creatures nonetheless. Created beings who began to exist, just like everything else.

Moses invites you to stop thinking of God as a created superhero. To stop thinking of God as some bearded mega-human writ large, with wings and bulging muscles. To stop thinking of the Creator as just the strongest creature among other creatures. To stop asking which of the gods is real, and start asking what the meaning of *is* is. To stop looking at the clouds to see which of the gods is hiding up there and to start looking at the God who is the source of everything everywhere. To stop debating which gods may or not be and bow before the one who is Being itself, I am.

[‡] The plague against male heirs was not aimed at children; the firstborn was simply the male who had inherited generational wealth, whether he was fifteen, forty, or seventy. Judgment on the firstborn male, as the inheritor of wealth and the spiritual head of the ancient home, likely symbolized judgment on the entire Egyptian economy, culture, and religion.

CREATION

Creation Begins ●
Creation Is Not God ●
Creation Is Good ●

FALL

Humanity in God's Image ●
Humanity Gone Wild ●

NATION

Abraham Finds Faith ● 2000 BC
Moses Meets I Aᴍ ● 1400–1200ish BC
Goodness Is Commanded ●
Beauty in the Promised Land ●
King David and His Boy ● 1000ish BC
Justice Exiles the Nation ● 586 BC

REDEMPTION

Jesus Is Born ● AD 0
Jesus Is Walking Around Saying Stuff ● AD 30
Jesus Is Dying to Meet You ● AD 33

CHURCH

The Spirit Arrives ● AD 33
The Church Begins ● AD 33
The Apostle Paul Converts ● AD 35ish
The Church Expands ● AD 300ish
The Church Today ● The Present

END

The End of the World as We Know It ●
Highway to Hell or Stairway to Heaven? ●

EIGHT

Goodness Is Commanded

FREE AT LAST! Thousands of Jewish families, carts, donkeys, and cows stream out of Egypt in droves, cross the Red Sea in dramatic style, then head for the Promised Land—the land promised to their ancestor, Abraham. Yet before they can get to their destination, they first need to make a pit stop. Marching through the desert, they see something rise like a sail on the horizon. The sloping summit of Mount Sinai grows ever nearer, stretching through the clouds to nearly eight thousand feet. Arriving, the people make base camp down below while Moses begins the long hike up above, barely taking a moment's rest. When Moses eventually reaches the top, God reaches down, booming out:

I AM the LORD your God, who brought you out of slavery in Egypt. . . .

Thou shalt have no other gods before me.

Thou shalt make no graven image. . . .

Thou shalt not take the Lord's name in vain. . . .

Thou shalt remember the Sabbath day. . . .

Thou shalt honor thy mother and father. . . .

Thou shalt not murder.

Thou shalt not commit adultery.

Thou shalt not steal.

Thou shalt not lie.

Thou shalt not envy.[1]

Moses has been to the mountain top—God has given humanity ten commandments carved in stone. These laws help reign in some of the more sinful of their fallen human impulses, shaping the Jewish nation for millennia, and eventually becoming part of the building blocks of Western morality and legal thought to this day. And yet, when it comes to, say, *not murdering*, we may rightly wonder whether humanity might have figured some of this out on our own. Was murder really all the rage before Moses went mountain climbing? Do we need God in order to be good?

〈 ▄ ▄ 〉

Do you prefer chocolate or vanilla ice cream?

Do you prefer coffee or tea?

Do you prefer morning or evening?

Do you think showing cleavage is immodest?

Do you think showing some ankle is immodest?

Do you think eating beef is wrong?

Do you think eating dogs is wrong?

Do you think torturing puppies for sport is bad?

Do you think love is good?

Do you think cold-blooded murder is bad?

Do you think slavery is bad?

Do you think there's a difference between the type of questions I first asked and the questions I'm asking now?

What is the difference?

Well, here's my final question, which we will explore throughout this chapter in more depth: Is morality *subjective* or *objective*?

Take ice cream, for example. What is the best ice cream flavor? Chocolate? Vanilla? Dairy-free salted caramel? Now, all of those answers are equally valid; there is no one right answer to that question. It's *subjective*. Some people like one flavor, other people like another. It changes from person to person, and even from one stage of life to the next (my favorite flavor used to be mint chocolate chip; it's now rum raisin). It's just a matter of personal taste. It's subjective—relative to the preferences of individual human *subjects* or persons or groups or times.

But what about morality? Is morality subjective or objective?* For example, modesty differs somewhat from culture to culture. One culture says most of your skin should be covered and that letting a little ankle slip out is quite scandalous. Another culture says you can show your legs and arms but not any cleavage. Another culture has men and women walking around bare-breasted, and no one blinks an eye. So, to some extent, modesty and mores are subjective, right? They are relative to an individual human *subject*: to a specific person, or time, or place, or culture.

But what about, say, slavery? Is slavery objectively right or wrong, or is that just a matter of personal taste and changing cultural values? Is stealing someone from their homeland, clasping them in chains, shipping them across the ocean in a matchbox of their own fluids and excrement, and then forcing them to do manual labor objectively wrong?

Now, at one point, slavery was everywhere, and the majority of human civilization was totally fine with it.† Millions of people believed slavery was not only useful but actually the right thing to do: that it provided stability and purpose for slaves, allowed for the evangelization of "savages," and was the natural and ethical hierarchy of things. And if we lived back then, we probably would have believed that as well.

So, is the morality of slavery just a subjective thing? One culture and ethics says one thing, another time and culture says something else, and no one is truly right or wrong? Is slavery like picking the best ice cream flavor, and we were just lame enough to pick vanilla? Most of us would (hopefully) respond: "*No!* Slavery is different. Slavery is objectively wrong, and if you don't agree, then you are wrong as well. And even if all the other humans in your culture think it's okay, they would still be wrong."

Great, I agree with you, my dialectical conversation partner who's actually me. Slavery is not just subjectively wrong in one time or place; it is objectively

---

*As a philosopher, I don't totally buy the language of subjective/objective. But as a teacher I think it can be helpful.
†Slavery is still everywhere, just not publicly endorsed anymore.

wrong in all times and places, regardless of what any person or culture thinks. Even when the majority of humanity got together and decided slavery was cool, it was still wrong. Which means that objective morality, if it exists, must be based on something higher than humans. For if it is possible for most of humanity and human society to be wrong about a moral issue, then there must be some standard of morality that is higher than humans. Objective morality, *if it exists*, must be higher than humanity, higher than society, higher than the changing cultural moment. Indeed, human culture and beliefs constantly evolve and shift with time. So if morality is to be at all objective, it has to be grounded in something beyond time, something eternal.

That is where God has traditionally come in. God has often been seen as this higher basis for objective morality. God is eternal and so does not change with time and society and evolution but can provide the objective, unchanging, eternal reference point for what is right. God is the ruler by which all moral measurements are made. Two humans may both look at a wall and make contradictory judgments about how big it is, but the ruler provides the objective measurement and standard by which one of those humans is objectively right and the other objectively wrong.

Now, God doesn't invent what is good; rather, God is *goodness itself.* The Bible does not say that God invents the idea of love; rather, it says, "God *is* love" (1 John 4). So don't picture God as Zeus in the clouds arguing with the other gods about the next batch of moral laws. If that were the case, then God's morality would be just as invented, subjective, and made up as any devised by human society. Goodness and love are not things God came up with at some point in time; rather, they are what God eternally *is*. In the last chapter we said God is not another created being but rather is Being itself. And in the same way, God does not just issue good commands but is *goodness itself*, forever and for always. Objective morality cannot change with time, seasons, empires, cultures, or human evolution but must be grounded in the one entity beyond those sands of time: God. God is the eternal and objective reference point. Human morals are good only inasmuch as they reflect the one who is goodness itself. God is not just a lawmaker but *is* the moral law.

But if God isn't real, then what is good is not eternally and objectively fixed from above but subjectively made up from down below. If God does not exist, then God is not the basis for the rules. *We are.* All of morality becomes a social construct, something humans invented. You might invent one morality, and I invent another. And since there is no higher, objective standard that one of us might be closer to or further away from, then morality becomes 100 percent subjective. It's just a matter of personal taste, like ice cream.

❮ ■ ■ ❯

Now, this doesn't mean you have to believe in God to be a good person. Not at all. There are atheists who will stop at nothing to defeat cancer, and priests who will stop at nothing to molest little boys. You don't have to believe in God to be good, in the same way you don't have to believe in gravity to stay on the ground. I'm *not* saying that you need to believe in God to be good. But rather that if God does not exist, there is no such thing as goodness. Atheists as people can be good, but atheism as a worldview has no objective basis for good. Nor does it have any objective basis for bad. Morality does not enter the picture one way or the other. If God does not exist, then to say I wronged you makes as little sense as to say a shoe wronged a puddle.

When this debate comes up about religion and morality, the Ten Commandments almost always gets dragged into it. One person says humanity needed God to tell us to be good, and another person says we could've figured out on our own not to kill each other, thank you very much. And while that may be an interesting discussion, it has absolutely nothing to do with what I'm getting at here. The reason I placed this chapter in the context of the Moses story is precisely so that I could clarify up front that this is *not* what I am saying. For the point I am making would be valid even if we did *not* have the Bible and even if God did *not* bother to give us the Ten Commandments. I am *not* saying we need God to yell down what is right and wrong but rather that we need God in order for *there to be such a thing as right and wrong.* We need an objective moral standard that is grounded in something higher than the subjective individual, higher than the changing mores of society, and higher than the shifting sands of time and space.

The moral predicament of humanity is like finding an old board game in the attic that you've never played before. The rule sheet is missing, so you and your friends argue about it, each coming up with your best guess for what the rules are based on clues from the board, cards, or pieces. And while no one can be completely sure they are right, at least at the end of the day one of those approximations is closer to the actual rules than the others, and so it wasn't a total waste of time to try to figure it out. But now let's imagine the game rules weren't just missing but never existed to begin with. It's not even a board game; it's just an old map with some rusty knickknacks you mistook for pieces. You thought you were playing a game with rules, but there is no game, and there never were any rules.

Now, if God is real, then different religions and worldviews may disagree on what the rules are, each coming up with their own Ten Commandments or five pillars or Hammurabi's Code. And while it might not be certain whose rules are the most correct, at least there actually are rules at the end of the day, and we are trying our best to figure them out and play the game well. But if God is not real, then there never were rules to begin with, and the person who tried to make sense of the game never got any closer than the person who flipped the board in anger, for there were never any rules to get closer *to*. In which case, you've totally misunderstood the nature of reality. There is no correct way to play the game of life. And that might sound thrilling when you're a teenager who wants your parents to stop telling you how to live, but it's a tad more chilling when there's no longer anything for human-rights violations to be a violation of.

❮ ■ ■ ❯

Now, this is one of those ideas you need to hear over and over before it begins to make sense (case in point: the first time I heard it, I called my freshman philosophy professor a moron). So let me explain it from a different angle by telling two different versions of where morality comes from: the religious version and the nonreligious version.

The religious version: In the beginning, morality already existed. Goodness is eternal, engrained in the nature of an eternally good God. God did not invent or create love. No, the Bible says God is love. Moral goodness and love did not begin to exist but are eternally grounded in the one who is eternal Being and love and goodness itself. Then God created the world, eventually bringing about humanity. God took these eternal, unchanging, objective morals and implanted them within our hearts. Romans 2:15 says that God's law is written on our hearts.

And though humans might disagree about what exactly is good and what exactly is bad, at the end of the day, good and bad really do exist underneath it all. We might not always be able to definitively prove which morality is the right one, but because God exists, there is an objective morality of some kind out there, which we can at least strive to unearth and abide by. Though some parts of morality may be cultural or subjective, and we may disagree on the particulars, underneath it all there is something objective about morality, something higher that is based in the eternal nature of God. Love is not just a social construct; love is something objectively good, a piece of eternity that has been placed in our hearts. God is moral goodness itself, and our human conscience is made in that image.

But let's see what happens when we remove God from the equation. . . .

The atheist version: In the beginning, there was nothing. No morality, love, goodness, or meaning. Then the universe banged into existence out of nothing. Slowly, inanimate matter turned into stars, planets, and single-celled organisms. At this point, there was still no such thing as morality or love or goodness; bacteria are not moral or immoral. If bacteria wipe something out, they're not being evil; they're just being bacteria.

Eventually, you got a species like a monkey (it's actually a common ancestor of monkeys, but for simplicity, I'm gonna call them monkeys). And they threw their poop at each other and if they got super hungry would sometimes eat their own children. But then something changed. The monkeys that were nicer and stuck together in a pack tended to live longer, because they had a network of protection working together as a group. Yet the monkeys who were naturally more independent and only took care of themselves started to die off. Since they didn't stick with the pack, they didn't get the same group protection as the others. And so they died more often and had fewer babies, and their genes became less dominant in the gene pool of the species.

So natural selection begins to engrain being nice and working together into our DNA. Because if you're not nice, you're left alone to fend for yourself, so you die sooner, and your genes die with you. Over millions of years, this common ancestor of monkeys evolved into human beings, and this sense of working together evolved into what we call morality. And so now we have this inner instinct to be nice, just like spiders have an inner instinct to build webs and to terrify my spouse so I have to stop writing this chapter and come home to gently scoop one up with a napkin and place it outside.

On the atheistic account, morality is not an absolute, objective, unchanging, eternal thing. No, it is a just a survival technique that was useful for the reproduction of our species, and over time it got so deeply engrained within us that now we're deluded into thinking it somehow means more than that. But it doesn't. Love is not a higher value. Love is not an eternal good. Love is just a survival mechanism; it's safer in pairs. Being nice and taking care of others isn't objectively good; that just happened to be useful to the gene pool at one particular moment in time.

That is the atheist story of morality. Our species adapted to its circumstances, and that led to these deep feelings within us that we call morality. But if our circumstances had been different, we would have evolved differently. What if we'd had fewer predators hunting us, and so our species didn't need to stick together to survive? Then we wouldn't have evolved to care about others, and our morality would be totally different. For example, there is a species of wasp that evolved in such a way that it lays its eggs inside the body of its prey. Then the eggs hatch and eat their pray alive from the inside out. What if we had evolved more like that? What if eating people from the inside out had become an acceptable part of our morality? A few small shifts in evolution, and all the things we think are good and moral would be radically different. That is the very definition of subjective. (Note that this does not mean evolution is incompatible with morality, just that evolution cannot be the *only* source of morality.)

And since evolution is an ongoing process that is still happening today, whatever we do becomes moral; whatever we do becomes part of the evolutionary process. People might not like my morality or how I live, but I'm just the next stage in evolution, so deal with it, baby! Cannibalism for the win.

I hate to use Hitler here, but the whole point of Nazism was to take control of evolution to produce a master race. Had the Nazis succeeded and killed off everyone who disagreed with them, then Nazism would not be immoral, because society would have evolved to be fine with it. If morality is *solely* the byproduct of our social and biological evolution, then whatever human society does becomes, by definition, the new morality. For there is nothing higher than us by which we can be declared right or wrong, good or evil—"If there is no absolute by which to judge society, [then] society is absolute."[2]

And any standard by which we could judge such a society—such as love or equality or tolerance—would itself be an invention and just as much an invented construct as anything they would say to us in response. Once a higher reference point is lost, it's not just antisemitism and patriarchy and White supremacy that become social constructs. Equality, love, tolerance, justice, and compassion would also be rendered social/biological constructs we've invented and can just as easily deconstruct. As C. S. Lewis writes, "If there is no objective standard, then our choice between one ideology and another becomes a matter of arbitrary taste. . . . A better moral code can only mean one which comes nearer to some real or absolute code. One map of New York can be better than another only if there is a real New York for it to be truer *to*."[3]

◄ ■ ■ ►

Usually by this point, I've convinced some people that there must be a higher, eternal reference point for morality. But you may still be left wondering why this higher reference point must be God. Why can't this eternal standard just be some moral law of the universe like the laws of gravity or thermodynamics? *Why bring God into it?* Great question, my convenient caricature of a conversation partner.

First, we've already argued that this (1) moral lawgiver must also be (2) eternal. For time and space constantly shift and change and evolve, and so any morality that is invented within the shifting sands of time and space will always be relative and changing and subjective. If the moral law is real, it can never have begun to exist but must be eternal. However, as the Big Bang shows, our universe began to exist—it is not eternal. So morality cannot be grounded in our universe or its laws, for morality must have existed eternally before our universe even began.

Yet what if something existed before the Big Bang? What if there was another universe before ours, and another universe before that? Perhaps each universe is born, then births another, then collapses in on itself in death. Perhaps everything begins and ends, with each thing caused by another thing caused by another thing, with no first source for it all. Perhaps there is no rock bottom, no ultimate source of everything; perhaps nothing is eternal. And maybe that's possible. Yet as we've argued, if morality really is objective, then something eternal *would exist.* And so there would be something that has always been there and could provide a rock bottom to ground everything else. If there is something eternal that grounds morality, then the universes don't have to keep going back and back in time with no ultimate explanation but could be caused by this one eternal thing. Since it has always been, it can create all that comes after. And so, it would make sense if this eternal moral lawgiver was also (3) the *Creator.*

Now, physical and material things are constantly changing. Material atoms fuse and break apart. Physical stars are born, burn brightly for a season, and then twinkle into that good night. Matter changes, but the moral law does not, and so the one cannot be grounded in the other. In turn, physical nature is full of animals killing their parents and lions eating their children, and so if morality is real, it must be higher than nature. The moral law cannot be grounded in the cruel vicissitudes of nature and the changing material world and so would seem to be (4) *nonphysical.* The LEGO instruction book is never itself made of LEGOs.

And it makes sense that moral goodness is not grounded in the physical world, because goodness is not a physical object but a concept, a notion, an *idea.* And ideas exist in minds, not in matter. It makes no sense to ask where the number five lives—it is not out there hiding somewhere in Alaska or in the outer reaches of sector six. For the number five is an abstract idea or concept that exists in minds. Likewise, moral goodness is an idea or concept and so must also dwell in a mind. And since we've already shown that true goodness cannot exist solely in ever-changing, subjective *human minds*, it must be grounded in an unchanging, eternal, objective, *higher mind*. Thus, we can argue that goodness is not an object in matter but an eternal thought in an eternal (5) *mind*.

Finally, the moral law is different from the impersonal laws of science. The laws of gravity apply equally to all things; it doesn't matter if you are a rock, a piano, or a person—if you are thrown from a rooftop, you are going down. But the moral law is not like that. Scientific laws apply to impersonal and personal beings alike, but the moral law only applies to personal beings. If I dropped a piano on someone, the piano wouldn't feel guilty about it, but I (hopefully) would. Saul repented for stoning Stephen, but the stones never gave it a second thought. The moral law does not seem to apply indifferently across the board to objects the way scientific laws do but only seems to apply intimately to humans (and perhaps other personal beings such as dogs, dolphins, elephants, etc.). Thus, the moral law is (6) *personal*.

You've probably realized where this is going. This (1) moral lawgiver would seem to also be (2) eternal, (3) the Creator, (4) nonphysical, and (5) a mind that is (6) personal. So even if you don't want to call this thing God, you've basically described something with the same attributes we normally think of God as having. You've described something personal like a human and conceptual like a mind but that is also eternal, nonphysical, and likely the creator of everything, as well as the giver of all meaning and morality. So call it what you want—call it spirit in the sky, the Numinous, Big Kahuna, Supreme Being, Eebowai, Sky Daddy, Jehovah, or Brian. Either way, if you think morality is objective, you basically end up asserting what billions of people across the globe assert in pews every Sunday.

◄ ▬ ▬ ►

What I'm arguing is not as controversial as you might think. Bertrand Russell, the most famous atheist of the twentieth century (and perhaps of all time), admitted, "Unless you assume a God, the question of life's purpose is meaningless."[4] Indeed, many of the greatest philosophers in the world have admitted that if God is dead, objective morality isn't real. And yet, many of those same philosophers do not believe in God. For simply wanting the world to have meaning does not mean it does. We might wish we lived in a moral universe, but that doesn't mean we do. I think we should have great respect for atheists who admit the death of morality and have the courage to face the void head-on. Of course, if God is dead, then the courage to face the void would be no more objectively good than being a coward. But let's not talk about that.

So, in the end, perhaps morality can't prove whether God is real. But what it does do is reveal the stakes of the question: religion is not just a matter of whether there is a bearded man in the clouds who sees you when you're sleeping and knows when you're awake. No, the God question is *the* question, without which morality and love and goodness lose any real meaning.

I often hear people say, "I can't believe in God because of all the suffering and evil in the world." But that assumes there is an objective standard of right and wrong in the first place. They are arguing there is no higher power because there is too much wrong with the world, but they can only appeal to higher notions of right and wrong if they assume a higher power in the first place.

I remember standing on the greened-over field of a mass grave at Dachau concentration camp in Munich (a scene eerily reminiscent of Jewish babies being thrown into the Nile en masse). And my first reaction was what kind of heartless God could have allowed such horror: humans herded like cattle, siblings shrieking in the dark, flame-filled ditches giving hellish flickers of what was to come, all while the trees and clouds and heavens watched on with indifference.

But then my reaction shifted, and I realized my repulsion at the scene hinted that we really do live in a meaningful cosmos. There really are objective standards, and the Holocaust really did violate them. We really do live in a world where what happened in those woods was wrong. *Truly wrong.* Not just wrong within my set of social constructs, not just wrong relative to my time and place and upbringing, but absolutely, eternally, fundamentally, cosmically, bloody wrong.

Only if a higher standard exists can I say the depths of human depravity falls short. Only in a moral universe can I say what was done in those German fields and Egyptian rivers was immoral. Only in a God-haunted cosmos can I say those acts were godless. And just like that, what once seemed the greatest disproof of divinity became the greatest source of my longing for an engodded earth.

So I don't know whether we need the Ten Commandments to do good, but we certainly need the one who commanded them—the one who is goodness itself.

❮ ❰ ❱ ❯

After receiving the Ten Commandments written on two stone tablets, an already exhausted Moses now has to carry these bloody things down the mountain. After days and days of trying not to trip and tumble down the hillside, Moses is ready to pretty much collapse and take a long nap. But as he nears base camp, he hears a raucous thundering, like a thousand voices singing in unison. Drawing closer, he sees the Jewish people bowing and praying to something shiny in the distance.

Moses has only been gone a month or so up on the mountain, yet in that time the people already got weary of waiting for God. So they forged a cow out of gold and made it their god. They began worshiping a creature—a cow—as if it were the Creator, bowing to another finite being as if it were Being itself, mistaking the goodness of gold with the one who is Goodness itself. This is not a great start for the young would-be nation. Horrified and heartbroken, Moses smashes the stone tablets on the ground. Yet in so doing, he does not smash the moral law itself, but only one created, stoney reflection of it. For the eternal law is not carved in stone by humans but written by God in our hearts—written in blood drawn from the one who is Goodness itself.

NINE

Beauty in the Promised Land

MY FIRST INTRODUCTION to religion was not at a church but when my parents sent us to a Christian summer camp on Gambier Island, Vancouver. Young Jonathan felt socially awkward in this new space with these new people and this new religion. And my social anxiety was not helped by the fact that I was chunkier and often labeled "the fat kid." I have a distinct memory of my cabin ganging up on me to spray bug repellent in my eyes. I also remember the most popular girl—with a whole group in tow—randomly taunting me by asking, "What did the whale say to Jonathan?" When I naively responded, "What?" she began singing, "We are family! . . ."

Yet her song was not the only one heard that summer. Every morning the camp had a service set in the outdoor chapel. I hated this because whom one sat with felt like a Victorian-era social procedure. Eventually, I gave up scrounging for friends among the chapel benches and started sitting twenty feet behind the chapel, alone in the woods, on an old stump. Throughout the week, multiple staff members tried to get me to rejoin the group, but they eventually gave up and let me stay among the trees. Which was good, because I had the better deal. As the worship leader up front began their song, around me the forest seemed to exhale and rustle with it, mossy vines twanging along, while the trees stretched above like elongated throats serenading heaven. On stage they had their old wooden cross, but mine was still growing and alive and rooted around and beneath me. Glancing beyond my veil of trees, I glimpsed the camp wharf in the distance, pining out into the Pacific. Riding those waves brings you to North Vancouver, where the ocean rises to forest that rises to glaciers then to the sky. My eyes and ears now entranced, my throat began to play along too, and soon I was singing, lonely but not alone in the wilderness. For a fleeting moment, I believed I could do this for a thousand years, while creation grew up all around and reabsorbed my song into itself. It was not just good but *beautiful*.

❮ ✖ ✖ ❯

The Jewish people left Egypt, got the Ten Commandments, fell in love with a shiny cow, lost the Ten Commandments, and then spent years wandering in the desert until they were truly ready to be God's people and follow God's laws. At long last, they were prepared, finally making it through the desert to the Promised Land. This was the land promised to their forefather Abraham as the place where his descendants would prosper, live, and grow as numerous as the stars in the sky. They described that land as *beautiful*:

> For the LORD your God is bringing you into a good land—a land with brooks, streams, and deep springs gushing out into the valleys and hills; a land with wheat and barley, vines and fig trees, pomegranates, olive oil and honey; a land where bread will not be scarce and you will lack nothing; a land where the rocks are iron and you can dig copper out of the hills. (Deuteronomy 8:7-9)
>
> . . . a land flowing with milk and honey, the most *beautiful* of all lands. (Ezekiel 20:6)

The Promised Land was gorgeous, good, and nurturing, giving them all they needed. For centuries they had just been *surviving*, first as slaves in Egypt, then later as wanderers in the desert. But now they had a home of their own, and *thriving* was finally on the table. Now that the nation had permanent fields for food, walls for safety, and hills for iron and copper, they could move beyond simply living to what life was worth living *for*. They could stop living off the land in desperation and start seeing its beauty in appreciation. In turn, they finally had space for poetry, art, architecture, song, dance, and culture to begin to flourish. Song of Songs, the Bible's collection of love poetry, was penned, exploring the spiritual beauty of sex and the human form:

Let him kiss me with the kisses of his mouth—
>for your love is more delightful than wine. . . .

Take me away with you—let us hurry!
>Let the king bring me into his chambers. (Song of Songs 1:2, 4)

Like a lily among thorns
>is my darling among the young women. (Song of Songs 2:2)

I am my beloved's and my beloved is mine. (Song of Songs 6:3)

Love is as strong as death,
>its jealousy as unyielding as the grave.

It burns like blazing fire,
>like a mighty flame.

Many waters cannot quench love;
>rivers cannot sweep it away. (Song of Songs 8:6-7)

How *beautiful* you are, my darling!
>Oh, how beautiful!

Your eyes behind your veil are doves. . . .
You are altogether beautiful. (Song of Songs 4:1, 7)

Such poetry was whispered in bedrooms and echoed through beautiful halls of architecture, such as the temple they later built in Jerusalem. This temple was full of ornate carvings, palm trees, flowers, decorative motifs, jewels, and elaborate porticoes. Its rituals were accompanied with feasts and sometimes (gasp) dancing.[1] In turn, music rang through every service, street, and household, for much of the Bible was not meant to be mumbled in monotone but sung aloud, such as the book of Psalms, which literally includes instructions for the music director before each psalm: "For the director of music. With stringed instruments" (Psalm 4). "For the director of music. To the tune of 'The Doe of the Morning'" (Psalm 22). These psalms include some of the most famous and beautiful lines in all of literature:

The LORD is my shepherd. . . .
Even though I walk through the valley of the shadow of death,
>I will fear no evil,
for you are with me. (Psalm 23:1, 4 ESV)

We will not fear, though the earth give way
    and the mountains fall into the heart of the sea. (Psalm 46:2)

Where can I go from your Spirit?
    Where can I flee from your presence?
If I go up to the heavens, you are there;
    if I make my bed in the depths, you are there.
If I rise on the wings of the dawn,
    if I settle on the far side of the sea,
even there your hand will guide me. (Psalm 139:7-10)

As the deer pants for streams of water,
    so my soul pants for you, my God. (Psalm 42:1)

The heavens declare the glory of God;
    the skies proclaim the work of his hands. (Psalm 19:1)

So, contrary to how the Bible is often depicted, poetry, pleasure, bliss, art, aesthetics, and natural beauty are not scorned in its pages. And when I thumb those pages, it is accompanied not only by the crisp flick of turning paper but by chanting, ringing, twirling; by sights, sounds, textures, tastes, and the perfumed splendor of nature. It croons that creation is not only objectively good but *beautiful*.

◖◗◖◗❯

In the previous chapter, we explored the idea that morality is objective and grounded in the eternal nature of God, who is goodness itself. A similar argument can be made for beauty. If beauty is a real, objective thing, then it cannot be a social construct but must be grounded in one who is beauty itself.

Now, on the one hand, there is obviously a cultural and personal subjectivity to beauty. Being skinny is considered beautiful today, while in the past what we now consider overweight was a sexy sign of wealth. Some cultures consider freckles to be blemishes, while others see them as constellations dotting an exquisite sky. And as a rather plump kid going through puberty before body positivity became popular, trust me when I say that I am deeply aware of the cruel relativity of changing beauty standards. There is undeniably a certain subjectivity and cultural relativism to beauty in the same way that morality around social etiquette is subjective and culturally relative. I would not deny that. Beauty is to some extent in the eye of the beholder.

Yet I would never say it is *solely* in the eye of the beholder. I still think there is something actually beautiful in the world that is *beheld*. Despite all those caveats above, I still encounter beauty to be as real as the ground beneath me. I encounter the unconscious poetry of

> morning mist rolling down the mountainside
> sun's rays skimming an unrippled sea at dawn
> an unadulterated smile curling on a newborn's lip
> the swirls of van Gogh's starry night
> the scent of burning firewood
> the sweat on your brow after a solid day's work
> a whiff of coffee beans from a freshly opened can
> handpicked strawberries in summer
> the right song coming on at just the right moment
> the ache in your bones from laughing too hard with good friends
> the stripped and leafless trees of winter that make me stop in my tracks to
>   exclaim, "Dear God, even their skeletons are beautiful!"
> even that wretched beauty of darkness, the intricacy of the spider's web, the
>   peaceful void of endless space—even the frightful parts of creation still
>   bear witness to an objective beauty, both horrifying and wondrous

While we may disagree about superficial and socially constructed definitions of it, I still believe that there is, at the end of the day, a real thing called *beauty*. It's not just a subjective illusion. And if there is such a thing as objective beauty, it must be grounded in an eternal and unchanging source of the beautiful, in one who is beauty itself. As the Psalms sing, "One thing I ask from the LORD, this only do I seek . . . to gaze on the beauty of the LORD" (Psalm 27:4).

Sadly, humans have often focused so much on our own beauty that we've missed the much broader question of cosmic beauty. To believe beauty is objectively real does not mean you can rank people according to hotness. All it means—minimally—is that you believe a life with music, art, food, nature, expression, pleasure, or bliss is objectively more beautiful than a life spent alone in a dull, empty room with none of it. Now, one might immediately think of the counterexample of Nelson Mandela in his prison cell, or Hellen Keller stuck in a chair and in her own mind. Yet they escaped precisely through worlds of creativity and words, and so they are not an example of beauty's subjectivity but of its triumph over even the harshest of odds. A blade of grass growing up through prison cement does not prove beauty is relative but that it can take root anywhere.

Different cultures and times may perceive different things as beautiful. Yet these perspectives need not cancel each other out but can bring out different facets of aesthetic reality. Indeed, while we can disagree about the *nature* of beauty, I think most of us, if we are being honest, still believe in its *existence*. In the same way, we might disagree about whether someone is guilty, how bad their crime was, and how many years they should serve, yet most of us can probably still get on board with the idea that cold-blooded murder is objectively wrong. And I can tell you from personal experience that if you talk to five different philosophers of science, you will get five different definitions of what matter and energy are—but most of them still agree matter and energy are real things. So why can't the same be said of beauty? Why can't we disagree about Taylor Swift or Richard Wagner while still agreeing that a life full of vibrant sounds, sights, smells, textures, and tastes is objectively more beautiful than a life without any?* And whatever counterexample you are trying to conjure up to show that beauty can be found in unexpected places doesn't show that beauty isn't real but simply that it doesn't play by our rules. I remember watching Brendan Fraser as a six-hundred-pound man in *The Whale*, and I kept thinking, "His eyes are so pure and beautiful."

So, what if beauty is real? Really real? What if it's not just a totally subjective illusion of the human mind? What if it's not just a changing social construct but grounded in something higher than humanity? What if,

---

*Of course, different things may *seem* or *not seem* beautiful depending on the person/perspective/context. This doesn't disprove my theory but is actually required by it, for no created thing is absolute beauty itself. Streams and setting suns and yearning lips can be beautiful, but they are not beauty itself—only *God is*. Created things will, like waves, rise up and reflect the light of the sun from one angle but not from another. And yet, this relativity does not mean there is no sun, nor that the light they catch, however briefly, is unreal. It just means they are *imperfect* and *fleeting* reflections of higher things that are *perfect* and *forever*. Likewise, humans may make good choices one day and bad choices another, and that does not mean goodness itself is unreal, nor that our good choices, while they were being made, were not actually good.

before our universe began, beauty and goodness danced in eternity, and, now begun, our universe reflects that glory like the moon reflects the sun? What if art is not just a way to pass the time but a way to touch eternity? What if religion is not just about ethics but *aesthetics*—about getting wider-eyed and closer to pleasure, beauty, bliss, and spasms of ecstasy? What if, in their Promised Land of milk and honey, the Jewish nation glimpsed the natural splendor of God? What if, in reading the Song of Songs, they caressed the face of a cosmic lover? What if, with their instruments and psalms, they struck a chord with the one who is beauty itself?

❰ ❰ ❱ ❱

One can see the type of case being made over and over in movement three: God is not just *a being*. God does not just happen to be *good*. God is not just occasionally *beautiful*. No, God is Goodness, Being, and Beauty *itself*. God is the absolute, objective, eternal, unchanging entity who grounds the deeper qualities of reality. These qualities—if real and objective—cannot be grounded in us, in human society and biology, for we are constantly changing and evolving. These things must somehow be grounded in something higher than us, something eternal and unchanging. Ideas such as goodness and beauty and love must dwell eternally and objectively in God, who does not change from day to day but is forever true. As such, the fleeting glimmers of beauty, love, goodness, and being that we encounter down here are reflections of the eternal ideas/absolutes/objective standards of God up there. As Emily Dickinson writes, "Beauty is not caused. It *is*."[2] Or as environmentalist John Muir writes, "No synonym for God is so perfect as Beauty."[3] This higher view of God as Being, Goodness, and Beauty itself is one of the key contributions of movement three and will be essential to our story moving forward.[4]

Now, this doesn't mean an atheist cannot appreciate beauty, any more than our last chapter meant an atheist could not be a good person. It simply means that if God does not exist, then there is *no such thing as beauty*. You might protest that your experience of beauty is still real, and I might concede that, but only in the same sense that the unicorn I once hallucinated was real. The atheist encounters a world of aesthetic and moral qualities—full of song, color, good, and evil—and must quickly reduce it to neurons firing in their brains, giving the subjective illusion of beauty and morality. The child points at the sky and says, "It's beautiful!" and their teacher might quickly correct them, saying, "It *feels* beautiful." The unspoken atheism of our age may allow something to genuinely *feel* like it's beautiful but cannot allow that it *actually is* beautiful. We've quietly decided beauty and goodness are not real things; only matter and atoms are real things. Beauty and goodness are not *things* but *ideas*, and ideas exist only in minds. And if there is no objective or divine mind that eternally structures reality, then such ideas can only exist subjectively in *our* minds. Your mind only invented—never discovered—beauty through the sill and song and mountainside. Beauty was not here before humans and will not be here once we are gone; beauty is a temporary human/personal/social/biological projection onto matter.

In contrast, the religious person looks at the world and does not see just material *quantities* but objective moral and aesthetic *qualities*—qualities that would be here with or without us humans to notice them. Ideas such as goodness and beauty exist eternally and objectively in the divine mind that forged creation in its image. Beauty is really *real*—it's not just in our minds but in *the Mind* that structured and upholds all of objective reality. Humans did not invent beauty but merely discovered it: "I found the poems in the fields, and only later wrote them down."[5] As such, the person who is moved to tears by the swaying forest sees truer than the person who sees only green things standing in their way.[6] The love of a mother is as real as her embrace; the beauty of the mountain is as real as its matter. When religious people say we've encountered God, we don't always mean there's a ghostly presence beyond what eyes can see. Just the opposite: we're seeing the daily, natural, normal course of this beautiful world and choosing to actually believe our own eyes.

So whether there is a Creator drastically affects the nature of the *creation* we are living in. Through the beauty and goodness of creation *down here*, we can begin to be drawn to the God *up there*, who is beauty and goodness itself. The Creator may not be creation, but the Creator can certainly be seen through creation, just as an artist can express themselves and be known through their art. In the words of Ralph Waldo Emerson, "Beauty is God's handwriting—a wayside sacrament; welcome it in every fair face, every fair sky, every fair flower, and thank God for it as a cup of blessing."[7] In which case God is not only felt in a church but in all of creation, wherever and whenever beauty chooses to undress. The Bible may reveal the God who is beauty itself, yet such beauty was present before it ever spilled upon the page, already carved into every tree, tapestry, song, star, story, sutra, canvas, wave, or willow of God's world. We humans have long been secret admirers who dared not look our crush in the eye, only catching secondary glimmers of her beauty reflected off a window, mirror, or glass.

Yet if all the world is a flirtation, then things really get going once we dare glance straight into the eyes of God and strike up the conversation more directly. If God is beauty itself, then the closer we are to God, the more we're enraptured, enticed, enthralled, seduced. Which is why many have read the love poetry of Song of Songs not only as a literal tale of two human lovers but as a metaphor for God's relationship with humanity. The one who is Being is also bliss, and in him we find our state of blissful being. Realizing this, we begin to near death like a wedding day, when the long engagement finally results in full intimacy with the divine. The closer we get in anticipation, the more tastes abound, colors swirl, trees sway and hold hands in the wind, sex arouses up to heaven, prayers begin to dance like poems and resound like songs, all orchestrated to the messy hum of creation. Standing in the presence of such beauty and feeling bowed down and small before it comes closest to what I think may be meant by worship.

❮❰❰❯

All those years ago at summer camp, the beauty of the trees, songs, and spilling waves gave me a taste of the one who is beauty itself. I didn't have a clue at the time, but I was slowly falling in love. Earth was the image heaven sent of itself to seduce me. Yet I was in no way the kind of person who had the strength or resources to reciprocate such a divine love or open myself up to it. We "need beauty because it makes us ache to be worthy of it," and I knew I was not worthy.[8] Nor was I on a trajectory to be so anytime soon, if ever. I did not know how to receive love, let alone how to give it back. When people say they're falling in love, at least they get the *fall* part right.

In the same way, while God did indeed begin to reveal God's self to the Jewish nation through songs, psalms, art, prose, and poetry, they would only rarely choose to reflect that beauty and goodness in themselves. More often than not, they would turn away from it, choosing to stay stuck in the same fallen generational cycles of sin and shame. . . .

TEN

King David and His Boy

Now that the Jews were out of Egypt and set up in the Promised Land, the nation really did grow and become *a nation*, just like God had promised their ancestor Abraham. With that nation came beautiful art, culture, music, psalms, and poetry, yes, but also government, infrastructure, bureaucracy, and an open spot at the top for someone to run things. However, God told them to leave that spot empty, to let it be filled by God, not by any mortal man.[1] God warned them that God alone was their true King—their true spiritual father (1 Samuel 8:7; Matthew 23:9).[2] God warned that a human king would tax them and take their sons for war and their daughters for brides. Yet the nation insisted, demanding a human male to rule over their Jewish homeland, a national father figure to nurture and guide and raise them up. . . .

〈 ▬ ▬ 〉

Once upon a crime, King David was enjoying the sunset from the palace roof.* The people had made him king of the Jewish nation a few years earlier, and he had done mostly all right in the role so far.

Suddenly, through the trees and streets below, David caught a glimpse of a woman bathing on her roof. The bathing woman's name was Bathsheba. Her *husband's* name was Uriah.

David glimpsed a peek for but a moment. Yet a moment turned to minutes, and minutes turned into a regular pattern of watching her.

---

*Scholars were skeptical that King David was real until 1993, when an enemy inscription from the correct period was found mocking David and his house. I try to keep that in mind whenever someone writes a scathing review of my books.

Her beauty in the moonlight overthrew him. King David requested Bath-sheba's presence at the palace (though given the power dynamics at play, it's not clear how much of a *request* it actually was), and you can surmise the rest. The king was giving in to the kind of temptations that so many men with power and responsibility over others seem to give into.

After the night(s) of passion, Bathsheba went home, and David returned to daily life. Days passed; months went by. David learned to suppress the shameful memory of that adulterous one-night stand. Until one day, a note arrived from Bathsheba. David opened it and saw the two words that could take down a king: "I'm pregnant."

David panicked. He tried to cover it up, but that only sunk him deeper into the lie. Eventually Bathsheba's husband got involved, and he was about to expose the truth. David reasoned he was left with no other choice, that there was only one way out: he had to secretly murder Bathsheba's husband and take her as his own wife. *Obviously.*

Bathsheba had multiple sons with David, one of which was a little baby boy named Solomon. Little Solomon was raised with everything. All the toys, education, and opportunities that you would expect for the son of a king. But Solomon likely didn't see his father very often. After all, David was king, distracted by all his kingly duties. Plus, David had a whole other wife and family. Multiple families, in fact. David seems to have done a bad job with all of them; one of David's sons raped one of his daughters, and David did nothing about it (2 Samuel 13). Another one of David's sons tried to kill him and steal his throne (2 Samuel 15). David's relationship with Solomon can't have been much better. Especially since Solomon wasn't originally the next in line to the throne (until after his brothers died) and so would not have grown up getting as much attention from the king as the rightful heir. It probably didn't help that Solomon and his mother were a living reminder to David of his murderous infidelity.

As he grew, Solomon likely learned to look for affection and praise in places other than his father. The Bible says that Solomon eventually became wise beyond measure, excelling in school and getting the praise of all his teachers. He became something of a ladies' man as well. As Prince Solomon, the future king of Israel, he had his pick of the litter. He fornicated with the foreign women of Moab. He loved the ladies of North Africa. He even slept with Pharoah's daughter—as in, the Pharoah of Egypt's daughter. Solomon was basically the Jewish Hugh Hefner, the playboy of the ancient world.[3] He went from one thing to the next, hoping that the next woman, the next endeavor, the next success would fill the hole in his heart.

Eventually, King David, Solomon's father, died. Within a matter of days the country celebrated a funeral and a coronation. He was no longer little baby Solomon but now King Solomon. His whole life he wanted to prove his worth, and now he was king. What's more impressive than that? Yet something was still missing. He still felt incomplete.

So Solomon redoubled his efforts. He built temples and gold towers unlike anything the world had ever seen before. He amassed a vast army of chariots. He read everything, learned all he could, became world renowned for his wisdom. And he took over seven hundred wives. He'd have to rotate through them, getting to see each of them for one day every two years. Which was ironically about the same amount of time his father had probably spent with him and his own mother, Bathsheba.

Solomon ruled for thirty-nine years as king. After his long reign, he looked back on his life and wrote these words in the book of Ecclesiastes: "Meaningless! Meaningless! Everything is meaningless!" (Yes, there's an entire book of the Bible traditionally attributed to Solomon, where he just rants about how life has no meaning. It is magnificent.)

Solomon writes, "I built houses, planted vineyards, made gardens, built reservoirs and temples, collected servants, had a harem of women, had all the gold and silver a man could count, had every pleasure, every accomplishment imaginable. Yet now I look back on all I've done, and what I achieved. And it's all meaningless, pointless, like chasing after the wind" (Ecclesiastes 2:4-6, 8-9, 11, my paraphrase). After all the construction, all the wars, wealth and women, Solomon realized that none of it ever filled the hole in his heart, ever quenched that thirst to prove himself, ever eased his childhood demons, ever made him whole again.

Which reminds me of a true story about an older gentleman. He was on a walk with a friend of mine. Even though the old man had a bad home life as a child, he'd gone on to become quite successful over the years, opened his own business, created a mini-empire. The old man was talking about all his achievements and the glory days. Then out of nowhere his eyes started watering a little, his voice got raspy, and in a rare moment of vulnerability, he muttered, "It was all for my father. All of it. Every dollar." Then he coughed, blinked the tears away, and went right back to talking as if nothing had happened.

That is the man I imagine in my head when I picture King Solomon. Reflecting on Solomon's life, I can't help but think there must be some connection between the pain of his past and the excesses of his adult life. It's as if the whole time Solomon was chasing his father's approval, as if every woman or brick laid was to earn David's affection. He was defined by the struggle and trauma he inherited from his father, just as his own father David likely inherited trauma from his father, and his father from his father, all the way back to Cain and his father, Adam.

❮ ▮ ▮ ❯

It's with this background in mind that I want to ask: Why is God called *Father*? Why, considering the epic history of bad fathers such as King David, is God so often depicted as a bearded sky-daddy?

Why is God referred to using parental imagery, given that nearly a third of grown children have cut ties with a parent (and countless more probably wish they could)?[4] Why refer to God as a parent, given that Sutton Trust recently did a study of fourteen thousand children and found that barely half had strong emotional bonds with their mother or father?[5] I mean, why choose a parental image that so many people associate with manipulation, disappointment, failure, neglect, anxiety, or even abandonment?

And if one is going to use a parental image, why father? Why not mother instead? Mothers are statistically much more likely to stick around or be highly involved in their kids' lives. And the Bible does use maternal and feminine imagery for God in a few places.† Yet most of the time, it refers to God as Father—the first person of the Christian Trinity.

Why? I mean, it's not like people in biblical times were oblivious to how much baggage could come with fathers. Obviously not. There is story after story in the Old Testament of fathers screwing up their children and passing on generational sin to their descendants. Sin is never just personal and private; it is social and communal, affecting those around you, especially those under your care. That's the whole point of Adam and Eve and the fall: sin gets passed on. King David is a prime example, passing his sin and shame and issues on to Solomon. The Bible is not oblivious to the generational failures of fathers. So why does it refer to God so often as Father?

Statistically, one in three children in the United States does not have their biological father in the home.[6] And even if your father stuck around, even if your father was physically present, that doesn't mean he was emotionally present. Some studies suggest that, on average, fathers give their children less than three to seven minutes of undivided attention a day. One person put it this way: "My dad never affirmed me as a man. He occasionally told me he was proud of me, but he didn't prove it with his actions. The main man in my life didn't want to spend time with me, didn't show me what it means to be a man, and made me feel that I wasn't worth the time of other men."[7] So why is God called Father?

I once heard a preacher tell the story of him and his six-year-old daughter in a pool. Across the other side of the pool, a twenty-something-year-old girl was flirting with a group of guys. They were all starting to touch her inappropriately, and she just laughed, enjoying the attention. Then the six-year-old looked up and said, "Her daddy must not love her very much." Now, that's one judgmental six-year-old.‡ But also, perhaps, an inadvertently insightful one. Statistics show that girls without a father in the home are seven times more likely to become pregnant as teens.[8] If you do not

---

†For example, both the apostles John and Paul are recorded as saying, "When I find myself in times of trouble, Mother Mary comes to me."

‡I don't want to be in the business of policing female sexuality, but the latent kernel of truth underlying the six-year-old's response is worth bringing up.

have a father in the home who loves you and affirms you, you will turn to people outside the home to fill that void. *So why is God called Father?!!?!*

I wrestled with that question for years. Then something occurred to me: *Perhaps God came to us as a Father because he knew there would be such a lack of them.*[9]

Perhaps God sought to fill the void in so many of our lives, sought to come as the parent you never had.

Perhaps God wants to give us a heavenly family that can fill in the gaps left by our earthly families, a heavenly parent who says to us the words our earthly parents did not.

Perhaps everything your childhood lacked, everything lost in the past, can be found in the arms of God.

Perhaps God comes to us as a parent not to trigger our painful memories but to heal them.

Perhaps God came as a loving father to a world that has many loving mothers but statistically fewer loving fathers.

Perhaps God came to be a father to those who, like Solomon, did not have much of a father.

Perhaps God came to be a "father to the fatherless" (Psalm 68:5).

Perhaps there was a reason God told them not to appoint a king and to leave that space empty, for the only true Father of the nation was God.

〈■■〉

Now, being a parent is one of the hardest jobs in the world. I'm a parent myself, and I'm trying to do my best. But I know I'm still messing my kids up in lots of ways, many of which I don't even realize yet. I have moments where I snap, say the wrong thing, or put myself ahead of my family. Even the best parents mess up. I know I do.

But God is not like that. God *is perfect.* God doesn't have off days. God doesn't lash out at you when he's frustrated. God doesn't get so caught up with work that he stops paying attention to you. God doesn't become emotionally distant when he's tired. God doesn't bring up your past mistakes and hold them against you. God doesn't leave. As Psalm 27:10 says, "My father and mother walked out and left me, but GOD took me in" (MSG).

Knowing that, you have a choice. You can ignore your past. You can just say, "My mom and dad were fine. My family was fine. I'm fine." You can repress and refuse to look within yourself and ask the hard questions. You can become consumed with anger and bitterness toward your family and whatever happened. *Or* you can start processing your past out loud with God, counselors, friends, mentors, pastors. Laying your pain and past at God's feet and inviting God into it, letting God heal those wounds, letting God fill that void in your heart, letting God forge new emotional patterns within you. Letting God be the mom or dad you never had, or (if you had decent parents) the heavenly parent that your earthly parents pointed toward.

Father is still not my go-to designation for God. I prefer lots of the other terms used for God in the Bible, especially less-gendered ones. Yet I've grown and gotten to the point where, when parent language is used, it no longer makes me snort but is another aspect of God that I can be comforted and enriched by. My journey might not be the same as yours; you might never quite get to that point in this life. But regardless of where you end up, I still encourage you to start the journey. Because the crummy thing is, if you don't start working through some of that baggage, you will eventually pass it on to your own children.

Are you ready to hear how the story ends?

Eventually, Solomon had a son as well. A boy named Rehoboam. Rehoboam went on to become one of the worst kings in Jewish history. Rehoboam was harsh, authoritarian, unwise, and emotionally stunted. He pretty much ruined the country, splitting the Jewish nation in half. Since Solomon never unpacked his baggage and generational sin, he passed all of it on to his son Rehoboam. And Solomon likely looked on in horror as he realized that he had done to his own son exactly what had been done to him.

CREATION

Creation Begins

Creation Is Not God

Creation Is Good

FALL

Humanity in God's Image

Humanity Gone Wild

NATION

Abraham Finds Faith ● 2000 BC

Moses Meets I Aᴍ ● 1400–1200ish BC

Goodness Is Commanded ●

Beauty in the Promised Land ●

King David and his Boy ● 1000ish BC

Justice Exiles the Nation ● 586 BC

REDEMPTION

Jesus Is Born ● AD 0

Jesus Is Walking Around Saying Stuff ● AD 30

Jesus Is Dying to Meet You ● AD 33

CHURCH

The Spirit Arrives ● AD 33

The Church Begins ● AD 33

The Apostle Paul Converts ● AD 35ish

The Church Expands ● AD 300ish

The Church Today ● The Present

END

The End of the World as We Know It ●

Highway to Hell or Stairway to Heaven? ●

ELEVEN

Justice Exiles the Nation

UNDER REHOBOAM'S RULE, the nation divides in two, with one ruler in the north and one in the south. For hundreds of years the hamstrung Jewish nation(s) hobbles on. They constantly turn on each other, shedding the blood of their Jewish brothers and sisters in uncivil wars. They vacillate between worshiping the great "I am" and worshiping the created beings of other nations and the goods they represent—gods of gold, war, food, and prosperity. They hoard wealth and oppress the poor, refusing to practice the year of Jubilee, when God ordained that all slaves and prisoners should be freed and all debts forgiven. In their desperation to be materially blessed, they begin offering child sacrifices in exchange for divine favor from other gods. They bow before bronze statues of Baal, then place their bundled babes on his sizzling tongue, letting them unravel down his throat to the fiery pit below.

For all their steps forward, the nation takes a dozen steps back, choosing to keep the same cycles of generational sin alive in their hearts. Abraham's descendants do indeed become as numerous as the stars in the sky, yet burn never as bright. God extends mercy to their nation over and over, yet the people keep swatting it away. God sends prophets to tell them to change their ways before it is too late, but they never listen. And after centuries of getting worse, it's finally time to pay the piper. What goes around is readying to come back around. Wrath is roused with impatience, hungry for her day of reckoning, eager to let loose the long-starved jackals of justice. . . .

A horn thunders in the distance, stirring the night. Husbands turn to their wives in bed, hoping for a look of reassurance that this was all a drill, planned and expected—only to see their own fear mirrored back at them. Looking outside, they see men with torches climbing the stone stairs, rising to the top of the Jerusalem wall, their flames circling the city like candles on a cake. The Jewish army is assembling, running to arms. But running where, assembling for what? Through cracks in the city wall, they glimpse ten thousand more torches marching toward the city like an army of fireflies. Then someone somewhere up above bellows, "They're coming! They're coming! Babylon is coming!!"

It was 586 BC, and the Babylonians were there to make war on the city of Jerusalem. Babylon sieged the walls so no food or supplies could get in, starving Jerusalem's citizens until they opened wide their gates and mouths. Inside, people started killing each other for a loaf of bread. They soon ran out of wood to cook whatever food they did have and so began using human feces as fuel. They were cut off from the dump outside the city, so garbage began stacking up in the street. Maggots, fleas, and sickness spread. Soon the starved, jagged, bloodied corpses began to pile up, so they threw them over the city wall, literally raining death on the Babylonians. Order in the city quickly evaporated, causing riots, looting, and murder. For nearly eighteen months, Jerusalem was locked inside with itself. By the end, it was said that mothers even began to boil and eat their own children (Lamentations 4:10).

Yet in hindsight, the Jewish nation did not think it had been abandoned or wronged by God. Quite the contrary. Looking back, they believed they had been treated rather fairly. Considering their own national history of abuse, greed, civil war, and child sacrifice, the consequences seemed only fitting to them. They believed that they were merely reaping what they had sown and that justice had been done:

> Because our ancestors angered the God of heaven, he gave them into the hands of Nebuchadnezzar the Chaldean, king of Babylon, who destroyed this temple and deported the people to Babylon. (Ezra 5:12)

I will punish ... them ... for their ways and repay them for their deeds. (Hosea 4:9-10)

The Jewish nation believed this was their just deserts: they had fed their children to Baal and so now were devoured by Babylon. They had ignored the years of Jubilee, belittling and oppressing the poor, and so were now made little themselves. They believed that what goes around comes back around, that we get what is coming to us. In other words, they believed the universe was governed by *justice*.

Now, you might be a little uncomfortable with the image of an angry God smiting and judging the nation. You may be imagining a street preacher yelling that hurricanes are punishment for your premarital sex. But perhaps divine justice is less about God losing his cool and more about the way the world works. If God is just, then God naturally would have created a just cosmos—a fair and balanced universe—where we tend to get back what we put out. You get what you give, you get served what you deserve, you take what you make. So perhaps justice is less God getting randomly annoyed and more the natural consequences of our actions coming back around to haunt us. It's less "Hurricanes are punishment for getting your swerve on" and more "Human industry and greed brought global warming on ourselves."

Yet even if these are the natural consequences, you might still feel like being besieged and starved by Babylon is a tad excessive or unfair. But notice that you are still consenting to the underlying point of the story, that things *should be fair*. It's precisely because you think justice is a real and important value that you think it was *unjust* for them to be punished so severely. So even if something within us rebels against the severity of the story, it rebels in the name of the underlying idea the story is trying to convey: justice.

Indeed, most of us have this sense that things should be just. Things ought to be fair. Something within us cries out at the injustice of Hitler going out on his own terms instead of facing judgment and a war tribunal. Something within us cries out against the injustice of billionaires getting away with paying less in taxes than the poor. Something within us cries out at the injustice of seventeen-year-old Trayvon Martin lying dead while his attacker walks free (and recently made $250,000 by selling the murder weapon as racist memorabilia). Something within us cries out against injustice even as early as the playground, when we see bullies prey on the weak without retribution.

But justice isn't only about punishing people who do bad. It's about rewarding people who do good. Our sense of justice is our sense that people *should be treated how they deserve to be treated*. If you work ten hours, you deserve ten hours' pay. If you give love, devotion, and service to your partner, you deserve love, devotion, and service back.

Justice is not only about punishment; it's about fairness. Justice is everyone getting what they deserve. That's why social justice isn't primarily about punishing oppressors but about liberating the oppressed and giving them the dignity and treatment and opportunities that they as humans deserve. It's only if we believe in fairness and justice that we can say every child *deserves* a childhood, that men and women *deserve* the same pay for the same work, and that everyone *deserves* the same opportunities regardless of skin color. So while some aspects of justice might make us more squeamish than others, at the end of the day, most of us are on board with the overall package. We'd rather live in a just world than an unjust one, a world where you get what you give.

Yet, looking around us, we see that most of the world is not just. Most people are not treated the way they deserve to be treated. There may be fleeting moments of justice being done, such as when Harvey Weinstein actually went to prison, but there are also moments of justice being undone, such as when Bill Cosby got out on a technicality. There may be shining moments of apartheid being undone and Nelson Mandela being justly released, but only after centuries of evil and decades unjustly shackled on Robben Island. For every village that gets clean drinking water there is another that does not, as well as a golf course wasting it away on greener grass. There may be a few moments when oppressors are overcome and the oppressed are vindicated, but those are rare and occasional sprinkles on a giant crap-cake of injustice.

This life is not just. So if justice is real, it must be in the next life. At least, that's the religious argument. If justice is a real and absolute value in our universe, then ultimately it has to be done. And if it's not done in this life, it must be done in the next. As one man said, "My name is Maximus Decimus Meridius . . . father to a murdered son. Husband to a murdered wife. *And I will have my vengeance, in this life or the next.*"[1] Or to quote a less bloodthirsty source, Martin Luther King Jr. once said, "The arc of the moral universe is long, but it bends toward justice."[2]

Vince Gilligan, the creator of *Breaking Bad*, who has spent his career exploring the mentality and gradual decline of criminals, says:

> I hate the idea of Idi Amin living in Saudi Arabia for the last 25 years of his life. That galls me to no end. I feel some sort of need for biblical atonement, or justice, or something. I like to believe there is some comeuppance, that karma kicks in at some point, even if it takes years or decades to happen. My girlfriend says this great thing that's become my philosophy as well. "I want to believe there's a Heaven. But I can't not believe there's a hell."[3]

Justice must be done. And it can begin to be done in this life ("Hello, Babylon!") or it can be done in the next ("Hello, Hitler! Today you will be recircumcised every hour by a Jewish mohel. Please take a seat next to Prometheus"). Either way, the universe will balance itself out. While different religions may disagree on the details, we tend to agree that the imbalances of this life will be made right in the next. If you are a jerk in this life, either you will be judged by God in the afterlife or you will reincarnate on earth as a dung beetle. We may disagree on the details, but the underlying virtue of justice seems to be darn near universal.

And it makes sense that different cultures and religions repeatedly hit on the same idea because there's a real and perhaps inescapable logic to the whole thing. You can either believe justice is an objective moral value in the universe, or not. If not, then throw out all this nonsense about fair treatment, accountability, social justice, wrongs being made right, or liberating the oppressed and reining in the oppressor. Those are just social constructs we've invented, and our social construct of love and justice is no better than our oppressor's social construct of dominance and power.

However, if justice really is an objective moral value in the universe, then that must mean it is an unchanging, eternal, absolute good. That must mean the very nature of existence and Being is *just*—that God is justice itself. In which case, it's not like justice can just *not happen*. It's not like God could have flippantly given the Jewish nation a pass. It's not like God could just as easily have woken up on the other side of heaven that day and been super chill about all their child sacrifices. And thinking of it that way shows you've stopped thinking about God as the eternal Being who grounds goodness and justice itself, and started to think about God the same way you think about the fleeting whims of finite *beings*.

Humans can be loving one day and inconsistently cruel the next because, thankfully, we aren't the eternal foundations for morality. A judge can treat a White criminal justly one day and a Black criminal unjustly the next because morality is higher than the fleeting moods and prejudices of an individual. Cultures can flip-flop on moral issues every minute, month, or millennia because they are not the eternal foundations of morality itself.

But God is. God is goodness, love, and justice itself. Asking God to be unjust is like asking two plus two to not equal four. It's asking existence to not be what it *is*. I don't even think it's logically possible for the one who is the objective ground of justice to choose not to be just. God is the one who grounds morality, so if God changes, then morality itself changes and so was never eternal or objective to begin with. Either justice is an objective value, or it is a social construct—you can't have it one way when it's convenient and another way when it's not. You can't belief in justice when it's giving an oppressed people the rights they deserve but not believe in it when it's giving the oppressor the comeuppance that they deserve.

Having heard all this, you might think God is the problem here. You might think that, if God is the one throwing a hissy fit and punishing everybody, then let's stop believing in the wrathful fairy princess above and avoid these issues altogether. However, it's the same predicament with or without God in the picture. Though I've argued in a previous chapter that it doesn't make sense, let us grant for the moment that there could be a just and moral universe without God. Yet in such a universe, justice would still need to be done—it just wouldn't be God doing it. The universe would still need to balance the books and pay back everyone what they are owed; it just could no longer outsource that task to God. Justice would simply be baked into reality as another one of the natural laws of the universe, in the same way as the laws of gravity or thermodynamics. So, karma. What goes around would still come back around: a murder for a murder and a punch for a punch; those who slaughter their infants would themselves be slaughtered when they're reborn. Keeping justice but getting rid of God wouldn't really change the equation much at all.

And in some ways, it makes the problem even worse. If no justice is deferred until heaven or hell, then all sins must be repaid here and now on this earth. And if literally everything that happens on earth is karma for a past life on earth, then if someone gets raped, it's because they deserved it. If someone is handicapped, it's because they did something in a past life to deserve it. If someone is from a lower caste, it's because they deserve to be there and deserve to be treated as lesser. By collapsing the way things justly should be into the way things unjustly are, some (not all, but some) versions of karma have only reaffirmed old hierarchies and injustices.

In contrast, the traditional afterlife still keeps these things somewhat separate, deferring ultimate judgment until heaven and hell. Yes, there can be moments of justice here and now on earth—like with Babylon—but these are few and far between. For the most part, things in this life are not yet what they are supposed to be and won't be made fully right until after we die. The poor person is not paying for a past life; no, they are just mistreated because greedy humans stink, and God will repay the poor but honest person with heaven and the greedy person with, well, let's save that for a later chapter.

Now, you might feel uncomfortable with the implications of all this, especially in light of the gory details of Babylon invading (I feel uncomfortable too, by the way). And you might feel doubly uncomfortable in light of the fact that you (like me) are a sinner, so justice coming for sins is not exactly great news for us. However, personal discomfort aside, I wonder which part of the logic you actually find fault with?

After a year and a half, Babylon finally broke through the walls of Jerusalem. Thousands of soldiers streamed through, meeting little to no resistance from the starving masses. They burned every barn, store, and street, casting light on every dark deed and desire. Many of those who survived the night were later dragged in chains to exile in Babylon.

Thankfully, Persia invaded Babylon half a century later (539 BC), and the Persians let all the Jews return home. But then the Greeks invaded Jerusalem (332 BC). And then later Rome took over the Promised Land (63 BC). Meaning that the Jewish people were never again the great nation they had once been—the great nation promised to their forefather Abraham. So they waited on God to save them. Waited on God to send a Messiah to free them from Babylon, free them from the Greeks, free them from the oppression of Rome. Waited for the third movement of nation to transition to a fourth movement of redemption.

And they are still waiting. To this day, they still leave an empty chair at their ceremonies and dinners, inviting the Messiah and his forerunners to come and sit down among them. They are still waiting on a Messiah from God to come and free them once and for all from the fire of their earthly enemies. Still waiting for a Messiah to definitively carve out the Promised Land of Israel and judge the other nations that bomb and rage against them. The chair is still empty.

For the true Messiah would not save them from their enemies *but from themselves.*

The true Messiah would not deal with the symptoms of Babylon *but the fallen disease of sin that led to it.*

The true Messiah would not slay Babylon or Rome but would *himself be slain.*

The true Messiah would not only bring justice but suffer justice once and for all *in our place.*

MOVEMENT IV
Redemption

MY SENIOR YEAR (grade twelve) was almost over, and I was exhausted and guilt-ridden from failing to improve and overcome my struggles. Plus, earlier that year my parents had gotten a divorce, and there had also been a death in my immediate family, so I wasn't in a great space emotionally. I was losing the struggle to generational sins as well as to some new ones I'd found all on my own.

A local youth pastor invited me on a spring break trip down to Mexico to help rebuild a small village, and I, hearing *Mexico* but ignoring the rest, thought this could be a relaxing vacation. Nope. I was sick and vomiting the whole trip down, which, due to our being too cheap to pay for a direct flight, involved multiple airplanes and an eight-hour bus ride from hell. Then we were put to manual labor in the Mexican heat. The first day on the building site I stepped down and a nail went through my left foot. A few days later, I broke the big toe on my right foot.

So now I was lying around in pain feeling sorry for myself. The youth pastor who organized the trip came and guilted me into joining the nightly worship service. Annoyed, I eventually gave in and got up, hobbling late to the church service on two broken feet. And in front of the whole church, I whipped out my middle finger and flipped that pastor the bird. Multiple gasps filled the room, and I sat down, pleased with myself for a second before my weariness and brokenness rushed back in, and I realized just how much I needed help. I'd been fighting a futile battle with myself that was two steps forward, two steps back, and I literally couldn't walk anymore. I was not going to be able to pull myself up by my own moral bootstraps—I needed goodness to come down and meet me where I was. I started praying, asking God to do what I could not. Until that moment I would have vehemently denied it, but what I really needed was someone to save me.

The third movement of the Jewish nation revealed God as Being, Beauty, Goodness, and Justice itself. Yet it also made us more aware than ever of how far we've fallen from those higher standards and of our desperate need for redemption. We are caught in cycles of generational sin and baggage (i.e., Solomon) and keep choosing what is bad for ourselves and for others (hence Babylon). If movement two showed we were sinners, then movement three showed this sin was not going away. Yet while it was two steps forward and two steps back for the Jewish nation, it was still through them and the ancestral line of Abraham, Moses, David, and Solomon that we eventually got to two of their descendants: a pregnant couple named Mary and Joseph. Through the Jewish people and nation, God did eventually bring about the one who would redeem humanity and undo the fall—a Savior to save us from ourselves. And it came not from a king or a military triumph but from a wailing babe in a manger. . . .

CREATION 🎯

Creation Begins ●
Creation Is Not God ●
Creation Is Good ●

FALL

Humanity in God's Image ●
Humanity Gone Wild ●

NATION 👑

Abraham Finds Faith ● 2000 BC
Moses Meets I Am ● 1400–1200ish BC
Goodness Is Commanded ●
Beauty in the Promised Land ●
King David and His Boy ● 1000ish BC
Justice Exiles the Nation ● 586 BC

REDEMPTION 🔼

Jesus Is Born ● AD 0
Jesus Is Walking Around Saying Stuff ● AD 30
Jesus Is Dying to Meet You ● AD 33

CHURCH 🏠

The Spirit Arrives ● AD 33
The Church Begins ● AD 33
The Apostle Paul Converts ● AD 35ish
The Church Expands ● AD 300ish
The Church Today ● The Present

END ❇️

The End of the World as We Know It ●
Highway to Hell or Stairway to Heaven? ●

TWELVE

Jesus Is Born

IMAGINE A WOMAN SCREAMING, perhaps at the top of her lungs, or perhaps at the bottom then increasing to the top like a crescendo. Imagine sweat trickling down like a summer rain, pooling at her base, along with blood and feces. Imagine fast breathing, like trying to blow the steam off a hot soup. Imagine this is all happening in a barn, with cows mooing, goats baaing, donkeys heehawing.[1] Imagine guests keep arriving and adding themselves and their gifts to the intensity of this moment. Then add in some final blood and bloodcurdling screams, a dash more animal acoustics, and you get the birth of our Lord and Savior, Jesus Christ. Weary of their bleating and baaing, Joseph finally glares at the stables and snarls, "Merry Christmas, you filthy animals."

Little baby Jesus was finally here after what must have been a truly dreadful nine months. It had started with Joseph trying to divorce Mary. It started with Joseph feeling betrayed, assuming (rather logically) that his fiancée had cheated on him and gotten pregnant with another man's baby. It started with a broken marriage, broken trust, a broken home, a brokenness so potent that only divine intervention could get things back on track. Only an angel literally appearing to Joseph could get him to return to Mary and see their marriage through.

Soon a census was called throughout the Roman Empire. Everyone had to return to the place of their ancestors to be counted for the sake of record keeping and taxation. Now, while all Jews were descended from Abraham, Joseph was descended from Abraham specifically through the distant ancestral line of King David. And since Bethlehem was thought to have been

David's home city, Mary and Joseph headed out on the journey to Beth-lehem to be counted for the census.

One can imagine people glaring at Mary and Joseph as they went to leave, whispering to themselves about the harlot and her enabler. The people Mary and Joseph had known their whole lives were turning on them, and even their own families may have been refusing to speak to them. Perhaps not everyone knew at first—which is why Joseph had originally planned to divorce her quietly—but news travels fast in a small town, and the bump on Mary's belly was becoming hard to ignore. The town was big with childish gossip.

After a sweaty, sun-scorched, four-day (or longer) journey through the desert, our bloated, disheveled, utterly overwhelmed, teenage mom-to-be finally arrived in Bethlehem. And she was greeted not by a resounding chorus of "Hark the Herald Angels Sing" but the news that there were no guest rooms available and they'd have to stay in a barn. Now, it's hard to imagine Middle Eastern hospitality not offering a proper place to a woman on the verge of birth, so perhaps she wasn't quite full term yet. Perhaps that's also why they were willing to travel. (I mean, who travels when you're nine months pregnant?) So perhaps it was not quite time; perhaps she was only eight or even seven months pregnant. Perhaps the God of eternity arrived early, terrifyingly early. Perhaps God was born into the world gasping for air, his mother unsure whether he would make it through the hour, let alone the night. Perhaps the omnipresent God of all space himself occupied little of it, arriving small, struggling, and premature.

Either way, whether early or on time, the moment inevitably did come. And it came in a world where death by childbirth was common, at a time where there was no modern medicine or painkillers. The birth of God was felt with Mary's every muscle, contorting and stretching to somehow squeeze heaven into earth. Mary was moaning and groaning, on and off, likely for hours. In the middle of a contraction Mary might have looked at Joseph and yelled, "*You* did this to me!" And he's like, "No, I didn't."

Suddenly, all the other noises ceased, silenced by a small cry, as baby Jesus emerged out of the womb and into the world for the very first time.

Not a Photoshopped, Hallmark, superhero baby, "no crying he makes." No, baby Jesus was fully human. Covered in blood and the fluids of an earthen womb, wheezing with fresh lungs struggling to expand for the very first time, steam rising off him, contrasting the cold night air.

It has begun. God has become incarnate. Literally, in *carne*. *Carne* means "flesh, body, meat." A *carni*vore eats *carne*, eats beef and blood and guts. Carnage at a battle is flesh flung about. God has become meaty, bloody, sweaty, aging, vulnerable *carne*. The spiritual has become material. Eternity and time have collided in this crib.

The Almighty has become helpless and human, like a strong man who ties his hands behind his back to make it a fair fight. The infinite has become finite, like a wave that's collapsed into a particle. Absolute has become particular, like the abstract concept of love suddenly embodied in another's kiss. The ideal has become real, like heaven on earth, like where clouds and mountains meet. The God of eternity has entered our timeline, like an author who's gone all meta and written themselves into their own story. The Creator has entered creation, like nothing that has ever happened before, like no creaturely example we could compare it to, like none of our metaphors and parables that stretch to fall short of a reality stranger than fiction. God has become incarnate and now dwells among us.

◖▰▰◗

There's a popular video you might have seen in which Brené Brown illustrates the difference between sympathy and empathy.[2] She imagines a scene where someone has tripped down into a deep, dark pit in the woods, a sunken hole of their own despair (bear with me, this will eventually lead back to baby Jesus).

Brown explains that *sympathy* is offering advice and support to the fallen person from outside the pit. Sympathy plants itself above the hole and yells down from a distance, "Hey you, you good? You want me to throw down like a sandwich or something?" Sympathy offers advice from the outside: "Hey, you should get out of there. It's way sunnier and warmer up here. You'll love it!" But empathy is climbing down into the pit yourself and sitting next to someone in their despair for as long as it takes until they're ready to climb back out. Empathy means descending into someone's pain and emotions, experiencing it not from the outside but from the inside, going through it with them. Empathy is mourning with those who mourn and rejoicing with those who rejoice. Empathy is hard because it "makes you vulnerable as well, for in order to connect with someone else's pain, you have to open up that part of yourself that has also felt those emotions." It requires you to actually go through a little piece of that pain yourself and to help carry their emotional load. That's hard to do, which is "why sympathy is so much more common."

Brown explains that we don't always know how to respond to someone else's emotions and struggles, so we try to find something sympathetic to say to fill the awkward silence. We try to give some piece of advice or try to find some silver lining to make them feel better as quickly as humanly (or rather, *subhumanly*) possible. Someone says, "I had a miscarriage," and sympathy responds, "I'm so sorry . . . but at least your baby is in heaven now, and you'll get to see them one day." Someone says, "My son is failing out of school," and sympathy responds, "Have you tried getting him a tutor? At least your daughter is a top student, though, so that's good!" Sympathy doesn't enter into the emotional experience of the other; it stands at a distance, lobbing advice at them from afar. We all know what it's like to have someone give you advice who clearly has no idea what you're going through. They might be well intentioned but they just don't get it. They haven't been there, they haven't gone through what you're going through, they haven't felt those things themselves, and instead of coming down into the pit and sitting with you, they just keep trying to pull you out before you're ready. They throw down a rope instead of coming down themselves.

But rarely does advice or sympathy actually make things better. What "makes things better is connection."[3] Relationship is what helps us weather reality. Most of the time, what people need is not just advice or sympathy. What they really need is someone to go through the experience with them, to feel like someone else gets it, someone else knows what it's like, someone else has been in the same place we are. Humans can get through almost anything if we know we are not alone in it.

And that is the beauty of Christmas. Christmas is the moment God descends into the pit of humanity, down into the struggles and mess and muck of *carne*. God didn't just shout rules and sympathy and advice at us from the heavens. No, God actually came down and experienced life with us, from the inside, as one of us—as a real, wriggling, baby of flesh and *carne*. Born not into some idealistic nuclear family but into near-divorce, scandal, and an unwed teen mother. Whatever relationship woes or family drama or public embarrassment I'm going through, Jesus gets it. He's down in that pit with me.

Christ was born not as a king in some castle in the clouds but as a peasant amid poverty, amid a manger, amid animals and stool and stench. And then as he grew up, he learned his father's trade as a carpenter, working long hours for decades to make ends meet. He was a working-class, salt-of-the-earth, wake-up-before-the-sun carpenter for thirty years before he was ever a preacher. Whatever struggles with finances, exhaustion, work, success, and security we have, God gets it. He's been down in that money pit.

Baby Jesus cried, laughed, smelled, stumbled and learned to walk; he grew up just as we did, going through all the pain of puberty and pimples and bullies and awkwardness. And if he *truly* was fully human, then the adolescent Jesus might even have had a crush or two. He might have known what it's like to be single and watch every one else get together in their seemingly perfect love lives. In fact, I imagine accepting his own singleness might have been one of the hardest parts of accepting who he was and his higher calling. We are never alone in our loneliness. God has been there. He's down in that pit with us, even when no one else is.

And as Jesus grew older, the inevitable decomposition of *carne* would have brought him face to face for the first time with death. But not his own. The Christmas story is the last time Joseph is mentioned by name in the Gospels. Joseph's absence, plus Jesus handing over care of his mother to the apostle John, make probable something that few have ever thought about: Joseph died. God knows what it's like to lose a parent, what it's like to grow up without a tree of past wisdom to lean on. That is the scandal of the incarnation, that the Father of all the universe has some sense of what it is to lose a father. That as we age and our loved ones begin to depart, God does not simply shout clichés at us from above: "Oh, but they're in heaven now." No, God knows what it is like to lose someone you love more than life itself. He's been there, held the weight of those emotions, felt that pit in his chest and known that almost nothing could ever fill it.

God is down here in the pit *with us*. And somehow, that matters far more than any advice or commands God might lob at us from above. Because at the end of the day, it is not sympathy that changes things—it's connection. It's intimacy. Empathy. Love. It's having others incarnate into our lives and loss. Like soldiers returning home from war, we find that no one really understands what we've gone through except those who've also gone through it. And Jesus has been down in those trenches next to us the whole time—he was born into them.

CREATION

Creation Begins

Creation Is Not God

Creation Is Good

FALL

Humanity in God's Image

Humanity Gone Wild

NATION

Abraham Finds Faith — 2000 BC

Moses Meets I Am — 1400–1200ish BC

Goodness Is Commanded

Beauty in the Promised Land

King David and His Boy — 1000ish BC

Justice Exiles the Nation — 586 BC

REDEMPTION

Jesus Is Born — AD 0

Jesus Is Walking Around Saying Stuff — AD 30

Jesus Is Dying to Meet You! — AD 33

CHURCH

The Spirit Arrives — AD 33

The Church Begins — AD 33

The Apostle Paul Converts — AD 35ish

The Church Expands — AD 300ish

The Church Today — The Present

END

The End of the World as We Know It

Highway to Hell or Stairway to Heaven?

THIRTEEN

Jesus Is Walking Around Saying Stuff

JESUS IS ALL GROWN UP NOW, and his first great act is to get everyone drunk at a wedding. He turns water into wine and respectable adults into relaxed, laughing, dancing, giggling children. Most hosts serve the best wine upfront and save the cheap wine for when everyone is too wasted to notice. But Jesus saves "the best for last." Meaning that at the point when most are about to pack it in, when your aunt's sliding off her chair, that's when Jesus shows up and really gets this party started.

It is amazing the somersaults teetotaling preachers do to deny this: "It was grape juice, not wine." "Alcohol was less alcoholic back then." "He made the wine but didn't drink it himself." This is indicative of how the rest of this chapter, and the rest of Jesus' life, and the rest of Christian history, will go. Jesus is way too big for any one person, one church, one philosophy, one cultural set of mores to accommodate all of him. We can get behind him on some things but nail him on the rest.

Jesus leaves the wedding and starts putting together his dream team.* He doesn't do interviews or seek out the leading religious scholars of the day to join him. Instead, he gets splinters under his fingernails from scraping the absolute bottom of the fish barrel. Walking along the Sea of Galilee one day, he sees two exasperated fisherman, Peter and Andrew, pulling in their nets after a long day of coming up empty. Jesus tells them to try again. They protest, but eventually they give in and indulge this weird guy on the beach.

---

*The Gospel writers ordered their stories differently to highlight different points, so I'm not going to be terribly concerned in this chapter with matching any exact chronology of events. I'm also gonna paraphrase a bunch of stuff. Please save your appall until the end.

This time, their nets bulge with wriggling fish, overflowing and tearing at the seams. They stare slack-jawed at the man standing on the sand, but Jesus doesn't clarify or elaborate or explain the trick. He just says, "Follow me," then starts walking away.

Peter, Andrew, and a few others are on board now, but already they are concerned about the quality of the new recruits. Jesus keeps hanging out with prostitutes, criminals, and (gasp) tax collectors. The nation had been invaded by Rome, and Jewish tax collectors are now working for the enemy, getting rich by collecting tax from their Jewish brethren and sending it thousands of miles away to Caesar. They are traitors to their own people, like Black slave owners or Jewish ghetto police. And here comes Jesus, like it's no big deal, saying to Matthew the tax collector exactly what he says to everyone else: "Follow me." And the bastard follows him, almost like he wasn't just a bastard anymore.

Matthew, the former tax collector, invites Jesus and his followers over to his house, where he cooks them a lavish meal using that tax-collector dough. The local religious leaders are outraged when they find out, whispering violently: "Why is Jesus eating with *tax collectors* and *sinners*?!" Jesus overhears this (he's an omni-hearer, obviously), and retorts, "It is not the healthy who need a doctor, but the sick." He's not interested in self-righteous church people, but sinners, sickos, traitors, and perverts—people who actually know they are broken and are willing to ask for help.

Even worse, there are women hanging out with him now. Human women! Only boys received synagogue education from a rabbi back then. Only men were allowed to sit at the feet of religious teachers and be mentored by them. But the Bible lists Jesus' female followers by name, including Mary, Joanna, and Susanna. Untethered from their homes, unconcerned with domesticity, they go vagabonding with Jesus from town to town, receiving spiritual instruction from him just like the men. Two of them are sisters, Mary and Martha. Martha busies herself preparing a meal and hosting, while Mary sits in the other room with the men, listening and peppering Jesus with questions. Martha tells her sister to slow her roll and come help with the housework like a good girl. Jesus says no,

Mary is exactly where she is supposed to be. "Mary has chosen what is better."

In one of the towns Jesus visits, there's a woman who's been discharging vaginal blood nonstop for twelve years, and so has been declared ritually unclean according to the same customs whereby a woman on her period has to sleep outside the city walls. This poor woman hasn't felt the warmth of another human in over a decade, for even to hold another's hand would be to make them ritually unclean as well. She's been abandoned by her family, by her husband, by her community. No matter what she does, she can't stop the bleeding or the pain or the smell. She's spent all her money subjecting herself to doctor's experiments and now begs on the street to survive. She hears there is a miracle man coming through and thinks, *If I could touch even just the hem of his robe, perhaps I might be healed.* But the crowd clamoring around Jesus is too great, so she crawls between their legs to get through. She reaches up and touches Jesus' robe from below, trembling with fear that he will rebuke her for doing so. Yet instead of backing away in disgust, instead of chiding her for making him spiritually unclean as well, instead of recoiling from the reek of womanly things, Jesus speaks to her like she's his child. "Daughter," he says, "your faith has healed you. Go in peace and be free."

Later on, there's a man with a shriveled hand he cannot unclasp. This probably prevented him from farming or doing basic labor, making employment—or even survival—uncertain. The man goes to the synagogue one day on the Sabbath, for it is the holy day of rest, when no work or even begging are allowed to be done. Jesus happens to be passing through, and he stands up and speaks in the synagogue. Mid-speech, Jesus randomly turns and reaches out halfway to the man, saying: "Stretch out your hand." It seems like a cruel joke at first, until the man actually reaches back in response, unfurling his fingers for the first time in years. Not only has Jesus just done another miracle, but he's done it on the Sabbath, the day of rest, when no one is supposed to do anything according to the religious laws. The holy men are furious, crying out that healing a hand is technically doing work on the Sabbath. Jesus retorts that "the Sabbath was made for man, not man for the Sabbath." You cling to your religious guidelines yet forget the people you are there to guide. The Sabbath was meant to help everyone chill out and relax and build a day of rest into the seven-day work cycle. But when you make it another thing to stress out about, it negates its original purpose. Policies were made for the sake of people, not people for the sake of policies. Bureaucracy doesn't matter, but the bureaucrat does.

Yet some of the religious leaders ignore his words and keep focusing on superficial stuff like Sabbath rituals and moral clauses and religious dress codes. They focus on the outer person, on the rituals and actions that can be seen.[1] But Jesus cares more about what is inside, what's unseen, what goes on behind the eyes instead of what lies before them. The religious leaders say do not murder; Jesus says "whoever hates has already murdered the person in their heart." The religious leaders say do not commit adultery; Jesus says if you repeatedly fantasize about having sex with your coworker, you've "already committed adultery with them in your heart." Watch your thoughts, for your thoughts will become your actions.[2] Behavior modification only deals with the symptoms; Jesus goes directly and surgically for the heart of the issue.

But behavior modification is religion's bread and butter, and if Jesus keeps this up he's gonna be toast. People don't like that this guy keeps questioning the powers that be and the whole social system. Even his own family is worried and weary of what Jesus is doing. They go to tell him to *stop preaching, be quiet, come home, stop embarrassing us and yourself.* Jesus' followers tell him his family is outside and wants a word, and Jesus responds: "Who is my family?" Then he points to his followers and says, "These are my family. Whoever is a child in the household of God is my brother and sister." Harsh words, but ones that many of us may end up uttering in one form or another, when the family we choose ends up more reliable than the family we were born into.

In fact, Jesus doesn't prioritize the traditional nuclear family nearly as much as you might expect (especially if you grew up with James Dobson and Focus on the Family). Jesus is single (a cultural oddity at his age) and tells people that the truths he brings are deeper than blood and likely to turn father against son and daughter against mother. And when a man uses his dying father as an excuse, Jesus responds with these harsh words: "Let the dead bury the dead." Try preaching that on Mother's Day. Jesus knows family is important and can bring us to God, but he also knows it can become an idol that gets between us and God. Much like nuclear power itself, family can be amazing, until suddenly it isn't.

Though perhaps Jesus' family was right to be worried, because the people in his hometown later try to throw him off a cliff, after he preaches a sermon proclaiming good news to the poor. Poverty is one of his favorite topics, by the way. He often says things like *blessed are the poor, for they will be rewarded in heaven*. And that might seem like religious opium—a drug to sedate and silence the masses so they'll be content with their poor lot on earth. Except that Jesus also tells the rich people they are going to hell. He says it is easier for a camel to fit through the eye of a needle than for a rich man to enter heaven, which is a fun, folksy way of saying *fat chance*. He tells stories about great banquets, where poor beggars are invited off the street to come and feast, while the royal court is locked out in the cold. Jesus says a day of justice is coming when the whole economic and social system will be inverted: "the first shall become last and the last become first." He tells the tale of Lazarus and the rich man. In this life Lazarus was a beggar at a rich man's door, but in the next life the rich man looks up at Lazarus in heaven, begging him to send down a drop of water to sooth his scorching tongue below. So if Jesus really is like a drug, he's not the kind that calms the masses down, but that makes them see things differently and want to flip the whole world on its head.

Yet finances are only one aspect of turning reality upside down. One day Jesus is teaching, and some children try to run up and see him, but his followers block them from getting near and interrupting the lesson. Jesus sees and cries out, "Let the little children come to me." Then he says to the crowd: "Unless you change and become like little children, you will never enter the kingdom of heaven. Whoever humbles himself like this child is the greatest in the kingdom of heaven." Remember back before you grew up, when you didn't use to take yourself so seriously? When you didn't assume you already knew everything there was to know, when each new second on earth still seemed to open wide the heavens with possibility instead of slamming them shut with a dull incuriosity that makes of everything a hell? Only grownups could ever possibly worry they would bore of eternal life. Perhaps it is no coincidence that in one of the earlier versions of Peter Pan, Neverland was actually heaven. Earth may be run by adults, but heaven belongs to little boys and girls. For Jesus, true maturity is to be reborn to the wide-eyed wonder and humility of youth, knowing the place for the very first time. The young will become old, and the old shall become young.

Another thing about little toddlers: they'll play with almost anyone. Jesus says to the crowd, "Love your neighbor as yourself." And the crowd cleverly retorts: "But who is my neighbor? You just mean my fellow Jew next door, right? Not all these other gross people, right?" In response, Jesus tells a story of a Jewish man traveling on a backwoods road from Jerusalem who gets robbed, stripped, and left for dead. A Jewish priest passes by but doesn't have time to carry the man to the nearest town (and was perhaps a tad worried that whoever did this was still nearby). So he went on his merry way. Later that day, another man from noble Jewish stock came across the dying body on the road. He too left and did nothing. Finally, a Samaritan came along. The Samaritans were often seen as foreigners in the land, abominations before God, half-breeds who perverted the Jewish lineage. Yet this good Samaritan (yes, that's where the saying comes from) has mercy on the man and stops to help him. He carries him to a nearby inn and pays for everything until the man is nursed back to health.

Having told the story, Jesus now turns to his Jewish audience, and says: "Which of these three men do you think was a neighbor to the dying man?" Perhaps annoyed, they eventually concede, saying, "The one who showed mercy to the dying man." And Jesus says, "Then go and do likewise." Go and be a neighbor to everyone, whether they be Jewish or Samaritan, Israeli or Palestinian, American or Russian, Christian or Muslim, Black or White, gay or straight, trans or cis, progressive or conservative. Jesus said all the clichés we post online, he just said them two thousand years ago in a Middle Eastern world that would eventually kill him for saying it. And he's the reason they are clichés today.

But Jesus doesn't stop there. He goes further. Don't just love those who are the opposite of you but those who are actively *opposed* to you. It's one thing to accept someone's handshake when they reach out to you across the aisle; it's an entirely different thing when they come at you with a machete. Yet Jesus says, "Love your enemies and pray for those who persecute you." Pray for the guy walking toward you with a Nazi tattoo; pray for your bully on the playground; pray for your abusive boss (report him, but also pray for him); pray for your predator of a landlord; pray for the man who keeps yelling over you; pray for the woman you think is ruining society; pray for the oppressors and the haters and the tyranny of evil men; pray for the pedophiles and rapists; pray for the suicide bomber as they are bombing you.

Jesus prays for the unprayable, sees the unseeable, and forgives the unforgiveable. He's not permissive; he still tells them to stop sinning in the future. It's just that he's willing to forgive them for their past. The crowd asks, "How many times should we forgive a person—seven times?" And Jesus responds, "Forgive them seventy times seven times." In other words, more times than you can imagine using mental math. In fact, don't judge others at all, he says; focus on making yourself better instead. Don't focus on the speck in your brother's eye when you've got a great big bloody log in your own.

Yet still, no one quite believes Jesus is serious about this, and they try to trick him into a corner and make him contradict himself or contradict the law (which could get him put away). They find a woman who has been caught in the act of adultery; perhaps she cheated on her husband, perhaps she helped someone else cheat on his wife. Either way, the crowd is yelling "Whore! Temptress! Home-wrecker!" and dragging her into the street to humiliate and then stone her to death, as is the accepted custom. They throw her at Jesus' feet and say, "Teacher, this woman was caught in the act of adultery. In our laws it says to stone such a woman to death. What do you say?" Jesus kneels down and starts writing something in the sand, barely even acknowledging the wrathful crowd and its self-righteous hullaballoo. He eventually looks up and says, "Alright. Whichever one of you has never sinned before can throw the first stone." Then he goes right back to drawing in the sand.

Dumbfounded, the crowd stands there, stones raised awkwardly, not sure what to do now. Then one by one they drop their stones and leave, the oldest first, perhaps because a lifetime's worth of mistakes now floods their memory, and they know better than anyone they're not innocent either. Finally, after every stone is left behind in the dirt, Jesus turns to the woman and looks up at her. She's the only person in the story he gives the dignity of looking at and speaking to directly. He says, "Where is everyone? Did no one condemn you?" "No sir," she stammers. "Then neither do I condemn you," he whispers. "Go now and walk a better path."

So it's pretty clear by now that Jesus is all about loving adulterers, criminals, social pariahs, and outcasts. He's all about praying for your enemies, opponents, and neighbors; pretty much for anyone but yourself. And when you do finally pray for yourself, he says to keep it simple, and live simply. Just pray these words: "Give us this day our daily bread." You just need enough food for your family today, not a yacht for next summer. In fact, this request for a yeast influxion is the only part of the Lord's Prayer that asks for physical stuff at all. The rest of it seems to be unbearably personal ways of talking with God—almost like he's a friend or loved one—starting with the intimate phrase "Our Father," better translated "Daddy" or "Papa." This is a snuggled-up child telling their parent about their day, not a brat telling Santa he wants a pony.

In fact, Jesus saves his juiciest wrath for those making religion about getting rich instead of about getting to know God. Heading for the big city of Jerusalem, he goes straight to the outer court of the temple—the only part of the temple that foreigners, non-Jews, women, and the handicapped are actually allowed to enter. The inner courts of God's presence are for male, Jewish, functioning eyes only. Jesus enters this outer court and sees it's been stuffed full of salesmen and gift shops and product placements,

trying to make money off the minorities they've condescended to let
through some, but not all, of the doors. Furious, he flips over the tables of
the money changers, violently knocking their coins into the dirt and
chasing them outside. He cries, "This was supposed to be a place of prayer
for all peoples of the world, but you've turned it into a den of robbers!" The
incarnate Christ embraces the full spectrum of human emotion—sometimes anger is the only appropriate response to injustice.

The religious leaders in the temple are furious, of course. They demand
to know what gives him the right to do these things: "By whose authority
are you disrupting our temple operations?!" Jesus doesn't really answer
their questions, except with more questions and riddles. Jesus later heals a
woman and tells her, "Your sins are forgiven." Again, the leaders demand
he explain himself, for who can forgive sins but God alone? (I like to
imagine Jesus amusedly shrugging here, giving them a look like "I think
you just answered your own question.") The leaders think they are the
rightful descendants of their forefather Abraham, heirs to the great holy
nation, and so owed an explanation from Jesus. Jesus never gives it to them,
responding that Abraham is not really their father. Indignant and confused,
they shout back: "What do you mean Abraham is not our father?!" And
Jesus replies, "Your only father is Satan."

As the days roll on, Jesus begins talking more and more about Father
Abraham, almost like he knows him personally, almost like he's an old friend
and not the long-dead ancestor of the entire Jewish people, almost like
Abraham died only yesterday instead of thousands of years ago. The listening
crowd retorts, "You're not even fifty years old! And yet you talk like you've
seen Abraham?!" Jesus responds, "I tell you the truth. Before Abraham was,
I AM." Immediately, without missing a beat, they all pick up rocks to stone
him to death, for Jesus has just said the one absolutely and utterly unfath-
omable thing for a Jew to say. He's taken God's name—I AM—and applied it
to himself. "I was here before Abraham," he essentially says, "before the nation
and the earth and time and space and light. I AM eternity; I AM Being itself."

Jesus escapes the temple just in time to avoid getting stoned. You might
think he would have learned his lesson, but instead he doubles—nay

triples—down. He's slipping this I AM statement into pretty much everything now. The people complain they are hungry, and Jesus responds, "I AM the bread of life." Someone makes the mistake of talking about the afterlife in front of him, and Jesus jumps in, saying, "I AM the resurrection and the life." Someone casually asks Jesus where he's headed next, and he says, "I AM the Way, the Truth, and the Life." So he's not being subtle about it. Jesus is clearly making the bold and/or bonkers claim that the God of Abraham and Moses—the God who is Being, Goodness, Justice, and Beauty itself—is incarnate in him.

Jesus is not claiming to be an elevated being, or another one of the gods, or a human being like Pharoah or Hercules who becomes a god; he's claiming to be Being itself. He's not offering another culturally relative take on what is good; he is Goodness itself. He's not another teacher helping guide us on our way to the truth; he is the Way, he is the Truth. Jesus is not claiming to be another character in the story; he's claiming to be the author. A character in a novel cannot escape their pages and take hold of the author's pen, but the author can go all meta and write themselves into the plot. Humans cannot ascend to God, but God can descend to us; a man cannot go back in time and become his own maker, but the maker can become a man. Mere beings could never usurp Being itself, but Being can incarnate among us, precisely because it already underlies and upholds all beings to begin with. Creation cannot back up and become its own Creator, but the Creator can enter their creation, like a father kneeling down into the playhouse he built for his children. We creatures exist on a totally different axis from the Creator—we chug forward in horizontal time while God's is a vertical eternity. And yet even on a grid the horizontal and vertical axis must meet in one, and only one, spot. Jesus is claiming to be that spot.

It is only once we understand the uniqueness and radicalness of this I AM claim that all the other things Jesus says begin to make any sense. He says, "He who is not with me is against me," which can seem a bit arrogant or harsh, until you realize that you're kind of either on team Love, Justice, Beauty, Goodness, and Being itself, or you're on team hate, injustice, badness, and nonbeing. All the good and love you've found elsewhere was not actually anywhere else but in him all along. You've always loved the song—now you know who sings it. Jesus' claim doesn't compete with any others as if he were down on the same level as them fighting for territory; no, he is the Goodness that other teachers, rabbis, lamas, imams, and gurus have unknowingly pointed to whenever they said anything good. And yet this expansiveness narrows out at the tip, because saying and doing good things does not actually seem to be fallen humanity's default. Broad is the path that leads to evil and destruction, Jesus says, while mine is the road less traveled through a narrow gate.

❰ ❙ ❙ ❱

The religious leaders have been trying to find a way to kill Jesus for a while now, but their timeline just leaped forward now that he's, you know, casually claiming to be existence itself. He will be dead within the week; they know it, he knows it, even the disciples suspect it. And yet Jesus' language is only getting harsher, more apocalyptic, more subverting of the reigning social order.

"Soon the sky will be darkened," he says, "and every stone of your Jerusalem temple will be knocked one from the other. I am leaving this earth soon, but will come again one day. On that day of my return, the first will indeed be made last, your social hierarchies will be hollowed out and filled with blood, and every injustice committed under the cover of darkness will be brought out into the light and made known. On that day, many will come before me," Jesus says, "and I will raise them up to glory, for they fed me when I was hungry and clothed me when I was naked. They will say to me, 'But Lord, when did we see you hungry and feed you, when did we see you naked and clothe you?' And I will say to them, 'Whatever you did for the poor and oppressed and hurting, you did for me.' Then others will come before me and be lowered down, and I will say to them, 'You did not feed me when I was hungry or clothe me when I was naked.' And they will reply in confusion, 'Lord! when did we ever see you hungry and not feed you? When did we ever see you naked and not clothe you?' And I will say, 'Whatever you did not do for the poor and oppressed and hurting, you did not do for me.'"

"Yet no one knows when this day of judgment is going to happen," Jesus says, "so don't bother with silly preachers who try to pin down the hour or day or year of my coming. Do not worry about tomorrow, just live your life here and now as if today was all you had, because it might very well be. I might return this very evening," he says, "unannounced like a thief in the night." Today might be your very last day to use your talents, to right a wrong, to care for the poor, to sit with the hurting, to be who you were called to be.

And you know he means it, because the next day would literally be his last on earth.[3] And what does Jesus do under his final moon? He washes feet. Ancient, sandaled, uncovered, dirt-trotting, hairy, unhygienic, bottom-dwelling, callous farms. All the disciples gather together for supper with their leader, Jesus. And usually, when you enter someone's home, a lower-level servant might run up, take your sandals off for you, then scrub your feet. But this night, Jesus is the one on his knees, taking their sandals and washing their feet. They had to walk everywhere back then in sandals, so those puppies are pretty disgusting, and everyone is pretty disgusted that their rabbi, their master, their great leader, is on his knees like a common servant scrubbing what is potentially the nastiest part of them. Some of them protest, crying out, "I will never let *you* condescend to wash *my* feet." But this has been Jesus' program of inversion all along: *the last will become first and the first shall become last.* All along he's been saying things like: *Those who exalt themselves will be humbled, and those who humble them-selves will be exalted. The greatest among you should be like a little child, and the one who wants to rule should become like a servant to all. I did not come to be served, but to serve, and to give my life for you.* The God, Creator and source of all Being and existence knelt down to earth to wash some poor, uneducated, filthy, fishermen's feet. *Now go and do likewise,* he says.

Done scrubbing their soles, Jesus says they are now clean, inside and out. Except for one of them, who will betray them this very night. Everyone glances at each other, trying to guess who it is. Judas stands up; he's been getting tired of the whole servant bit for a while now. He always expected the Messiah to bring power and wealth, not poetry and a wash bucket.

Judas storms out of the room to go and tell the religious leaders where they can find Jesus and kill him. With hindsight, we picture Judas as a sniveling Smeagol plotting all along in the back of the room. But Judas was so respected among the community that when he gets up and suspiciously leaves right in the middle of the traitor discussion, no one even bats an eye. No one thinks to imagine the traitor is Judas. He's the one they trusted enough to hold the money bag for the whole group, and so they assume he's just going off to pay the meal tab. Judas is one of the spiritual heavyweights among the disciples, that leader you always trusted and wanted to be like and never thought would be capable of something like this. His is not the betrayal of a Smeagol but of a Saruman.

Peter stands up now. He feels the need to say something, to force everything back to normal, to drown out great fear and flux with an equally exaggerated confidence. He declares boldly: "I would never betray you, Lord. Never." Jesus' heart sinks, for Peter is his closest companion, his Samwise Gamgee. Jesus sighs, saying: "Oh, Peter, before this day is over you will betray me not once but three times." And Peter collapses in on himself in horror and shame.

Guards come for Jesus later that night, led to his whereabouts by Judas. Judas works out a way to signal to the guards in the dark which person in the group is Jesus, walking up and giving him a customary kiss on the cheek. Jesus looks into Judas and truly sees him, saying, "Oh, Judas, do you betray me with a kiss?" Dozens of soldiers then run up and clasp him in chains. "Are you Jesus of Nazareth?" they demand, wanting to confirm their catch. "I am," Jesus replies, slipping that phrase in one last time.

Watching his whole life for the last three years fall a part in one night, Simon Peter tries to grab control of the situation, drawing a sword and slicing one of the attacker's ears clean off. Jesus cries out, "Peter! Sheathe your sword. Those who live by the sword will die by the sword." Jesus hobbles over to the wailing, bloodied man who had been arresting him moments earlier. He places his hands on both sides of the man's head, looking him in the eyes like a mother calming her child. The screaming stops and so does the blood. Jesus withdraws his hand, revealing an ear of flesh returned from nonbeing. His last miracle is healing his own oppressor. Amidst the shock and awe, the disciples manage to slip away into the night.

Dragging Jesus through the streets, they lead him into the city for a quick mockery of a trial. But they can't actually execute him without the empire's consent, so they escort him along to Pontius Pilate, the Roman governor of the area from AD 26 to 37. Meanwhile, Peter sneaks back into town, trying to find out what's happening. He sits down in one of the inner courtyards near the trial, warming himself comfortably by the fire. But a girl soon recognizes him, saying: "Aren't you one of Jesus' followers? shouldn't you be in jail with him?" Peter responds casually: "You must have me confused with someone else. I don't know anyone called Jesus."

Governor Pilate doesn't like meetings this early in the morning, but the local religious leaders are really worked up this time, saying they've got a rabble-rouser who's threatening to usurp Rome's power and make himself king. Pilate relents and lets them bring their petition. In hobbles a shackled Jesus, looking like any other peasant or criminal Pilate has deigned to deal with in his decorated career. He tells the guards they can go—he's not scared of this chained sack of bones.

"So," Pilate says, "you're claiming to be king of the Jews?" "Did you come up with that all by yourself," Jesus replies, "or is that just something you've heard from others?" Caught off guard, Pilate retorts indignantly: "I'm not a Jew! I don't care about your petty religious squabbles. Your own people brought you here to me. What is it you've done? How are you a threat to me and to Rome?" "My kingdom . . ." Jesus breathes back, "is not of this world." "You are a king, then!" Pilate retorts, hopeful he's finally getting somewhere." "If that's what you say," Jesus responds. "But all I say is that I came into the world to testify to the truth." Pilate mutters back rhetorically, "What is truth?" and sends Jesus away to be flogged.

Stripped down and tied to a post, Jesus is whipped with animal leather tipped with jagged bones and lead. Two men, one on either side, take turns with the lashing to pace themselves and to make sure they get both sides of the meat evenly. There are surface wounds, his skin torn like a shirt, but the deeper muscles and tissue are also incorporated into the process, either through the digging of the whip or through deep-tissue bruising from the sheer force and relentlessness of it all. Jesus had walked to the whipping post but would need to be dragged away, brush stroking red behind him.

Meanwhile, back in the courtyard, another person has recognized Peter, yelling: "Hey! you're one of them!" Peter responds, skittishly: "I'm not, I tell you. I'm not!" But a third person recognizes him now too, so Peter cries out definitively: "I don't know what you are talking about! I don't know this Jesus! I don't know him!!" His voice peters out with this final betrayal, momentarily harmonizing with the overlapping crow of a rooster at dawn. The sun rises upon Peter weeping, realizing he has indeed betrayed Christ not once, but three times. Elsewhere, Judas is looking on that same sun, scorched by that same remorse. He goes off alone and kills himself.

On their way back to Pilate, the guards twist together some thorns to weave a crown atop of Christ. They slap him but the crown stays thorned in place, so they bow before him, mockingly crying, "Hail! King of the Jews!" Returning, they deposit him like garbage at Pilate's feet. Pilate is hopeful that this debacle will satisfy the wrath of the angry mob, parading Jesus in front of them. "Here is the man," Pilate announces, but they want to degrade him further, beyond anything recognizably human, and so they cry back, "Crucify him! Crucify him!" Shocked that one man has stirred so many to anger, Pilate brings him back inside, questioning him again: "Who are you? Where do you come from?" But Jesus just stares straight ahead, saying nothing in response to one of the most influential leaders in the land. "Are you actually refusing to speak to me?! Don't you realize I have the power to either free you or crucify you?!" Jesus' frayed body remains motionless, but his eyes flicker toward Pilate, as he states, "You have no power over me, except what has been given to you by God."

Pilate is not used to feeling like this. He's supposed to be over this man, but somehow the psychology of their interaction doesn't play that way. He doesn't know what to make of him, but he doesn't think he deserves death either. So Pilate tries to flee the burden placed on him and make it someone else's problem. He learns that Jesus is technically from King Herod's territory, so he tries to pawn the case off on him. But Herod sends Jesus right back to Pilate's door, where outside the wailing mob is only getting louder: "Crucify him! Crucify him!" Pilate doesn't want to rise to this moment in history and make the choice it presents him with; he wants to delay it with whippings and stall tactics and appeasement; he wants someone else to bear the weight of this decision; he wishes Jesus had never come to him, that none of this had ever happened; that Being, Goodness, and Truth had never hobbled through his door and told him there was a choice to make. And so instead of making it himself, Pilate has a bowl of water brought to him in front of the crowd and dramatically washes his hands of the whole situation, announcing, "I am innocent of this man's blood. I hand this responsibility over to you; you do with him what you will." And the crowd takes Jesus away to crucify him.

Being is now unto death. Christ carries his own cross, a great big hulking half-log, through city streets lined with gawking, gossiping, relishing eyes. The people aren't quite yelling "Shame!" as he passes, but the effect is similar. This is the conquered being paraded through the streets; this is the bullied teenager being forced to walk through the crowded halls in nothing but the panties they left him in the locker room. Jesus stumbles and staggers through miles of crowded Jerusalem streets, till he's led outside the city to a site known only as Golgotha, the place of the skull. The guards strip him naked and divide his clothes among themselves. Contrary to sanitized cinema, there's no loincloth, no rag to hide that which is most private and personal, no single thread of dignity left. Perhaps he instinctively tries to cover himself up, but his hands are no longer his, the guards grabbing and stretching them to their outermost to reach the premade crucifixion holes in the wood, as if it were a medieval rack. The nails go down, and the cross goes up, high upon the horizon, with a mock sign above his head saying, "King of the Jews." Here is your humiliated king, here is your dying God, here hangs Being itself, unmade.

We tend to assume this was a somber event, with dark clouds in the sky and downcast faces all around. But in the American lynch mob years, newspapers often advertised a lynching ahead of time, barbeques and games were arranged, pictures were taken of people smiling while pointing up, and postcards of the lynching were sold.[4] (Similar things happened in Europe with beheadings and the guillotine.) That's how I imagine this scene. A fair going on around a corpse; the carnival tent held up by a wooden tree with a man hanging on it. People sharing food, popping in and out to get things, taking bets on how long he'll last up there, commenting how this one hangs funny. It's the same unnoticed, culturally endorsed, quotidian suffering that happens every day, with one part of the world feasting on a party bus and the other half crushed beneath the wheels. Most of the crowd is having the time of their lives; it's just Jesus' mother, Mary, who won't shut up and enjoy herself. Jesus looks up from the cross and cries out, "Father, forgive them, for they know not what they do."

Crucified on either side of Jesus are two common criminals. Trying to pass their pain onto another, one of them snarls at Jesus, "You're the Messiah?! Ha! If you were really who you said you were, you'd save yourself now—and us while you're at it!" But the crucified man on the other side wails back: "We deserve this! You and me, we deserve to die for what we did, but this man hasn't done anything wrong!" Justice must be done; someone deserves to die, but it is not this man. It is not him who should be up here.

A crowd begins to form at the foot of the cross, joining the other criminal in shrieking at Christ: "You could save others, but you couldn't save yourself! If you're the son of God, have daddy come and save you now!" But the camera isn't at a wide angle, viewing the unruly crowd from above or from the outside. No, we're close up, seeing through the eyes that glare at Christ, cursing through the same lips that condemn him. I'm there screaming all the wrath that's been screamed onto me. I'm lashing out at him at the parent teacher conference. I'm squishing him in my fist instead of crushing my colleagues. I'm punching him at the gym to prevent myself from going insane after a long day. I'm grinding his bones in my teeth to get through an anxious night. I'm kicking him because I forgot to let the dog out and there's crap everywhere. I'm cutting him instead of cutting myself. I'm raging at the screen in *1984*. I'm blaming foreigners and Middle Easterners and Jews for all my problems, and Jesus just happens to be all three. In an ideal world he shouldn't have to take it all, but in an ideal world there wouldn't be an *all* to take; he's just carrying what has to be carried, by the only one big enough to carry it.

After hours and hours (crucifixion victims could sometimes take days to die) of publicly broadcast horror, Jesus finally cries out, *"My God, My God! Why have you forsaken me?"* People disagree about what's going on here, and I have no way to make sense of it philosophically. But I wonder if, in this moment, Jesus is taking the full weight of the human condition upon himself, experiencing our existential dread in its purest form, being alienated from God the Father in the same way our sin has alienated us all from our Maker.[5] He's allowed himself to be torn by sin, just as reality has been torn by it, and so he now knows what it is like to be one of us on the other side of the chasm, separated from Beauty, Truth, Goodness, and Love itself. *Forsaken* by all that is right and good and lovely. God has allowed a rift within himself, allowed our cracked glass to fracture all the way up to him. He's reaping the death and nonbeing we've sowed. He's sucking out the poison by taking it into his own mouth. He's listening and letting us vent and vomit all of our emotional burden onto him. Whatever it is that happens on a human level when one person gives up some part of themselves for another, God's doing that too, except on a cosmic, ontological, metaphysical level. God's diving in front of the bullet, jumping on the grenade, taking the fall so his lover can escape prison. He's donating his organs so we can have them. He's killing himself so we can cannibalize his corpse. He's giving up his candlesticks so Jean Valjean can see the light; he's whoring out his own body to pay for Fantine's medicine. He's offering himself in Edmund's place; he's dying to save the *USS Enterprise*; he's volunteering as tribute. What goes around is coming back around, except upon him instead of us. Justice is being done, except on his body instead of mine.

Christ cries out his final agony, then hangs his head. It is finished. God is dead. And we have killed him.

〈 ▮ ▮ 〉

The guards tip the cross over and peel off what they can. Then they wrap what's left of him in linens and carry it down to the tombs. Rigor mortis may already be kicking in, making the corpse inflexible and hard to carry. Occasional spasms simulate and mimic life, but these guards have seen it all; they know the dead like to get settled in, their former limbs flailing about as blood resettles, muscles relax, and gases shift. Someone has purchased Jesus a half decent tomb, so they head over there and roll a proper burial stone in front, as much to keep the smell in as to keep the grave robbers out. Not that this Jesus fellow had anything on him worth stealing; "a king indeed," they chuckle.

Then the world moves on. It's Passover weekend, so people are already distracted and busy making preparations. The disciples, however, cannot just move on, for they have nowhere to move on to, having spent the last three years following a failed Messiah to the grave. Jesus' mother is inconsolable, his closest followers are confused and upset, and Peter is coming to terms with the fact that the very last thing he'll ever have said or done to Jesus was betray him.

Three women, perhaps used to having to put the needs of others before their own, push through their sorrow to go and tend to Jesus' tomb. They come by candlelight with spices and oils and all the things needed to prepare his body for passage into the next life. They leave early Sunday morning, when it's still mostly dark and you can't quite tell if it looks like the sun is rising or falling. Nearing the burial site, one of them turns to the others, feeling like a fool, for she's realizing they have no way to roll open the tomb themselves. It required several large men just to get the stone in place to begin with. Yet the issue becomes moot before they ever settle it, for upon arriving they see the rock has already been rolled away. They assume there must be a simple explanation, but no one else is there to explain things, so they plug their noses, bend down and crawl into the tomb to investigate for themselves. Their candlelight flickers, revealing linens lying flat upon the ground instead of conforming to a human corpse. They gasp in shock, inhaling the aromas not of decaying flesh but of the earth. The body is gone.

Dazed and confused, they crawl backward out of the hole and into the newly risen sun.[6] After a stunned moment soaking it all in, two of them get up and hustle to where their fellow followers are staying, sounding the alarm: "Somethings happened! It's gone! His body, it's, it's just . . . gone! They've taken our Jesus away!" Waking eyes share looks of confusion. But Peter gets up and sprints headlong to the tombs, perhaps ready to fight for the body, perhaps just to witness the emptiness for himself, perhaps because he doesn't know what else to do but knows he has to do something. Practically diving in, he plunges straight through the hole into the tomb. He can't see much now, his body blocking most of the light from outside. He feels around in the shadows, touching for the textures of the dead, but finding only empty cloth with nothing to clothe.

Forlorn, Peter returns to the group. Yet everyone is gathered together now, standing around Mary Magdalene, who's weeping tears of joy. "They didn't take him! He was there all along! He never left!" she cries. Perhaps Peter pushes through the group, taking her by the shoulders more firmly than he might have wished in hindsight, barking out: "What is this? What are you saying, Mary?! You saw him?" She responds, perhaps saying she stayed behind after the other two women left. She stayed and wept at the empty tomb, and in her weeping someone said her name, and she knew before turning it was him, the one who knew that name before the earth was born. And then turning, she saw and was seen. He is alive. Jesus is alive!

She must have just left right before I got there, Peter probably frets to himself. *I can't have missed Jesus by more than a minute! Was he still there in the graveyard, hiding in the shadows the whole time, watching me panic? But I betrayed him. Of course, he doesn't want to have anything to do with me*, Peter probably thinks. Indeed, for some of us, it is harder to believe God actually wants us than to believe he's risen from the dead.

Weeks pass, and more and more people are claiming to have seen Jesus, but Peter is still not one of them. Even doubting Thomas, who declared, "I will not believe unless I actually stick my finger through the nail holes," has had his penetrating mind blown by a visit from the resurrected Christ. And after weeks of waiting and hoping and longing, Peter gives up. He returns home to the Sea of Galilee, accepting that he is no longer one of God's chosen and that all he is good for is catching fish.[7] Long into the night he fights the storms and scarcity of the sea, punishing himself with wind and waves and chill.

Peter returns ashore early one morning after another fruitless haul. As he's skimming alongside the shore, a man on the beach over a hundred feet away yells out, "Bad haul?" Peter mutters back, annoyed at being reminded of the evening's failures. "Why don't you try just one more time?" the voice yells again. "Ha. Fine. Whatever." Peter relents, not yet catching on. He casts his net back over the side. But when he tries to pull it back in, his arms can barely hoist it out of the water enough to see it's teeming with fish. Peter stares at the shoreline, and he suddenly knows. Without saying another word, he leaps fully clothed into the water, leaving behind his boat and lucrative haul, and swimming to shore as fast as his tired limbs will allow. When he gets there, the man has a small fire going. Peter wants to run and tackle him with his embrace, but the man says, "Go back and get some of the fish for our breakfast." Barely able to hold himself back, Peter eagerly runs/swims back to the boat, dragging his netful of fish to the fire. He squats down, unsure what to do or say but not giving that anxiety a care in the world, for all that matters is that he knows, without asking, without seeing the nail holes, who this is. This is Jesus.

Then they sit. And eat. And munch and sip and burp and bask. There's no theatrics or light flares or heavens opening up to sing. There's just Jesus and Peter, eating together like they used to. Our daily, digestive, bodily, human need for sustenance meeting the eternal, spiritual, sustaining Bread of Life itself. And it was Good.

The meal coming to a close, Jesus says, "Peter, do you love me?" And Peter giddies back without a second thought, "Yes, Lord! You know I love you!" "Peter," Jesus repeats, "Do you love me?" Again, Peter hurries the words, saying, "Yes! Of course! You know I do." Yet again, Jesus asks, "Peter, do you love me?" And Peter is cut to the core, for Jesus asks a third time, as if undoing each betrayal in turn. Mustering up a response fully from his heart, saying what he knows to be true even though he doesn't know how to live it out, Peter cries, "Lord, you know all things. You know I love you." And Jesus makes their love new, offering again the same words, the same hope, the same invitation he'd offered Peter on that same beach all those years ago, long before any of this had ever happened: "Follow me."

Jesus did many other things as well. If every one of them were written down, I suppose that even the whole world would not have room for the books that would be written.

FOURTEEN

Jesus Is Dying to Meet You

OUR STORY HAS COVERED A LOT. We've covered how creation was made and called good, and how we used our freedom to fall from that goodness into sin and shadow. We talked about how God planned to fix the fallenness of creation and how the line of Abraham, Moses, David, Solomon, and the Jewish nation eventually led to Mary, Joseph, and baby Jesus. In the previous chapter, we learned about how this Jesus controversially claimed to be the I AM. Yet we fallen humans have made ourselves inconsistent with the one who is Being, Goodness, Beauty, Love, and Justice. By sinning, we have put into the world much that will boomerang back on us in the name of justice. We're often told that Jesus' death somehow solves this conundrum and absolves our souls—but how? How does movement four resolve the plot and conflict set up in movement two? How can humanity be raised back up after the fall?

These are difficult questions. And so far, I've mostly been pushing *you* to wrestle with them. But in this chapter you'll get to watch *me* wrestle with them. My brain tends to work in conversations, scenes, debates, back-and-forths—very much like there are two little Jonathans on either shoulder maniacally whispering into my ear. As such, this chapter is going to be a different genre from the others. It is a—likely unasked-for—invitation into my mind as I debate with myself whether Jesus dying for our sins makes any sense, or whether it, like his hands, simply doesn't hold water.

❮ ▪ ▪ ❯

Jonathan: It is an honor to be here with you all tonight debating the topic "Did Jesus really Die for My Sins?" Thank you for inviting me, and thank you to my colleague, Dr. Johnny, for joining me on stage.

Dr. Johnny: Thank you, Jonathan. It's an honor to be here with you. And may I say, you look absolutely stunning tonight.

Jonathan: Why, thank you, Dr. Johnny. You as well. That girl who rejected you in college was an absolute nutter and surely now regrets her decision on a daily basis.

Dr. Johnny: Agreed.

Jonathan: Well, let's get to it, then.

Dr. Johnny: Indeed, let's. To start, I'd like to remind the audience that when we talk about the crucifixion of Jesus, we are not talking about a mythological or fairy tale figure like Zeus or Rumpelstiltskin. For Jesus is historical, in the same way Napoleon, Alexander the Great, or Buddha were historical figures who actually existed. As Cambridge professor Graham Stanton writes, "Today, nearly all historians, whether Christians or not, accept that Jesus existed."[1] Likewise, atheist historian Bart Ehrman writes, "We have more evidence for Jesus than we have for almost anybody from his time period. I'm not saying this as a Christian—I'm not a Christian. I'm saying this as a historian. . . . Virtually all scholars of antiquity agree [that Jesus] was crucified."[2] So, when we debate Jesus' death, we are not debating *whether* this historical event happened. The real question is, What does this event *mean*?

Jonathan: I grant that Jesus historically existed and was crucified. I just don't think his death was *for our sins*. Deep down, we all know there's something slightly off with the Christian story. They say God made us. So if we're stupid and cruel, it's because God made us stupid and cruel. It doesn't make sense for God to punish us for simply being what he made us to be. And it certainly doesn't make sense for him to kill his own kid in our place.

Dr. Johnny: Well, God didn't *make* us stupid. No, God made us with free will. Most of us just choose to use our free will *to be stupid*.

Jonathan: Ah, but see, then someone might just as easily use their freedom to choose to do good, and so a good person wouldn't need God's forgiveness, right?

Dr. Johnny: Well, perhaps in theory. And if you happen to be morally perfect, then great. But I know *I'm* not. I make the same stupid mistakes over and over again. I say and do things that hurt the people I love most. Even my most selfless decisions tend to have some ulterior motive lingering in the background.

Jonathan: Yeah, okay, people make bad decisions. But that doesn't mean they're bad people.

Dr. Johnny: But what do you define as bad, then?

Jonathan: I mean . . . like, murderers, pedophiles, rapists.

Dr. Johnny: What a convenient definition.

Jonathan: How so?

Dr. Johnny: It's convenient to imagine a world where the bad people are all far away in a maximum-security prison or hatching plans in a dark cabin in the woods. How convenient to have this view of evil that's so fabulous, so extreme, so removed from the hustle and bustle of everyday life . . . so removed from *yourself.*

Jonathan: I mean, obviously, we all have our own struggles and ways we could improve. I'm not saying I'm perfect. But I'm not evil, either.

Dr. Johnny: I'm not saying *you* specifically are evil. I'm just saying, I know myself, and I know that if I'd had different parents, or a different childhood, I totally could have been one of those people.

Jonathan: But you *weren't.*

Dr. Johnny: Yeah, but I very easily could have been. And it wasn't like I made good choices to turn out okay. Mostly it was just luck and other people looking out for me. I mean, sure, I'm delightful *now.* But strand me on an island somewhere, having to fight with others to survive, and things are gonna get *Lord of the Flies* pretty darn quick.

Jonathan: Okay, so what are you saying? That everyone's secretly Hitler?

Dr. Johnny: No, not everyone's Hitler. But it wasn't just Hitler who made the trains of flesh run on time. There were tens of millions of normal, everyday German citizens who supported that regime. I'm talking farmers, bakers, nurses, mail carriers, builders. I'm talking about the people who painted the walls of Auschwitz and the milk carriers who walked the fence every day to drop milk for the officers. I mean, at least with Hitler you knew what you were dealing with—what you see is what you get. But this thing we call polite society, these civilized smiles between polite people—that's what scares the crap out of me. It's not just the people with guns and knives who are terrifying; it's people with knives and forks sitting across from you at the dinner table.

Jonathan sighs and chuckles to himself

Dr. Johnny: Did I say something funny?

Jonathan: No, it's just . . . this is what religion always does. Makes everyone feel horrible about themselves. But there is still light and love and hope here. Hold a baby, kiss your wife, go for a walk or something, and see that the world is not all bad, that we don't all need saving.

Dr. Johnny: It's not that there isn't love and goodness here. *There is.* God created the world and called it good. But part of what makes goodness *good* is that it is not forced on you; part of goodness is freedom. And wherever there is the freedom to do good, there must always be the freedom to do evil. Humanity used our freedom to pervert what was good within us. We fell.

Jonathan: But I don't believe the story of Adam and Eve and the talking snake!

Dr. Johnny: But surely you must believe the point it was trying to make? None of us is innocent, least of all the one who thinks he is. As Thomas Carlisle said, "The greatest of faults is to be conscious of none." You don't think you need a savior because you don't think you need saving. But you might be willing to look to the cross, if you first looked yourself long and hard in the mirror.

Jonathan: I guess I just have more faith in humanity than you do. Look at all the strides we're making as a society, all the progress and technology and medicine, all the steps we're taking toward human flourishing and science, toward liberated, equal, democratic, tolerant societies. *You may say I'm a dreamer, but I'm not the only one.*[3]

Dr. Johnny: I just . . . I don't know how you can possibly think that. I mean, in the 1800s people believed humanity was getting better, yeah. But then the myth of progress was shattered by two world wars, gas chambers, gulags, and an atom bomb. Sure, a couple decades later we forgot again, and so in the 1960s our parents believed things were getting better, marching for peace and civil rights. But guess what, it's the third millennium now, and we're still struggling with the same bloody things. I'm not saying we're all bad; I'm just saying things aren't all good either. Something isn't right, not right in me, not right in you, not right in us. You can call it sin, you can call it injustice, greed, evil, or stupidity, but whatever it is, it's there. And time and science and progress don't seem to be making it go away.

Jonathan: Well . . . even if there really is something wrong, that doesn't mean God is how we fix it.

Dr. Johnny: I think God can fix it. But he's got to forgive us first.

Jonathan: Ha. Just when I think you might be saying something interesting, you go straight back to the God who cries wrath and repentance. Can't we get past all the sin and forgiveness stuff and talk about how to actually make the world a better place?

Dr. Johnny: How can we make the world a better place if we don't deal with the root of the problem? You have to admit you're sick before you're willing to go to the doctor.

Jonathan: You have to admit you're sick, but you don't have to apologize to the doctor for it.

Dr. Johnny: You might if you infected him and all his patients. And that's what sin does. Our brokenness doesn't just hurt us; no, it hurts everyone around us.

Jonathan: Yes, you should apologize to the doctor if you infect him, but you don't need to crucify him!

Dr. Johnny: And the metaphor is dead.

Jonathan: Really? I thought I nailed it. Anyways, what I'm saying is that even if we are all sinners, and even if we do need forgiveness, I have no idea why that means God had to crucify some poor Middle Eastern Jewish guy.

Dr. Johnny: Well, I don't know whether he needed to be Jewish or Middle Eastern. Those details are secondary to the more primary fact that in some way or other *justice* had to be done.

Jonathan: But why?! . . . Why does *justice* have to be done? Why believe in this wrathful, sin-punishing, sex-hating, Sodom-smiting, point-tallying, hell-sending, angry umpire in the clouds? If Jesus had to die because your God is a jerk, *then maybe you should believe in a God who's not a jerk.*

Dr. Johnny: You think a just God is a cruel god. But I think it's the opposite. If God is not just, then he doesn't care enough to respond to the abuse of young children or the raping of every last cent from the poor. A God without justice is a God who doesn't give a crap.

Jonathan: Okay, that kind of justice would be nice. *But it's precisely what we don't see.* Look around—the world is not a just place. Abusers die peacefully in their sleep all the time, but I can't even get out of a parking ticket.

Dr. Johnny: Exactly! There is no justice in *this life*. Which is why we believe it must be coming for us in the next.

Jonathan: Ha. Wishful thinking.

Dr. Johnny: It's certainly not something I *wish* for. It's just the result of believing in a moral, rational, just universe. If we believe in a meaningful, moral universe, then evil can't just get away with it in the end. And so if it seems to get away with it for a time in this life, then the universe must balance the books in the life to come. That conclusion just *inescapably* follows.

Jonathan: But it's not *inescapable*! Obviously not. That's why none of the religions can agree about what happens when we die.

Dr. Johnny: Actually, they kind of do agree. I mean, not in all the details, but in the underlying idea.

Jonathan: What?!

Dr. Johnny: In Christianity, we call it justice. But in many other religions they call it karma. What goes around comes back around. You do bad in this life, and you come back in the next as a flea clinging to a dog's butt hair.

Jonathan: But reincarnation is totally different from hell and God's wrath!

Dr. Johnny: It's different in the details. But the underlying virtue of justice is the same. Both believe that justice is coming for us in the next life.

They disagree on what that next life consists of—whether that's the afterlife or another life on earth. Nevertheless, we agree that the universe is a moral, rational, meaningful whole where justice ultimately wins out, whether in this life or the next.

Jonathan: I guess . . . I just . . . don't believe in a moral universe, then. I think words like *justice, love,* or *goodness* are social constructs. Things we invented to police society but not true of the universe as a whole.

Dr. Johnny: And you can go that route. You can think these are just things that evolution tricked us into caring about, or society invented to control us. But then stop pretending that right and wrong are real things. Stop pretending that justice is a real objective value, that the oppressed really do deserve to be liberated, or that oppressors really do deserve to be put in their place. Stop acting like *any* of this has any meaning.

Jonathan: Hmm . . . so, if religions are united about a meaningful and just universe, then why can't you all just get along?

Dr. Johnny: We agree justice demands a debt be paid; we just disagree about who can pay it. Some try to pay off their *own* karmic debt. Whatever sins they commit must be atoned for by them in their next life. And whatever sins they commit in the next life are paid off in the next *next* life. And on it goes. I've heard some people say they've gone through millions of years of reincarnations, trying to be good enough, yet never quite getting there on their own.* Never quite escaping the cycle of justice, sin, and guilt.

Jonathan: Yeah, and like Christianity isn't all about guilt too. . . .

Dr. Johnny: Oh, it totally is. Guilt is the soul's way of letting us know that we've done something wrong—that we have a debt to pay. It's just that in Christianity, *we* are not the ones who pay it. Jesus pays it for us, dying in our place. Guilt leads us to Jesus, and Jesus leads us away from our guilt.

Jonathan: But how can it be justice for *someone else* to be punished and die in *my* place? That seems positively unjust!

---

*This is a broad generalization. E.g., not all believe that they pay off their karmic debt but rather simply realize the cycle of samsara is unreal. However, such models may be fully loving, but it is questionable whether they are still fully just. See our interview with Tyler McNabb on *The Spiritually Incorrect Podcast,* "Who's Afraid of Buddhism?," April 4, 2024, 1:08:36, https://www.spirituallyincorrectpodcast.com/podcast/episode/20d0cf46/whos-afraid-of-buddhism.

Dr. Johnny: It would be unjust if God *forced* someone else to go through it. But God freely chose to go through it himself. God is like anyone who chooses to help carry the load of another. God is like a father who pays off his son's legal fines or a friend who pays their roommate's rent. Things are made right, justice is done, the accounts are settled, our debt is paid. It's just not *us* who has paid it. And that's what Jesus did on the cross; he paid the debt that all of us justly owed.

Jonathan: But how can one dude's death cover billions of people?

Dr. Johnny: Because Jesus was not just any dude. Jesus is God, is infinite Being itself. In the Old Testament, people sacrificed one finite animal to cover the finite number of sins from that week. And with karma, you might pay for one finite life's worth of sins by suffering for another finite lifetime. A finite sacrifice for a finite number of sins. But Jesus is God, and God is infinite. A payment of a thousand dollars might cover your debt for a month, but a payment of infinity covers it once and for always. The sacrifice of Being itself covers every individual being.

Jonathan: But the crucifixion was done in a day. And yes, perhaps Jesus descended into hell for three days, but then he rose again and went to live with God in a big, big house where he could play football. I fail to see how one dude's bad weekend pays off the sins for all humans for all time.

Dr. Johnny: But what is time to an infinite entity who is outside time? Is the suffering of an eternal entity not in some sense eternal? Some people (though not me personally) would even go as far as to say that some part of Jesus is eternally being crucified for us, is eternally in hell for us, is eternally shedding his blood for us.

Jonathan: Okay, this is getting a tad macabre and medieval and bloody.

Dr. Johnny: It is, isn't it?

Jonathan: So you just sort of concede that, then?

Dr. Johnny: I concede that the Western world has so sheltered and sanitized itself, so exported elsewhere the messes that prop up our empire, that we've forgotten the cycle of life and death we're caught up in. We've forgotten our burgers come from carcasses and our houses from dead trees. Even vegetarians need food grown from fields, and those fields displace animals, uproot woodland homes, and shatter ecosystems. Our privilege is another's pain; our salvation is another's suffering. If the cross is bloody and macabre and medieval, it is no more so than the reality it came to redeem. The difference is that while reality is littered with those passing their burdens onto others, the cross is where God takes all of our burdens on himself.

Jonathan: But the cross is only further perpetuating that cycle of blood and violence and death!

Dr. Johnny: No, Jesus is ending the cycle by throwing himself under the wheels. Once sin enters the world, it gets passed around like a game of hot potato. But Jesus eats the potato and ends the game.

Jonathan: Okay, but if he wants to end the game, why not just forgive us? Why go through the whole song and dance of crucifixion? Just forgive and forget.

Dr. Johnny: Because that would be impossible. We humans may act inconsistently all the time, our actions and beliefs flip-flopping depending on what we had for lunch. But God is justice and goodness itself—he can't just pick and choose when to be just and when not to be. If he is just, he is always just and cannot suddenly change who he is on a dime to be something else without negating the very foundations of morality itself. So you can't have it both ways; you can't have justice one day and then contradict yourself the next. God is either justice itself or not just at all.

Jonathan: But you don't need to cut yourself in order to forgive others. Mature adults just forgive, and that's that.

Dr. Johnny: Okay, but think about what forgiveness entails. Imagine when someone hurts you. There is this initial moment where screaming out in retaliation would vent your own emotional and physical burden back onto them and thereby lighten it for yourself. When someone smacks you, it always feels less painful if you smack them right back. When someone insults you, it's always less embarrassing when you have a clever retort. You can always seek relief by returning the burden of sin to the sinner so that they get a taste of their own poison. *Or* you can choose not to seek relief, not to pass that negative energy back, but to swallow and bear it all yourself, letting the cycle die in you. So even in forgiveness someone is always suffering for the sin; it's just you instead of the sinner. You are choosing to grin and bear it yourself. Forgiveness is suffering what is sent rather than sending it back. And that's what the cross is: it is God taking all the negative energy of the world and letting it die in him rather than spitting it back on us. We crucified him, and instead of shrieking back insults at us from the cross or banishing us all to hell or sending down lightning bolts, he just hung there and took it. Some people think the cross is what God does *instead* of forgiving us, but I think the cross is precisely what forgiveness *is*.

Jonathan: But you know other religions just have the gods forgive us, and that's that, right? Thor punishes Loki sometimes but forgives him others. You don't need to make it any more complicated than that.

Dr. Johnny: Yes, other religions may have gods who sometimes forgive, but they have no way to make sense of *why* they forgive. Their gods may be full of wrath and fury some days and then merciful other days, and there's no rhyme or reason to it. They act justly when they feel like it and unjustly when they feel like it. But in Christianity, our God makes sense. He is what he is 100 percent of the time. Since God is justice itself, what goes around must always come back around. But since God is also love itself, God lets it come back around on him instead of on us. Divine justice means that sin must be buried somewhere; love means that God lets it remain buried in him. In this, God is both fully loving and fully just—true to both sides of his nature. Our God is what he is absolutely and always, never flip-flopping or being inconsistent. *Our God actually makes sense.*

Jonathan: I get what you're saying, but I just don't think I could ever embrace a God of wrath who simply *has to spank us.*

Dr. Johnny: Well, some Christians would actually agree with you—they'd say it's Satan who punishes sin, not God. They'd say that when we sin we're basically selling our souls to Satan or to evil. And Jesus offers himself in our place to pay off the debt we owe Satan and get us back. In the Chronicles of Narnia, the White Witch has a claim on Edmund's soul because he selfishly betrayed his brothers and sisters. But Aslan ransoms Edmund back from the witch by offering to die in his place, thereby repaying his moral debt. The payment and punishment here is not demanded by God but by the satanic witch figure.

Jonathan: Okay, well, that's different.

Dr. Johnny: Well, it *is* and it *isn't*. Because the end result is the same: Jesus has to die for us. And the reason he has to die is also the same: it is only because justice is real that Satan has any legitimate claim on sinners. Justice was the deep magic that gave the White Witch her right. Justice must still be done; it is just done through a different delivery boy. It's outsourced. So, our broader point here about justice could remain the same across multiple atonement models, even ones where God doesn't do the punishing.

Jonathan: But all these theories and models just feel, so, so . . . unnecessary. You're trying to solve a problem that doesn't exist if we simply choose not to believe in God or in Satan. Can't we just have a moral universe and get rid of God and Satan, and so avoid the need for this whole retributive song and dance?

Dr. Johnny: But that wouldn't solve anything! Conceding, for the sake of argument, that you could have a moral universe without God, what would that accomplish? If it is still a meaningful, moral, just universe, then sins would still be naturally punished. Perhaps in the way of karma, where it's just the nature of things that what goes around comes back around. But a just universe can't stop being just any more than it can stop obeying the laws of gravity or thermodynamics. So, there would still be justice in what you're proposing; the only difference would be that there would no longer be a God to save us from ourselves, so we'd have to bear the brunt of the punishment on our own.

Jonathan: Okay, but this is all getting so . . . complicated. You're talking about God's nature and wrath and Satan and Hitler and thermodynamics. Your religion is like a math equation, and if even one decimal place is off, you get the answer wrong. Is this really what faith is for you? Is this really what God expects the whole world to figure out?

Dr. Johnny: I mean, if you take any belief and break it down to the nuts and bolts, it's gonna get complicated. You're asking hard questions, so I'm giving hard answers. But that isn't all that faith is—this isn't how most people encounter Jesus. No, they encounter him on their weeping knees, begging God for a second chance they know they don't deserve. They encounter it when they finally confess their deepest, darkest secrets and find God still waiting, arms open to forgive them. They find the cross in the simple words of a former slave driver, "Amazing grace, how sweet the sound, that saved a wretch like me." They glimpse it in the end of *Pulp Fiction*, when Samuel L. Jackson confesses he is the tyranny of all men and needs forgiveness and a fresh start. We feel it when we finally admit we are *fallen* and need Christ's helping hand to get back up.

Jonathan: Now it's my turn to say, "How convenient." How convenient that you can do anything, you can even be a slave driver, *apparently*, and God will forgive you for it. How convenient that you can go all Quentin Tarantino and kill a bunch of fools, and God will still forgive you for it. How convenient that mobsters and pedophile priests have done unimaginable things, then gone to confession and cleared their conscience before going out and doing it all over again.

Dr. Johnny: Yes, some people use the cross as a get-out-of-jail-free card. But those people clearly don't get it. Because if you truly understand that God loves you enough to die for you, truly understand that you are valued despite your failures, despite your past, despite your shame—if you truly get that, that changes you. That makes you a better person.

Jonathan: But how?! If you're loved despite what you do, then you can go out and *do* whatever you want. The rules no longer apply to you.

Dr. Johnny: Rules don't change people—love changes people. I mean, why do you think kids act out and do bad stuff? Is it because there aren't enough rules? Or because they are looking for love, attention, affirmation, identity? You think we need more rules to create a world of love. But I think that if people know they're truly loved, they'll start to follow the rules.

Jonathan: Yes, okay, obviously kids need love. But they also need structure, discipline, accountability, rules and, and, and—

Dr. Johnny:—and justice?

Jonathan: Yes . . . *that*.

Dr. Johnny: You're right. People need love, but they also need justice. And most worldviews can only provide one half of that equation. But at the cross, justice and love come together. Justice must be done. And because God loves us, he lets it be done upon himself in our place. There is only one worldview that provides a just, moral, rational, and loving universe all at once, only one corpse in history that does not crumble under the weight of it all.

MOVEMENT V
Church

JESUS CAME TO EARTH AND DIED FOR OUR SINS. But that was two thousand years ago. After Jesus left, his followers banded together to form tight-knit communities that would come to be known as the church. But who leads the church now that Jesus is gone? Did God abandon us down here to figure things out on our own? What are we supposed to do now?

After my hell trip to Mexico, I decided I truly wanted to follow Jesus. If anyone was worth living for, it was the one who thought I was worth dying for. But it's one thing to follow Jesus, and another thing entirely to do so with other people, especially when they're just as messed up as I am and when our fearless leader seems nowhere to be found. Movement five explores the nature of the church, and who is steering the ship now that Jesus is no longer incarnate on earth. A few chapters into this movement, we may even get into some of my own personal struggles with church. . . .

CREATION

Creation Begins

Creation Is Not God

Creation is good

FALL

Humanity in God's Image

Humanity Gone Wild

NATION

Abraham Finds Faith — 2000 BC

Moses Meets I Am — 1400–1200ish BC

Goodness Is Commanded

Beauty in the Promised Land

King David and His Boy — 1000ish BC

Justice Exiles the Nation — 586 BC

REDEMPTION

Jesus Is Born — AD 0

Jesus Is Walking Around Saying Stuff — AD 30

Jesus Is Dying to Meet You — AD 33

CHURCH

The Spirit Arrives — AD 33

The Church Begins — AD 33

The Apostle Paul Converts — AD 35ish

The Church Expands — AD 300ish

The Church Today — The Present

END

The End of the World as We Know It

Highway to Hell or Stairway to Heaven?

FIFTEEN

The Spirit Arrives

JESUS CAME BACK FROM THE GRAVE . . . for forty days. He had just
enough time to see a few people, eat some fish, then take off again. The Bible
casually informs us, "[Jesus] was taken up before their very eyes, and a cloud
hid him from their sight" (Acts 1:9). And he hasn't been back since. Jesus
ascended up to heaven and left the disciples looking up, wondering, *Wait,
is he coming back?! Has God abandoned ship? Are we all alone down here?*

〔▰▰〕

Ten days after Jesus ascended and went away for good, the disciples sat
down to eat together on a day that would come to be known as Pentecost.
This is what the Bible claims happened next:

> When the day of Pentecost came, they were all together in one place. Suddenly
> a sound like the blowing of a violent wind came from heaven and filled the whole
> house where they were sitting. They saw what seemed to be tongues of fire that
> came to rest on each of them. All of them were filled with the Holy Spirit and
> began to speak in other tongues as the Spirit enabled them.
>
> When they heard this sound, a crowd [of Jews from every nation] came to-
> gether in bewilderment, because each one heard their own language being
> spoken. Utterly amazed, they asked: "Aren't all these who are speaking Galileans?
> Then how is it that each of us hears them in our native language? Parthians,
> Medes and Elamites; residents of Mesopotamia, Judea and Cappadocia, Pontus
> and Asia, Phrygia and Pamphylia, Egypt and the parts of Libya near Cyrene;
> visitors from Rome (both Jews and converts to Judaism); Cretans and Arabs—
> we hear them declaring the wonders of God in our own tongues!" . . .
>
> Some, however, made fun of them and said, "They have had too much wine."

Then Peter stood up . . . and addressed the crowd: . . . "These people are not drunk, as you suppose. It's only nine in the morning! No, this is what was spoken by the prophet Joel:

"'In the last days, God says,

I will pour out my Spirit on all people.' . . .

"Repent and be baptized, every one of you, in the name of Jesus Christ for the forgiveness of your sins. And you will receive the gift of the Holy Spirit." (Acts 2:1-4, 6-11, 13-17, 38-39)

So Jesus left, but he didn't leave us alone. He left us his Spirit—that elusive third member of the Christian Trinity. Now, you might have heard that Christians believe God is Father, Son, and Holy Spirit. And yet Christians also believe there is only one God. Three but also one. One but also three. Confused? Good, that means you're getting it. If you're not confused, then you haven't been paying attention, because it *is* confusing. Hold on to that confusion for a later chapter, where we will address more fully whether any of this three-and-one business makes any sense. For now though, just nod along with me, assuming that the Spirit is God. Are you nodding? *Good.* Let the confusion flow through you.

Back to Pentecost. So, this divine Spirit thingy shows up and blows everyone's mind. But contrary to how it may seem, *the Spirit is not new.* The Spirit "was hovering over the waters" (Gen 1:2) during the creation story and descended on Jesus like a dove at his baptism. So the Spirit was in play even before Pentecost, just more in the background, pulling strings. But now that Jesus has ascended offstage (with some very impressive wire work), the Spirit really gets a turn to run out and take a bow. The Old Testament focused more on the Father, and the Gospels more on the Son, Jesus. But now, with the dawning of the fifth movement, the focus will shift somewhat to the Spirit, who inspires and guides the church. Jesus may no longer be physically available to us for hugs and crucifixions, but his Spirit is still with us, leading the way.

Part of what distinguishes the Spirit from other gods in mythology who are off fighting Titans or lounging on Mount Olympus is that the Spirit is not somewhere out there in the world or up in the clouds. The Spirit is not just next to us, above us, behind us, or twenty miles north of us. Rather, the Spirit is within us. "The Spirit of God lives in you" (Romans 8:9). In the ancient world, people made great stone temples to their gods, hoping their gods would come and live inside the temple. Yet our God is not off sitting on a throne in some stone temple, is not some distant dictator ruling from a mountaintop, not some absent father who created us and then abandoned us to go chill in the clouds of heaven. No, our God is within us, close, personal, intimate. *We are God's temple.* "Your bodies are temples of the Holy Spirit" (1 Corinthians 6:19).* Even when you are lost in a forest, you are not alone—God is within you. Jesus may have left, but he didn't leave us alone; he sent us his Spirit.

Yet his *Spirit may not even be a "he."* Many languages give words a gender, and in Biblical Aramaic and Biblical Hebrew, the word for "Spirit" is feminine. Now, I wouldn't want to make too much of this (just because in French *pencil* is masculine and *eraser* is feminine doesn't mean they need to be stored separately in coed boxes).† I don't know whether the Spirit is a he or a she, but what I can say with certainty is that the Spirit is not an "it." The Spirit is a personal *who*, not an impersonal *what.* The Spirit is not an impersonal field like the electromagnetic or gravitational fields. Rather, Scripture has the Spirit feeling personal emotions, including getting angry or sad, or feeling grief (Ephesians 4:30). The Spirit loves (Romans 15:30), prays (Romans 8:26), comforts (John 14:16-17), teaches (John 14:25), and can even feel personally insulted (Matthew 12:32). So regardless of sex, the personal pronoun *he/she* is closer than the impersonal *it.*

Yet while the Spirit is personal like a human, the Spirit is also more than that. The Spirit is like wind. In the Bible, the Greek word for Spirit is *pneuma. Pneuma* could also be translated as "wind," "air," or "breath." Which is why at Pentecost the Spirit's arrival is initiated by a "sound like

---

*Movement one may have made it clear that the creatures are not the Creator, but that distance is held in tension with movement five, where the Spirit of God literally dwells within us. I may not *be* God, but God is within me, in the same way I may not literally *be* my lover, and yet our two flesh is intimately intertwined. We may not be the same as God, but God is near us all the same. The mystical closeness people have sought through turning nature into God's body can just as well be captured by the Spirit nesting in ours.

†Additionally, the Spirit can sometimes also be referred to as a he, such as in John 16:13.

the blowing of a violent wind" (Acts 2:2). *Pneuma* can even be translated "life," because air and breath are the wind within us. Our life begins with our first breath and ends with our last breath, when the *pneuma* finally leaves our bodies. In Genesis, when God first created the world, it says God took raw matter, the dust of the earth, and breathed into it, gave it the breath of life.

It is fitting that *pneuma* is also translated "wind," for the Spirit is much like wind. You can't quite grab wind—no sooner do you reach out to capture it than it slips through your fingers. And if anyone said, "Where is it? Prove it to me, show me this Spirit," you'd have nothing to hand them but empty, invisible air. Yet when wind comes coursing over you, it sets hair flying, clothes flapping, and arms chilling. Wind is good yet terrifying; wind can fly kites and down planes; wind can power countries and destroy cities. Wind is a lover, yes, but a lover you don't want to cross. The *pneuma*, the Spirit, is a comfort, a guide, a friend, a helper, but can also conjure great tongues of fire. The *pneuma* dwells within us yet fits in no mortal box, surrenders to none of our human ways of thinking. John 3 says, "The wind blows wherever it pleases. You hear its sound, but you cannot tell where it comes from or where it is going. So it is with everyone born of the Spirit" (John 3:8).

As soon as we try to control or pinpoint or reach out and grasp the Spirit, the Spirit slips through our fingers, like grasping for the wind. There have been times I thought I felt the Spirit comforting me within so powerfully that it brought tears to my eyes. Yet as soon as I tried to pin down that feeling and recreate it, it slipped through my fingers, and I was left wondering, *Did I just experience God, or was that an overblown stomachache?* There have been times when I was singing or hiking or swimming when I felt like God was pulsating through me. Then, when I was back in my comfortable couch at home, I began to doubt it. There was even one time when I saw the Spirit with my own eyes, like a great ball of fire (no tongues, though, sadly) rushing out of me. Then, as weeks and months passed and the memory faded, I was left wondering, *Was that God, or just a hallucination?* People ask, "How do you know the Spirit is there, how do you know it's God and not something else, how do you know what the Spirit wants you to do?" And I don't have a generic, one-size-fits-all, cookie-cutter answer to give them. *The wind blows wherever it pleases.* As soon as someone seems to have a patent on the Spirit, like they've figured God out once and for all, that's when you know that person is full of it (and I don't mean the Spirit).

And so, fittingly, the Spirit is universal. The Spirit is not limited to any particular person, ideology, culture, framework, place, time, ethnicity, or language. The Spirit is present everywhere to everyone all the time. That's what those crazy-sounding tongues of fire were about at Pentecost: "How is it that each of us hears . . . in our native language? Parthians, Medes and Elamites; residents of Mesopotamia, Judea and Cappadocia, Pontus and Asia, Phrygia and Pamphylia, Egypt and the parts of Libya near Cyrene; visitors from Rome; Cretans and Arabs—we hear . . . the wonders of God in our own tongues!" (Acts 2:8-10). You may not have a map in front of you, but the Bible just did a 360-degree circle, listing places from every single direction on the world map—Phrygia, Pamphylia, Cappadocia, and Pontus in the north; Elam, Mesopotamia, Parthia, and Media in the east; Egypt, Judea, and Arabia in the south; Libya, Cyrene, Crete, and Rome in the west. No longer will the world be divided into warring tribes and local deities; everyone everywhere can hear the call of the one Spirit and know that voice, regardless of country, class, race, or language. While the third movement was limited to the *physical nation* of Israel—to the ethnically Jewish and Middle Eastern—the fifth movement drastically expands out to include the whole world in a *spiritual nation*. For while we all speak our mother tongue, the Spirit is mother of us all, speaking tongues of universal fire.

And with that tongue, the Spirit whispers the way to goodness. The Bible talks about the result of having the Spirit within you: "The fruit of the Spirit is love, joy, peace, forbearance, kindness, goodness, faithfulness, gentleness, and self-control. Against such things there is no law" (Galatians 5:22-23). Notice that the text explicitly rejects the idea of this being about the Spirit making us follow the law or rules or moral customs. The point here is not ethical but relational. We become who we spend time with. My wife has made me more empathetic, and I have made her more susceptible to bad puns. If we spend time with the Spirit of God, with the one who is goodness itself, then that goodness will eventually begin to rub off on us. The Spirit loves us, rejoices in us, has patience with us, is kind and good and gentle with us. And the more we are around that kind of goodness, the more good and kind we will be. The more God rejoices in us, the more joy we'll have in ourselves and in others. The more time we spend with the *Spirit*, the more *spiritual* we'll become; indeed, the one term is literally the origin of the other.

Yet this spirituality, this intimacy with the Spirit, would not be fully possible without the other parts of the story happening first. One cannot skip to the Spirit in movement five without movement four (redemption) first addressing the fallout from movement two (fall).

For sin creates this separation, this loss of intimacy, this chasm between us and the God from whom we've fallen. Likewise, if I were to cheat on my wife or backstab a close friend, that would come between us and create emotional distance. If the Spirit of God is going to come near us again, the sin that got between us must first begin to be dealt with by Christ. Now, it's not that you have to be perfect before you can have a good relationship. Just the opposite. We can only have a good relationship once we admit we are *not* perfect and are willing to start addressing the stuff that inevitably comes between us. As with other humans, so with us and God. We can't have movement five–type intimacy with the Spirit without admitting the need for a little movement four–type redemption.

Plus, logically speaking, God is supposed to be goodness itself, so how could goodness be one with our badness? Goodness can only stream through us to the degree that our badness has been cleared out; clean water cannot flow through clogged pipes. Which is why in his speech earlier, Peter said, "Repent and be baptized, every one of you, in the name of Jesus Christ for the forgiveness of your sins. And [then] you will receive the gift of the Holy Spirit" (Acts 2:38). Many of us today want to be spiritual without all the sin and repentance talk, yet from a sheerly logical perspective, I cannot become one with goodness itself unless I first begin to address whatever badness is in my own self. That's why the Spirit comes only *after* Jesus. Of course, wouldn't it just be lovely if the perfect relationship suddenly entered our lives and made everything bright and good all the time, without requiring us face or even admit our own failings? But that's not how intimacy works, and the imagery of the Spirit literally *entering us* is nothing if not intimate.

So, we cannot talk about the Spirit without first talking about Christ. Yet we also cannot finish talking about Christ without talking about the Spirit. For the Spirit carries forward the work Jesus began. Jesus bore the guilt and justice of our sin, yes, but it is the Spirit who helps us actually stop sinning. Many are those who ask Jesus' forgiveness, then go home and drunkenly yell at their spouse all over again. It is one thing to get forgiveness for a mistake, and another thing entirely to stop making that mistake. Both aspects of our fallenness must be addressed if the fall is to be undone. As such, the Spirit of God comes alongside and within us on a daily basis, guiding us ever closer in our actions, thoughts, impulses, and desires to the one who is goodness itself. Jesus may have left, but he did not leave us alone—the Spirit has arrived.

❮❰❰❱❯

Now that this chapter is nearly over, I'll admit I really struggled to write it. It's not the last chapter in the book, yet it's the chapter I ended up writing last, because I just couldn't muster myself to it. And I finally admitted to myself why: I'm embarrassed by it. I am quite content discussing philosophy of religion and objective morality and a theoretical God of eternity. But I get rather uncomfortable when that God wants to enter time and space and flamboyantly disrupt the natural order like the Spirit does at Pentecost. I can stomach God the Father as long as he's somewhere off in the clouds. I can even stomach God as Jesus, because at least he's tucked away far enough in the past to have that distant glow of ancient and unquestionable things. But Christians are supposed to believe the Holy Spirit is still living and active in the church *today*. It's one thing to say there's a God in heaven, yet quite another to believe he's busy doing things on earth. I know God is technically my father, but it's awkward when he wants to get involved and embarrass me in front of my friends. Yet if you believe in God and believe we can access or experience this God—that God has not left us alone down here but is somehow present with us—then it inevitably follows that something at least vaguely like the Spirit exists. And is probably more embarrassed of us than we are of it.[‡]

Now, I think there are two major sources for this embarrassment some of us feel. First, we live in a scientific age that somewhere along the way decided nature was a closed system, that every natural effect must have a natural cause, and that nothing from above can interrupt the clashing of matter and flesh and atoms below. There doesn't seem to be room for the Spirit between the gears and cogs of the natural machine. However, the more I've looked into it, the more I've realized this is not necessarily the case, and there are a number of good arguments for why science and the divine interventions of the Spirit need not be at odds:

1. Even if nature is a closed system, we still need to explain what caused that system, and that might mean appealing to something outside the system itself. Once the dominoes get going, they may naturally take care of themselves, but someone still needed to tip the first one over. And if that someone could tip the first one over, there's no reason they couldn't directly tip any of the others over as well. If God created nature, then why can't God also interrupt it?

2. Science tests for what is repeatable and what normally happens. Miracles and the supernatural are supposed to be things that *don't* normally happen. So, this is kind of beyond science's purview. Science hasn't added anything new to the equation, because even in the ancient world people knew that tongues of fire didn't *usually* descend from the sky. They knew it was odd and noteworthy, which is why they noted it. The Bible is not saying these things happen every day— it's saying they happen maybe a few times a century, and that's why it bothered to record them when they did.

[‡]See how easy it is to slip into impersonal "it" language.

3. If God created the universe and the laws of nature, there's really no reason why God can't also violate those laws or rewrite them at will. I break the rules I set for my diet all the time. But in God's case, they wouldn't really be violations anyway, for if God violates them, then they can't have truly been *laws* to begin with, just human observations about what normally tends to happen (and those kind of observations get overturned all the time). What we call the laws of nature would just be what God *usually* does, and what we call miracles would just be what God *occasionally* does.

4. Precisely because divine intervention is rare, the religious person is free to believe that nature usually runs a tight ship and that natural science can still tell us a heck of a lot about the world. The supernatural need not negate the science of the natural, and so we can remain open to following the evidence wherever it leads. However, the opposite is not true for the atheist, as G. K. Chesterton notes: "The Christian is quite free to believe that there is a considerable amount of settled order and inevitable development in the universe. But the materialist is not allowed to admit into his spotless machine the slightest speck of spiritualism or miracle."[1]

5. We became embarrassed of the supernatural during the eighteenth and nineteenth century because science began to depict nature as a deterministic machine where every little cog and wheel interlocked, and every physical effect had a physical cause, without remainder or room for divine intervention. But quantum physics basically shattered this deterministic machine image in the twentieth century, and mainstream science never bothered to go back and rethink its past philosophical assumptions. We got rid of the machine but kept the mechanistic worldview. Oops.

6. Skeptics have rigged the game from the outset against divine intervention. They say that if the Spirit needs to miraculously interrupt nature to get things back on track, then God can't have designed nature very well to begin with, for it constantly needs fixing. So God

doesn't exist. However, if nature doesn't need tinkering from the outside and is a closed and perfect system, then it can run on its own without need for a God. So, God doesn't exist. Damned if you do, damned if you don't. Skeptics haven't weighed God and found him wanting but wanted to get rid of him and so weighted the scales against him. Maybe it's not just Christians who should feel embarrassed.

The second source of my embarrassment is the *when* and *where* of the Spirit's interventions. Why does the Spirit show up with tongues of fire or to miraculously provide funds for the church roof but drop the ball on the Holocaust or the Black Death? If God's Spirit *can* intervene, why not more often, especially in the midst of great suffering?

Now, I started to put together another list of retorts to this. But then I threw out the list, because I don't have a good enough answer to this question. I don't know if anyone does. Maybe ours really is a tale told by an idiot, full of sound and fury. Or maybe I'm the idiot and I just don't understand yet. Now, I could remind you that only if there is a divine reference point for morality can we call something like the Holocaust objectively wrong. But that only helps us continue to believe in God, not understand his utter lack of involvement when it counts. I could point out that many people have kept or even found faith in the midst of trauma and terror and death. But that doesn't explain God's absence; it just shows they were able to forgive it.[§] I could point out that we are never alone in our sufferings, for Christ is on the cross next to us, and the Spirit is going through it with and within us. But that only addresses the emotional problem of suffering, not the intellectual problem of it. I could tell you the *end* justifies the *means*, that perhaps the Spirit can only intervene when the situation doesn't overwhelm the greater end of human freedom, or that the Spirit intervening in some cases might create even darker timelines later on.

[§]Holocaust survivor Elie Wiesel writes, "I reject all these answers. Auschwitz must and will forever remain a question mark only: it can be conceived neither with God nor without God. . . . Let us make up, Master of the Universe. In spite of everything that happened? Yes, in spite. Let us make up: for the child in me, it is unbearable to be divorced from you so long." Elie Wiesel, "A Prayer for the Days of Awe," *New York Times*, October 2, 1997, www.nytimes.com/1997/10/02/opinion/a-prayer-for-the-days-of-awe.html.

But the problem with those end-justifies-the-means arguments is that we don't know what the end is. The story isn't over yet; we're still in movement five today. We don't know how it all ends or what it's all building to. Trying to solve life before it's over would not just be talking out one side of my mouth but out of another orifice altogether. The sixth and final movement has not even begun, let alone finished, and I have no idea how it's going to (or how it even possibly could) resolve the threads of this sprawling, manic, terrifying, beautiful, barmy, madcap story. It's one thing to say I trust my surgeon knows what she's doing, and another thing entirely to say *I know* what she's doing. The Spirit moves in mysterious ways; the wind blows where it will.

CREATION

- Creation begins
- Creation Is Not God
- Creation Is Good

FALL

- Humanity in God's Image
- Humanity Gone Wild

NATION

- Abraham Finds Faith — 2000 BC
- Moses Meets I Am — 1400–1200ish BC
- Goodness Is Commanded
- Beauty in the Promised Land
- King David and His Boy — 1000ish BC
- Justice Exiles the Nation — 586 BC

REDEMPTION

- Jesus Is Born — AD 0
- Jesus Is Walking Around Saying Stuff — AD 30
- Jesus Is Dying to Meet You — AD 33

CHURCH

- The Spirit Arrives — AD 33
- The Church Begins — AD 33
- The Apostle Paul Converts — AD 35ish
- The Church Expands — AD 300ish
- The Church Today — The Present

END

- The End of the World as We Know It
- Highway to Hell or Stairway to Heaven?

SIXTEEN

The Church Begins

RIGHT AFTER THE SPIRIT IS INTRODUCED, the Bible says in the very next verse:

> All the believers were together and had everything in common. They sold property and possessions to give to anyone who had need. Every day they continued to meet together in the temple courts. They broke bread in their homes and ate together with glad and sincere hearts, praising God and enjoying the favor of all the people. And the Lord added to their number daily. (Acts 2:44-47)

So when the Holy Spirit shows up, it doesn't just make individuals feel tingly inside; no, the Spirit begins to reshape whole communities and entire social landscapes. The Spirit brings lonely individuals into selfless community, fellowship, accountability, intimacy, and connection, into a community that shares what they have with one another, that eats and rejoices and prays and grows together. At first, this Spirit-led community meets in the streets and temple courts. But Christianity is soon outlawed in the Roman Empire, and its adherents often persecuted, so they can't meet in public anymore. Instead, they huddle together in each other's homes, risking their safety and security to be together. Later on, the laws are changed, and they start to meet in actual buildings designated for their community of faith. God continues to add to their numbers each day, month, year, decade, century, and millennia, until that ragtag bunch of a few dozen Spirit-led Christ-followers grow into two billion diverse people today, held together in a common unity calling itself *church*.

Yet for some people today, church is the last place they would ever want to go. For some of us, it would almost be easier to believe the Spirit showed up with great balls of fire than to believe God has anything to do with what is going on at the local church down the street. . . .

〈 ▨ ▨ 〉

When I was seventeen, my high school had all the graduating seniors write a blurb to go along with their picture in the yearbook. For mine, I quoted John Lennon:

> I don't believe in Bible
>
> I don't believe in Beatles
>
> *I just believe in me.*[1]

I don't need the rest of the band—I just need myself. Expressing the same sentiment but in nonmusical form is Jean-Paul Sartre, who writes, "Hell is other people."[2] Sartre was a famed philosopher who placed the individual's existence above the attempts of society, morality, the church, or other people to limit and define us. Man is born free, but everywhere he is chained by the moronic mores of the social machine. First off, we are born to parents who never cease overbearing us. Sure, you eventually graduate and move out, but your deference to your parents only transfers from them to your employer, your overbearing boyfriend/girlfriend, your country, your ideology, your church, your pastor, your favorite authors and podcasters and pundits and like-minded groupthink-ers. Everything you've done, you've done for others or copied from others or repackaged from others. *Everyone is the other, and no one is themself.** Hell is other people, and you are too afraid to leave their warmth to carve your true, authentic, solitary self from the frost.

And at seventeen, I could already see how the community was destroying individuality. They say society is a melting pot, but what that actually means is all differences are melted down and overwhelmed into a homogenous, bland broth. As soon as we are placed alongside others, they begin

---

*As if to prove the point, I stole that sentence from Martin Heidegger, *Being and Time*, trans. Joan Stambaugh, rev. Dennis Schmidt (Albany: University of New York, 2010), § 27.

to grate against our edges until we are sanded down into good little boys and girls who fit the mold. Boyfriends change for girlfriends; wives change for husbands; children become who their parents want them to be; teachers mold us into carbon copies; peers fold to pressure; congregants conform to their congregation and denomination and pastor and God. Indeed, the church is almost a punch line today, representing the last place that unique individuals with unique identities and proclivities might wish to go. Congregations stampede over any individuality or uniqueness or diversity, flattening us into cardboard cutouts of formerly full individuals. As soon as your spiritual journey needs the approval and input of others, it ceases to be *your* spiritual journey. The *self* gets swallowed up in the *other*.

These sentiments define the Western world in which I was raised. We value freedom, autonomy, and self-determination; consider our formative revolutions in England in the 1640s, America in 1776, and France in 1789. We prize independence, individualism, and pulling yourself up by your own bootstraps; consider any modern political debate about almost any issue, from welfare to capitalism to vaccinations. We value individual authenticity and being yourself; consider the perfume commercial I watched yesterday that went, "*Bleu de Chanel*—a fragrance for an individual who is deeply themselves." We believe our purpose on earth is to find out who we are and stay true to it; just watch any Disney movie ever. We listen to our own heart and mind over the wisdom of others, family, society, authority, and tradition; just read Dr. Seuss, who writes, "Be who you are and say what you feel, because those who mind don't matter and those who matter don't mind."[3] We think the meaning of life is not at the bottom of a bottle but at the bottom of ourselves, and if we could just dive deep enough, meditate long enough, psychoanalyze inwardly enough, we would finally return to the hearth within, knowing the place for the very first time. Our modern age is the age of the individual self.

This is perhaps why so many in today's culture define themselves as "spiritual but not religious." It's a way of saying we have a personal sense of the divine but don't pursue that sense in a communal or church setting. As Deepak Chopra writes, "Religion is belief in someone else's experience. Spirituality is having your own experience. . . . You should be totally independent. . . . You should have faith in yourself."[4] Spiritual guru Ram Dass reiterates this, saying, "The spiritual journey is individual, highly personal. It can't be organized or regulated. . . . Listen to your own truth."[5] Or, as Eckhart Tolle states, "I cannot tell you any spiritual *truth* that deep *within you* don't know already. . . . The real spiritual awakening [is] when something emerges from within you."[6] Growing up, these kinds of sentiments were very much my world. As mentioned earlier, less than 3 percent of people in my hometown, Vancouver, attend a weekly religious service. Yet more than half the population still believes some sort of divine entity exists.[7] Which means we're still spiritual but want to get away from religious communities, churches, clergy, dogma, groupthink, and so on. The problem isn't God but his people.

❰ ▦ ▦ ❱

Growing up in Vancouver, I read *Walden* in my high school English class, one of the defining texts of the modern Western canon. It condenses the true story of Henry David Thoreau escaping civilization to live alone in the woods for two years. How wonderful that sounded to me, to cease being a social animal and simply be an animal, alone and scrounging in the wild. I got giddy with introversion. *Oh, to get away from the whining and fighting and etiquette and gossip and insults and passive-aggressiveness and cruelty and complications of others and civilization. One-way ticket for one, please!* I thought to myself.

The only problem, which I realized later, is that Thoreau was, and I'm quoting here, a "miserable a**hole."[8] He once visited the site of a shipwreck that killed a hundred people days earlier and commented on how he felt pity not for the lost souls but for the wind and waves that had to deal with them. He was well known for being a puffed-up, sour, judgmental, cold misanthrope. The irony, then, is that Thoreau fled the evils of society, only to bring them all along within him. He escaped society but was still stuck with his miserable self. The fall follows us wherever we go—it's not just *social* but *individual*. The problem isn't just out there; it's in here. It's in me.

Isolate me in the woods and I'm not going to get better but, if anything, worse. My inner demons will finally have me all to themselves. My thoughts will bounce around incestuously in the echo chamber of my own mind, with no one to bring me back down to reality. Sure, I may have less social anxiety at first, but my existential dread and cosmic isolation will slowly begin to toy with insanity and suicide. No one will be there to stir me awake from my nightmares. My basic need for touch, conversation, and intimacy will funnel itself into increasingly deranged fantasies. I will begin to talk to myself and the walls. I will find a round object, smear it with my own blood, and call it Wilson. Sartre may have been right that hell is other people, but hell is also yourself, raveling further in forever.

Humans are inescapably social creatures, even the weird ones. Which is why Christopher McCandless, an Emory grad who fled society in 1992 to go live alone in the Alaskan wild, later scribbled next to his dying corpse, "Happiness only real when shared."[9] According to the World Health Organization, loneliness is equal health-wise to smoking fifteen cigarettes a day.[10] These effects can be so detrimental that some countries have even appointed an official minister of loneliness to address it.[11] And a Harvard medical study following the health of 168 men over eighty years found that medically the "only thing that really matters in life are your relationships to other people."[12]

What is more, community isn't just essential for the health of the individual but for their existence to begin with. Sorry, Rousseau, but man is not "born free." No, he is born umbilically chained to another who is not disposable but rather essential to the whole birthing process. Then we are raised up, nursed, potty-trained, given a common language, and shown the way of the world by others, in the lengthiest dependency period in the entire animal kingdom. Kangaroos only depend on others for half a year, humpback whales for a year, and giraffes for a year and a half. In contrast, humans are dependent on others for a decade or two, and this dependency has been linked to our higher brain functions and abilities (so at least in this case, the more dependent we are, the more empowered). We do not exist first as individuals and only later get placed into relationships. Rather, we are in relation from the very get-go. We are conceived through an act of intimacy, carried to term inside another, and then raised up by the community. No others means no self.

The fantasy of personal independence has only been plausible for a few centuries and only for wealthier countries. It now feels possible for an individual to stock up on groceries, work from home, never come out, and live in total isolation and independence. Yet the groceries do not magically appear on the doorstep but are placed there by another human, who is a member of an intricate social system requiring dozens if not hundreds of others to be working together in unison, both at the store itself and at the app company that processed your order, as well as the bank that forwarded the money and the internet provider through which they forwarded it. And don't even get me started on household electricity, water, heat, and so on. The contemporary creature comforts of isolation are only made possible because of the social and economic communities we exist in and benefit from. A thousand treaties had to be struck in order for you to treat yourself. Even Thoreau popped into town to get groceries.

This illusion of physical independence has been coupled with intellectual independence. The creed of the Western Enlightenment was "Think for yourself." This is ironic, because what we define as valid thinking was itself the result of thousands of years of communal reflection and tradition. While we tend to think of our individual self as the one thing that hasn't been hand-fed to us from the outside by others, our Western individualism is arguably what is most unique to our specific community, culture, time, place, and tradition. Even science is not just thinking for yourself but thinking with others; one of the main causes of the scientific revolution was the printing press allowing scientists to widely disseminate their work to others and thereby converse and learn from the global community of scientists. Most of what the individual scientist believes is not because they've done all the experiments for themselves but because they trust the scientific community. A marine biologist doesn't have time to double-check every single conclusion of past marine biologists, let alone those in their parallel discipline of astrobiology, and certainly not an entirely distinct field such as astrophysics. You can't rebuild from scratch the entire history of thought on your own any more than you can retile every time you go to the bathroom. This is why Isaac Newton, arguably the most important scientist in history, said, "If I have seen farther than anyone else, it is only because I have stood on the shoulders of giants."[13] You cannot think for yourself unless you first think *with others.*

One might point out similar issues with the "spiritual but not religious" crowd, which tends to believe it is thinking, feeling, meditating, journeying in isolation from the system and tradition and community and dogma. Yet we inherited these New Age and individualistic sentiments from our parents and grandparents in the sixties and seventies, and they themselves appropriated these ideas from Western individualists and Eastern religious communities going back thousands of years. So even when you are meditating or reading alone in your room, you're not escaping the human race or tradition or social system.

Remember those New Age thinkers I quoted a few paragraphs back, who said to set out alone on your own spiritual path? Well, Deepak Chopra and Eckhart Tolle both have a net worth of around $70–80 million.[14] What they should have said was, "Pay me to tell you to think for yourself." The "spiritual but not religious" crowd is still part of a collective system, economy, and ideology. They are still putting coins in the coffer, just not at church. They still have gurus and teachers and yogis, and so still have corruption and infighting and sexual abuse, just without the accountability or appeal process of a more established religious denomination. They still tend to meet in groups, and as soon as you start meeting with any regularity you start to get the trappings of religion, so perhaps they should accept that and just try to do religion better than others have done it. They still have their dogmas, except no one else is allowed to question them because their spiritual journey is deeply private and all that matters is what's *true for you.* And they only believe that to begin with because they've inherited it from a spiritual community of thought and practice, which likes to fancy it has somehow evolved beyond the communal nature of religion and humanity. But it's not less communal; it's just less aware of the social privileges that allow them to play at being authentically themselves, while not actually making the world a better place for anyone else. And if you are reading this and think that's an unfair caricature (which I'm sure for some people it is), then great; I am so happy to hear you *actually are* deeply embedded in spiritual communities of support. I'm glad we agree that's important.

Because it really is important—more important than I could have realized at seventeen. Luckily, my spiritual community did not give up on me even though I had given up on it. A small group of Christians met together during the week for food, games, conversation, debate, and prayer, and I'd begun to join them regularly. The way they did church constantly challenged my assumptions. With them, church wasn't about the building; we often met at McDonald's, the beach, or someone's house (just like the early church). With them, church wasn't a pastor telling us what to think; it was a pastor listening to me rant and process everything *I was thinking*. Church wasn't about force-feeding me dogma; it was a lively discussion and late-night debates about whether we have free will and other crazy questions. The fire of my own thoughts became infinitely larger and more provocative for having been stoked and kindled by the thoughts of others. Church wasn't about hiding who we were as individuals but opening up the doors and letting others see us fully, sharing and confessing and processing together—I told them things about myself I'd never told anyone. Church wasn't about money; I was a teen with no job or money to give, and I later learned the youth pastor made only $500 a month.[15] Yes, that church was bound within a system, tradition, and community, yet it wasn't bogged down by it. Rather, it was buoyed up and given breath and life and songs and potlucks by it. I could feel the Spirit *through* the community. I was no longer alone in the wilderness trying to track down God; other lights were gathering around me in the night, and the brighter we were, the easier it was for God to find us. I was a *self* who had encountered an *other*.

So I got special, last-minute permission to change my yearbook blurb after the deadline. I didn't take anything away. I kept the quote from John Lennon. I just added something after it:

"I don't believe in Beatles.

I just believe in me."

—*John Lennon.*

I love you John, but in the past year many things have changed. I don't think I am ready to turn my back on it all, on hope for the world. There's cud yet to be chewed here.

❮ ▮ ▮ ❯

I had a good experience with church. I was lucky enough to see what a good and healthy spiritual community could look like. Yet I am not naive enough to think that everyone is so lucky. Some of the most egregious desecrations have occurred in church basements and Sunday schools. Some of the worst oppressors and most terrifying ideologies have found shelter in the church. For some of you, just reading a chapter about church has likely been a triggering experience, and justifiably so. I wouldn't want to argue with any of that. It's all true; in fact, the truth is probably even worse than what we know about. I swear this chapter is not about trying to get you to go back to a specific church, such as perhaps your childhood church. I'll take your word for it that it's terrifying, backward, repressive, and xenophobic. I've been to churches like that myself over the years. I have no interest in pressuring you to go back to that particular church, denomination, or cultural movement (because sometimes it's not just a few bad apples but the broader systemic tree). If someone gave you this book as fuel for further gaslighting, then use it to instead drive as far away from them as you can to a healthier spiritual community.

I'm not saying you should go back to any specific church. Rather, I am simply suggesting you don't give up on the general idea of church *as church*—as spirituality pursued socially with others. Now, it makes sense if you don't go to church because you think Christianity is untrue or harmful. But that's a problem with the Christian beliefs explored in churches, not a problem with the idea of communal spirituality itself. That's a problem I need to address in all my other chapters in this book on Christian thought but not here in this chapter on church. And it makes sense if you don't want to go back to your particular church because it's terrifying and traumatizing. But that's not necessarily a problem with spiritual community in general but with a specific church, denomination, or cultural movement.

It makes sense if you've been burned, hurt, or even abused by the fallenness of others. But you can't escape that by ditching people altogether or going to live in a cabin in the woods. It makes sense if you've had some rough experiences and need to take some time away from church to reset. But while those may be healthy rhythms, they can't be the end of the song. For to give up on church *as church*, not for one of those other reasons I listed above but because you are tired of dealing with other people *as other people*—as complicated, messy, fallen mortals—is to give up on humanity itself. To paraphrase Bob Marley: other humans are always going to hurt you, you just have to decide which ones you're willing to suffer for.

〈 ▨ ▨ 〉

Despite everything I just said about community, I still go on personal retreats. I still take off on my own for a few nights every other month just to read, write, pray, sleep, and walk alone. I would still say that if you're in an unhealthy community, you as an individual should push back against that and possibly consider leaving. And I still disagree with my church community about a lot of things; in fact, I'm often the one pushing the envelope. As you might have noticed from reading my book, I'm not exactly a quiet, polite wallflower who just fits into the Christian mold. No, I'm eccentric and ridiculous and refuse to surrender my individual personality. For while it would have been easy to go from the one extreme to another—from holding the individual self above the community to holding the community above the self—I believe the truth is in the tension. We are not just individual persons or just our relationships. Rather, we are persons-in-relation.

When community overwhelms the individual, we get conformity, homogeneity, assimilation, abuse, cover-ups, groupthink, mob mentality, *1984*, and totalitarianism. People repress and hide whatever parts of themselves don't fit into the social box. Diversity, difference, and otherness are sliced away, leaving only a homogenous unity and artificial oneness. People stay in harmful marriages, submit to unhealthy churches, and suppress their personal qualms for the sake of the whole. Yet on the opposite end, when the individual trumps the community, we get selfishness, narcissism, broken communities, broken families, isolation, loneliness, anarchy, and so on. Individuals place themselves above others, or isolate themselves from others, avoiding some pain but also avoiding all the joys, support, and accountability of community. So, individuals without community doesn't work. And community that overwhelms, stifles, and homogenizes individuals doesn't work either. Can't live with them, can't live without them. Hell is other people, and hell is also yourself.

But heaven is yourself-with-others. My seventeen-year-old individualistic self wasn't lost but balanced out by a church community that loved and supported and challenged and refined me. Rising up as fully myself, I came face to face with others who saw me, challenged me, pushed me, supported me, enjoyed me—who made me more than I was and all that I could be. I only came to know myself fully through seeing myself reflected back in their eyes. In turn, I challenged and supported them. I pushed them on some of their views and dogmas, and they pushed me on some of mine. I called my community out on ways it could do better, and it called me out too. I would not be who I am today without the community that shaped me, and that community would not be fully what it is without me and the other individuals within it.

There is no whole individual without their community, and no community without the individuals that comprise it. Problems arise when we try to make one side of the equation bigger or more dominant than the other. I truly believe everything I said in the first half of this chapter, but I also believe it is incomplete and lopsided unless balanced by everything said in the second half. Humans are not just individual persons or just our relationships. Rather, we are persons-in-relation.

〈▉▉〉

That said, let's conclude with this easy and totally-not-unsolvable question: Is God a person or is God a relationship? Is God an individual or a community?

Now, if you say that God is primarily an individual, then God was lonely and isolated until later on, when God invented community and love and relationship. In which case, individuality would be more fundamental to existence than community. At the heart of reality would not be love or relationship or intimacy but a solitary, self-sufficient individual. Community and relationship would not be eternally good or grounded in the nature of a communal and relational God. Rather, they would be later inventions and social constructs, deviations from the initial individual. As argued throughout this book, what we define God as is also the ground for objective morality and meaning. So, if God is fundamentally unsocial, then it is hard to make the case that love, relationship, family, intimacy, and connection are inherently good things we ought to cultivate. In turn, God cannot be love itself, for how can there be love without someone *to* love?[†] Being is now individual. The absolute is alone. God is isolation. The heart of the universe does not quicken for another. The only good is the self.

Yet if you answer the other way, then that means that community is more primary to existence than the individual. The community is the only absolute. In which case, it's the same problem in reverse. Your personal needs ultimately disappear in the collective—our individuality really should dissolve like a drop in the ocean. Your personality, uniqueness, and individual identity should all be consumed by the Leviathan of family, marriage, church, society, government, and God.

Of course, most worldviews have only one or the other of those at their core. They either emphasize manyness or oneness, diversity or unity, individuality or community, persons or their relationships. They bite the bullet and choose between one side or the other. But the brilliant and/or bonkers thing about Christianity is that it calmly and without sarcasm answers *both*. Is there only one God? *Yes.* But your God is also three persons: Father, Son, and Spirit? *Yes.* So, is your God an individual or a community? *Yes.* How does that make sense? *Yes.*

Christians believe there is only one God. And yet they also believe that God is three persons, Father, Son, and Spirit. The Father we talked about

---

[†]Perhaps God might simply "love Godself," but such a love would only be a homogenous and self-focused love, which does not reach beyond itself to embrace an *other* but only that which is like itself and an extension of itself.

with David and Solomon is God. And Jesus is God. And the Spirit is God. Yet there's only one God. God is three, and God is one. God is united as one in relationship yet distinct as three individual persons. Or perhaps you could see it another way and say God is one as an individual and yet three as a community. Either way, the two sides of the equation are held together in tension. God is individual and communal, one and many, person and relations, persons-in-relation. And if that sounds confusing to you, good, you're getting it. If that sounds as bewildering as trying to figure out your relationship to your church or the family dynamics at Thanksgiving, then good, that's exactly the point.

For the Christian, we are made in the image of a God who is three *and* one, individual *and* communal, person *and* relation. And so we too are persons-in-relation. Hence, when one side of that equation trumps the other—when the individual is swallowed up in the church community, or the church community is trampled over by the individual—we fail to live up to the divine image within us. We are failing to be fully human, for we are failing to reflect the Trinity who is persons-in-relation. The church, as a community of persons-in-relation, balances out the image of God on earth. The individual is not more basic than the church community, nor vice versa, for at the heart of all existence is not one or many but both, held eternally in tension. Three and one, one and three. One God, three persons. Father, Son, and Spirit.

As I've been contending this whole book, what is good down here must be modeled off what is good up there. It is objectively and morally better to be good because God is eternally goodness itself. So, if we are called to be in relationship, it is because God is relationship. If we are called to be whole and unique individuals, it is because God is a wholesomely unique individual(s). If we are called to love others, it is because God is love itself—a forever community who eternally gives and receives love from one another. If our most basic definition is as persons-in-relation, then we must be made in the image of one who is persons-in-relation. The three and one, one and three—Father, Son, and Spirit. As Jesus says to God the Father, he came so that humanity "may be one as we are one—I in them and you in me" (John 17:22-23).

Now, you might have heard of the problem of "the one and the many," which is perennial in philosophy. Some philosophers start with oneness but then can't explain the manyness and diversity and differences of our world. Other philosophers start with manyness but then can't explain the oneness underlying and interconnecting the universe and how it all holds together as one whole. In contrast, Christianity starts with oneness and manyness held in tension, postulating a trinitarian God who is three *and* one, one *and* many. The absolute at the heart of existence is not just one or many but *both*. And while we cannot necessarily explain how that works, it can then explain all the overlapping oneness and manyness we see in the world around us. None of these philosophical approaches can make sense of everything, yet one of them must somehow be true at the end of the day. So pick your poison. I've chosen the poison I can drink and toast with others, the one that makes sense of my human needs as a person-in-relation.‡

---

‡If you want to know more, check out my book on the Trinity, titled *MonoThreeism* (Portland, OR: Cascade Books, 2021). Is that how I'm going to end a chapter on community? With self-promotion? Yes, I think it is.

CREATION

Creation Begins ●
Creation Is Not God ●
Creation Is Good ●

FALL

Humanity in God's Image ●
Humanity Gone Wild ●

NATION

Abraham Finds Faith ● 2000 BC
Moses Meets I Aᴍ ● 1400–1200ish BC
Goodness Is Commanded ●
Beauty in the Promised Land ●
King David and His Boy ● 1000ish BC
Justice Exiles the Nation ● 586 BC

REDEMPTION

Jesus Is Born ● AD 0
Jesus Is Walking Around Saying Stuff ● AD 30
Jesus Is Dying to Meet You ● AD 33

CHURCH

The Spirit Arrives ● AD 33
The Church Begins ● AD 33
The Apostle Paul Converts ● AD 35ish
The Church Expands ● AD 300ish
The Church Today ● The Present

END

The End of the World as We Know It ●
Highway to Hell or Stairway to Heaven? ●

SEVENTEEN

The Apostle Paul Converts

LED BY THE SPIRIT, the early church meets in each other's homes in this radical social experiment. They share whatever they have with one another, carrying each other's burdens and rejoicing in one another's successes, learning and loving together. Yet the local religious and political elites are not thrilled that a vibrant community is forming around a criminal who had been officially crucified by the powers that be. The early church is seen as a threat to the religious establishment because they worship Jesus as their God, and a threat to the Roman Empire because they worship this God above Caesar. The Roman government and local religious leaders begin hunting down church members. In this chapter, we meet one of the hunters.

〈 ▬ ▬ 〉

It's a boy! He's finally here! And on the eighth day after the birth, all the family and friends gathered around to circumcise him and give him a beautiful Jewish name: *Saul.*

Saul was raised in a devout Jewish family who followed the Jewish laws to a T. Yet they were living among Gentiles. If you don't know what a Gentile is, then you almost certainly are one. *Gentile* means anyone who is non-Jewish. I'm a Gentile. Brad Pitt is a Gentile. Barack Obama is a Gentile. Adam Sandler isn't, but I've heard his agent is. Of the world's people, 99.7 percent are Gentiles.

There was an ancient Jewish prayer that went, "Thank you, God, for not making me a Gentile, a woman, or a slave."[1] So, back then Jewish people didn't exactly have a high view of Gentiles (and vice versa). Gentile nations—for example, Babylon, Rome—had constantly been attacking and invading the land, and so Jewish communities and families took extra-special care to preserve their Jewish identity amid foreign invasion and cultural oppression. Saul's family would have worked hard to preserve his Jewish heritage and raise him like a Jew, not a Gentile. He would have gone to Jewish night school and learned Hebrew so he could read the Hebrew Bible in its original language.

Saul showed unique promise in this regard, mastering his religious studies and shocking his teachers. He quickly rose to the top of the local religious government, becoming a Pharisee and a close associate of the Sanhedrin, an ancient council of holy men. And as the early church began to gather and grow, the Sanhedrin started to get uncomfortable. So they appointed Saul to police and track down church members. On one such occasion, Saul helped haul a churchgoer named Stephen in front of the Sanhedrin for sentencing and execution. The Bible says Saul was right there, giving approval to his death (Acts 8:1), close enough to jeer on the crowd and see the life go out of Stephen's eyes as he disappeared behind a sea of stones.

Stoning Stephen really got things rolling, with Saul now going from house to house, dragging churchgoers to prison, or worse. His reputation spread, and the church scattered for protection, forcing Saul to travel farther away to catch them. On one such journey, he had to take the long and winding Damascus Road (which you can still walk today, by the way). Somewhere along the way, he saw someone he did not expect. Or rather, he heard someone he did not expect. For his eyes were suddenly surged with light till they seemed to pop and flicker out altogether. Darkness ruled the day, and a throatless voice pierced the newly fallen night: "Saul, Saul, why do you persecute me?" (Acts 9:4).

Blinded, Saul turned every which way, frantically trying to pinpoint that omnipresent pitch. But to no avail. He suddenly felt very small in the arms of something very big. Falling back, he sobbed to the sky, "Who—who are you, Lord?" And upending everything Saul knew, believed, and had been about to do, a whisper breathed back, "I am Jesus, whom you are perse-cuting" (Acts 9:5).

Saul froze, cringed, crumpled, collapsed—did whatever someone does when they realize it's over, that they've stumbled into the enemy camp. Saul waited for death, for revenge, for the boomerang of justice, for his former prey to prey upon him, for what goes around to come back around, for the first stone to strike his skull, fair and true. Instead, the voice calmly instructed, "Get up and go into the city, and you will be told what you must do" (Acts 9:6).

The Bible does not describe Saul's reaction or thought process here. We don't know whether he broke down in tears, or whether he apologized for the souls he had sent on early to the grave, or whether he suddenly felt a wave of forgiveness, having a very literal come-to-Jesus moment. Maybe all that and more. What we do know is that Saul was never the same again. Once in the city of Damascus, he was led to the house of a churchgoer, Ananias, who taught Saul more about Jesus. Saul soon regained his sight, while also growing in faith, becoming very wise and much less murder-y. While many of us grow in fits and spurts, Saul was one of those rare few who had a vision and then seemed to change almost overnight.

Of course, you might not buy that, and neither did the early church. They heard that Saul was now claiming to be one of them and assumed it was an undercover tactic, an attempt to infiltrate their operation from within. No one was willing to believe that this murderer and persecutor of the church could really change and, even if he had, that Jesus would really want someone like him.

But then Saul starting publicly preaching about Jesus in the streets and synagogues of Damascus, leading to a wave of new people joining the church. Saul quickly became the target of the persecution efforts he had until recently led. Saul's old Sanhedrin friends were furious; they couldn't have one of their own turn on them so publicly. They began to plot his death. Things got so bad in Damascus that Saul had to be lowered over the city wall in a basket to escape. The one who martyred Stephen now faced martyrdom himself; the one who stormed into house churches now hid in them; he who once guarded the walls was now being lowered down them in a basket. If it was all an act, Saul was playing his part a little too well.

Eventually, after much debate and reticence, the early church became convinced that Saul was the real deal and welcomed him in. The arms of the cross now spread wide enough to embrace a murderer.

Saul continued traveling, telling any of his fellow Jews who would listen about Jesus and meeting with the other Jewish Christ-followers. Note that I didn't say *Christians*, for at this time there technically were no Christians. The earliest churches were just Jews going around telling other Jews that their long-awaited Jewish Messiah had arrived. They didn't think they were starting a new religion called Christianity; they just thought Jesus was the fulfillment of the Jewish beliefs they already held. They still thought of themselves as the chosen people, and the Gentiles as forsaken. Or at least they did until Saul got involved.

Saul's ministry kept expanding bigger and bigger until he began telling even non-Jews about Jesus. The arms of the cross now spread wide enough to embrace the Godforsaken Gentiles. Saul even started going by the name Paul, because Paul sounded more like a Gentile name, and he wanted to connect better with his non-Jewish audience (like someone named Hiroshi Yamamoto changing their name to Gary to fit in in Kansas). So Saul was actually the apostle Paul, the same Paul that St. Paul's Cathedral and seemingly half the hospitals in the world are named after.

So the apostle Paul/Saul (try saying that five times fast) started traveling far beyond the Jewish land of Israel, spreading the church throughout the broader Gentile world. He traveled north into Asia Minor (modern-day Turkey), visiting the city of Ephesus. In Ephesus, people worshiped Artemis, the titillating goddess of fertility who had more than a dozen breasts. The Ephesian streets were lined with vendors who sold little idols of her for people to keep with them (a bosom buddy, if you will). Now, Artemis was one of many gods and was herself created, born to Zeus and Leto. So Paul told them about the "I am" God who is Being itself, in contrast to their created gods of mythology and wooden idols whittled by mortal hands. Many people seemed to be buying Paul's message, which meant they weren't buying idols anymore. The local craftsmen were losing money, and the local religious leaders were losing out on gifts and donations to Artemis.

They began rioting in the streets, beating local churchgoers and chanting, "Great is Artemis of the Ephesians!"

Not wanting to cause more trouble for the local church, Paul fled Ephesus. But he continued to write letters back and forth with the church in Ephesus for many years. We still have one of these letters; it's the biblical book of Ephesians. In fact, much of the Bible is simply Paul's letters to various people and city churches. Which is why they often include hilariously specific and personal side notes, such as:

> Do your best to come to me at Nicopolis, because I have decided to winter there. Do everything you can to help Zenas the lawyer and Apollos on their way and see that they have everything they need. (Titus 3:12-13)

> Demas . . . has deserted me and has gone to Thessalonica. . . . Only Luke is with me. Get Mark and bring him with you. (2 Timothy 4:10)

Another such community Paul wrote to was the church in Philippi, Greece, which Paul visited between AD 49 and 51 and from which we get the name for the biblical book of Philippians. In Philippi, a demon-possessed slave girl chased behind Paul, screaming prophecies and profanities at him wherever he went. She kept this up for days, so long that the Bible gives us this enjoyably human moment: "Finally Paul became so annoyed that he turned around and said to the spirit, 'In the name of Jesus Christ I command you to come out of her!'" (Acts 16:18). The girl calmed down, suddenly freed of whatever inner demons had long haunted her. But there was a problem. Her master made money from people paying for her demonic prophecies and fortunetelling. Her possession was what made her profitable; now she was just a normal girl. Furious, the rich master had Paul whipped and thrown in prison for property damage.

The jailer fastened Paul's feet in stocks, leaving him lying in a pool of his own blood, drained from his freshly thrashed back. Paul had no strength left to sit up, yet lying back put pressure on his mangled torso, shooting pain along his spine. Yet around midnight, Paul somehow began praying aloud and singing to God. His voice was pathetic, constantly interrupted by gasps of pain. But he kept on singing anyway, as if propelled forward by something deeper than circumstance, as if the Spirit was erupting through him. The other prisoners listened in to this ancient jailhouse rock, stunned at the shredded body whose soul yet rejoiced.[*]

Now, objectively, Paul's time in Philippi sucked. Yet years later, when Paul wrote a letter to the church in Philippi, he used the word *joy* sixteen times in barely a hundred verses. He writes of a joy one can have even when one is locked "in chains" (Philippians 1:7). If we strive for external happiness and status and comfort, we'll never get it for long, never quite reaching our goal or wanting just a little bit more when we do. But true joy is learning to resound in the midst of instability, insecurity, layoffs, recessions, prison, disease, death, and aging. When the things of this world pass us by, the only joy left us must be otherworldly, supernatural, divine.[†] As Corrie ten Boom said of her time in the concentration camps, "You may never know that Jesus is all you need, until Jesus is all you have."[2]

Paul soon escaped Philippi, moving on to the city of Athens, the birthplace of philosophy. Paul immediately got into a discussion with some of the local philosophers, even quoting some of their own Greek intellectuals

---

[*]"Even in the mud and scum of things, something always, always sings." Ralph Waldo Emerson. See Clellan Coe, "Multiple Things," *The American Scholar,* January 13, 2021.
[†]Indeed, one of the fruits of the Holy Spirit I listed a few chapters back was joy.

back to them. The arms of the cross were now spreading wide enough to embrace the philosophers, doubters, and skeptics. Yet while Paul used philosophy, he also knew its limits. Looking around, he saw the Athenians had erected a monument dedicated to an "unknown God." Philosophy is great at showing you how little you know, but it's not always great at giving you something in its place. Their reason helped them deconstruct the Greek mythological gods but left them with nothing solid on which to reconstruct. On its own, human reason gets you Münchhausen's trilemma, an unknowable universe, and an "unknown God." Trust me, I've been pulling at that thread my whole life.

When I was younger, I thought if I could just learn enough, I'd finally figure everything out. So I went and did a PhD in philosophy of religion at Cambridge University. What I found is that the smartest humans on earth cannot agree about almost anything. At Cambridge, some of the most brilliant philosophers in the world were Christians, and some of the most brilliant philosophers in the world were atheists. So it's not like if you just study some more you're going to figure out something they haven't and finally settle this issue once and for all. Even at the very top, no one is quite sure what's going down. Human reason can only get you so far. Which is why, having been to Athens and seen the very best that human reason has to offer, Paul later wrote, "Where is the philosopher of this age? Has not God made foolish the wisdom of the world?" (1 Corinthians 1:20).

Paul soon moved on from Athens. Somewhere around this time, he wrote a letter to the church in Rome. We still have this letter today; it's called the book of Romans. In Rome, many of the Jewish Christ-followers were refusing to accept the Gentile Christ-followers as legitimate. They still thought of Jesus as a Jewish Messiah sent by a Jewish God solely to save the Jewish descendants of Abraham. They assumed that Christ-followers must still be circumcised, eat kosher foods, and follow all the Jewish laws and customs. They thought of their faith in Jesus as something strictly for those who were ethnically and culturally Jewish. Now, they were willing to allow some non-Jews to join, but only on the condition that they became Jews first, only on the condition that they circumcised themselves and observed all the other Jewish customs. Which, as you can imagine, was not something many adult males were willing to do.

Paul wrote to the Jewish and Gentile church in Rome to address these issues. He told them that God's love was not the sort of thing they could earn by following Jewish customs and moral laws. God's mercy is given unconditionally, without our ticking off a checklist of good deeds, or getting circumcised, or eating kosher foods, or being from the right tribe or nation or ethnicity. Anyone who thinks they've earned a ticket to heaven through how awesome and respectable they are only reveals how self-righteous and un-self-aware and not-awesome they truly are. None of us can climb to heaven on our own strength alone but need to be carried on the lashed back of Christ. Jesus died for our sins precisely because *none of us* were awesome or respectable or moral enough to make it on our own. The cross is the great equalizer of humanity. All of us are fallen, and so all need the love and mercy of God. If God could accept Paul—a murderer—into the church, then surely God can accept Gentiles as well. As Paul writes, "There is no difference between Jew and Gentile—the same Lord is Lord of all" (Romans 10:12). The arms of the cross now spread wide enough to embrace both the sinful Gentile and the self-righteous Pharisee. (So for all my uncircumcised readers, you can thank Paul for really saving your skin.)

Yet Paul believes this is the fulfillment of the Jewish faith, not its negation. Opening things up to the Gentiles doesn't mean negating the Jewish nation and Abraham and everything that happened earlier in the story. For what made Abraham close to God was never that he was ethnically Jewish (which would be redundant, as being ethnically Jewish originally meant descending *from Abraham*). No, Abraham was close to God because he had faith in God. So if the Gentiles now have faith in Jesus, then they too are following in Abraham's footsteps. They don't have to be from his biological line to be his spiritual successors.

More importantly, recall what God said to Abraham in the first place: "I will make you into a great nation! . . . *All peoples on earth will be blessed through you*" (Genesis 12:2-3). So God chose the Jewish people, but never for their own sake alone. The goal was always to bring about—through them—the blessing of "all peoples on earth." Which obviously includes the Gentiles. Jesus wasn't an off-ramp from the Jewish road but the destination that Abraham, Moses, and the Jewish nation had been driving toward all along. Jesus, the Jewish descendant of Abraham, was finally going to undo the fall and bring humanity *as a whole* back to the original goodness of creation.

Letting the Gentiles in didn't make the church less true to its Jewish roots but more. Some in the Jewish nation thought the world should have to shrink to fit their borders, but Paul was expanding the borders of the nation to include the whole world. God's people would no longer be limited to a *physical nation* of those ethnically Jewish but expanded into a *spiritual nation* called the church—a church led by the Spirit, whose tongues of fire can be understood by everyone everywhere.

Around when Paul wrote to the Romans, he also went and visited the Greek city of Corinth, from which we later get the name for the books of 1 Corinthians (you know, that one that always gets trotted out at weddings: "Love is patient, love is kind . . ." [1 Corinthians 13:4]) and 2 Corinthians. In Corinth, Paul met a couple named Priscilla and Aquila. Paul soon put Priscilla in positions of authority in the community and, contrary to ancient convention, almost always lists her before her husband. In fact, in one chapter alone, Paul mentions over a dozen women who were important leaders in the church, including Priscilla (whom he calls his coworker), Phoebe (whom he calls a deacon), and Junia (whom he likely calls an apostle).[3] In line with this, Paul later wrote these wall-shattering words: "There is neither Jew nor Gentile, neither slave nor free, nor is there male and female, for you are all one in Christ Jesus" (Galatians 3:28). Indeed, sociologist Rodney Stark argues that one of the major reasons the early church grew so rapidly was that it appealed to every demographic of society, including woman and slaves, who had previously been excluded from religious life and practice.[4] The arms of the cross now spread wide enough to embrace every woman, minority, and second-class citizen.

So, Paul was a socially radical, exciting, and explosive thinker. Yet he is often seen today as a source of sexism, slavery, and social hierarchy. I'll admit, it's easy to cherry-pick of few of his words out of context; there are things he says that part of me kind of wishes he hadn't. But what is crucial here is that the places where Paul most upsets our culture today are where he was most trying to appease his culture back then. Yes, there are places where Paul talks about slaves submitting to their masters, wives submitting to their husbands, and citizens submitting to their government (e.g., Ephesians 5:21–6:9). Yet this was standard stuff in the ancient world that pretty much everyone already thought and assumed.

What's interesting is not where Paul sticks with the ancient party line but where he breaks with it. Yes, Paul tells women to submit to their husbands, but in the verse next to it he tells all Christians to submit to one another regardless of their gender and says husbands must daily lay down their lives for their wives like Christ did on the cross (a rather submissive act in itself, and very much *not* something that was expected of husbands in the ancient world). Yes, Paul says we are to obey the government, but Paul himself was constantly disobeying the government and getting whipped and imprisoned for it. Perhaps what Paul means is that we should obey the government in most things so that when we do disobey it actually means something; you can't go to marches and commit civil disobedience if you're already in jail for tax fraud. And yes, Paul says slaves should obey their masters, but his audience was slaves who were trying to stay alive in difficult circumstances, not masters wanting to legitimate their oppression (they never would have thought they needed such legitimation anyway, nor read it as such, for slavery was ubiquitous and assumed in the ancient world). Perhaps Paul is less like a White man telling his slaves to obey and more like a Black father telling his son not to give the cops any reason to shoot.[‡] And Paul is clearly not for slavery, elsewhere writing the most passive-aggressive letter ever in hopes that Onesimus would embrace his escaped slave, Philemon, "no longer as a slave, but . . . as a dear brother" (Philemon 1:16).

[‡]This is debated, and I can certainly appreciate the response of those who are uncomfortable with Paul due to how his words were used when slavery was legal in the US. Black theologian Howard Thurman's grandmother, who was born into slavery, wouldn't read Paul for this reason. See Lisa Bowens, "It's Complicated: Confronting Complex Scripture," Pittsburgh Theological Seminary, August 6, 2020, https://ptsem.edu/about/the-quad/news/news-its-complicated-confronting-complex-scripture/.

So we tend to misread Paul through the oppressive lens that he has been misused by the powerful throughout history, forgetting that he was himself a persecuted minority writing to fellow persecuted minorities.[§] I suspect that many religious disputes—at least in my own community—have come from trying to *directly* apply the nuanced texts of an ancient and oppressed people to a modern, Western context, without appreciating that we are part of the wealthiest and most powerful empires in the history of the planet, and that Paul is not one of us. Paul was a second-class Jew in a Roman-occupied land, who was then cast out by his fellow Jews after he converted, spending his life in and out of prison for his beliefs. Paul was constantly in danger, and to question the accepted hierarchy of *God over emperor over nation over father over mother over child over slave* would have been to foolishly threaten the entire social and political order (which Paul was totally willing to do, but only when necessary). Perhaps Paul was toeing the line, not drawing it. We should be very cautious about overemphasizing the ways in which Paul strategically fit into the social norms and hierarchies of his time, while paying special attention to where he shatters them. As his own story demonstrates, it didn't take a lot back then to get your head cut off.

Paul eventually returned to the Holy Land, preaching to the people of Jerusalem about the same Christ they had crucified as a criminal. A furious crowd formed—some of them likely Paul's former Sanhedrin associates, who had been publicly humiliated by his betrayal. They dragged Paul away, beating him and crying out, "Get rid of him!" Some Roman soldiers in the area caught wind of what was going on, putting Paul in prison then later shipping him off to Rome to await trial. The Bible ends Paul's story with him imprisoned under house arrest in Rome for two years. But we know from history that the Emperor Nero eventually had Paul publicly beheaded. We also know that Paul did not waste a minute of those final years. He couldn't go anywhere, but neither could his guards. They were a captive audience, and many of them came to believe in the Christ that this prisoner would not shut up about.

[§]Yes, Paul was also a Roman citizen, but citizens can still be oppressed.

EIGHTEEN

The Church Expands

PAUL DIED. HE WAS EXECUTED under the authority of the Roman Emperor Nero somewhere around AD 64–68. Likewise, nearly all of Jesus' remaining disciples were executed by the religious and political authorities over the ensuing decades. Peter was crucified upside down. James and Nathaniel were beheaded. Thomas was speared in India.[1] Going to church in those early years meant putting your whole life on the line. It meant risking all social status and worldly affirmation, risking leaving your life and loved ones behind. Yet the early church kept meeting in homes and huddling together to pray and worship even though they knew it might cost them everything. They loved Jesus enough to die for him because Jesus loved humanity enough to die for us.

One of the worst persecutions of the church occurred later on, from AD 284 to 305, when Emperor Diocletian ordered the destruction of churches and the arrest and torture of anyone who would not renounce Christ and pledge their worship to Caesar. Yet Diocletian was succeeded by Emperor Constantine, who—through a crazy series of events involving a battle and a psychedelic vision—somehow became a Christian himself. The early church suddenly went from a persecuted minority to having the ear of the most powerful man in the ancient world. And things have been complicated ever since.

The Roman Empire slowly became Christian, making the church one of the most powerful and widespread institutions in the world. Over the centuries, the church expanded into the centerpiece of the social world, functioning as a hub that connected all the other aspects of communal life.

Political deals and alliances were shaken on in the pew and approved by the papacy. Marriages went through the priest, under the steeple, and out the church doors. Communal gatherings were oriented around church holidays, festivals, feasts, and saints' days. The community marked each individual life through the rituals of baptism, confirmation, and, eventually, a church funeral. For thousands of years, you could not be a full part of your local community unless you were part of the local church. Whereas going to church once meant being hated by the world and broader society, it now meant fitting into the social system. Within such cultural Christianity, it became possible to attend church solely for community rather than for Christ.

I recently heard someone say, "I'm not sure what I believe about all the God stuff. But I go to church for the community." This makes complete sense. As we talked about a few chapters ago, individuals need community and connection and love, and that's hard to come by today. Much of our modern social order was originally built around the church as its centerpiece, and society has been struggling for the last few centuries—with only occasional success—to find secular equivalents to replace it (social media and online dating are some of the more recent options). So it makes complete sense that many people go to church today because they are lonely or because that's where their connections, friends, and family are. Yet this sentiment would have made rather less sense in an age when people were getting their heads cut off for going to church. If the apostle Paul had just wanted friends, he would have been better off going to a Roman spa, gymnasium, or country club. Being part of the early church meant potentially forsaking social status and cultural capital, not gaining it. The early church was about community, yes, but a specific type of community grounded in something higher than itself. The early church didn't just meet because of their love for one another but because of the love of God.

〔▮▮〕

We're all looking for love, affirmation, identity—that's almost too obvious to bother stating. The real question is: Where should we look?

Sometimes religious people will desperately find their whole value and identity in their spiritual community: What does the pastor think of me? Did my out-loud prayer sound holy and wise enough? Will people glare at me if I walk into church wearing *this*? How will my cookies compare to everyone else's at the church bake sale? Could they detect my unholy annoyance in that email? What if everyone finds out what I did last summer? What if everyone finds out what I did *last night*?

Sometimes we struggle to earn the love of our church community. And sometimes, in turn, the church struggles to be worthy of *our* love. Sometimes when we lean on the church, it crumbles beneath us. Like every community, the church is full of finite, fallible, fallen people. People who say senseless, hurtful, soul-crushing things, often out of what seems to them like the best of intentions. Faithful yet flawed friends who gossip about us when we're out sick but also bring soup by the house, whose love often warms and scalds in equal measure. Which is why church friends and pastors and people in the pews cannot be our absolute source of identity and value. *We are looking for love in all the wrong places.*

Some of us sidestep that narrow church identity, only to then spend our whole lives trying to prove ourselves to society at large. We try to succeed and get external validation through school or through career, clout, cars, houses, achievements, causes, social media, likes, and so on. But what happens when you say or do something stupid and everyone finds out? What happens when you fail socially—when your voice cracks in public, you forget someone's name or hit "reply all" by mistake? What happens when the thing that tethers your social status fails—what if the stock market or your business crashes, and your worth crashes with it? What happens when you get laid off and feel like a failure in the eyes of everyone around you? What happens when you get older, and you can no longer use your fading looks to get the affirmation of others? What happens when your muscles dissipate, your back aches, and you can no longer prove your dominance to others on the court? What happens when the things you've used to get affirmation, love, and identity from social society all fail or begin to fade?

I remember how proud I was when I got my first professor job at a university. I felt like a million bucks having people address me as Dr. Lyonhart or Professor Lyonhart. Professor jobs are almost impossible to get nowadays, and, having got one, I strutted around campus feeling like I was finally somebody in the eyes of society. I found a confidence I'd never had before and a sense that surely everyone must be clinging to my every profound word. I posted online about my new role every chance I could get, finding ways to awkwardly slip it into conversations. I rode that high for almost nine months—until the university announced it was closing near the end of my very first year. And I completely collapsed. It wasn't just a job I was losing; it was my whole identity. I was afraid to tell people what was happening, that I wasn't going to be a professor anymore, that I'd already fumbled and lost my newfound social status. I felt weak, embarrassed, emasculated. I spiraled into depression and began struggling with my old vices again. My wife says that I was a shell of myself for nearly a year.

Building our worth on what we do in social society—on our careers, cleverness, abilities, titles, status, looks, or whatever it is—has always been shaky ground. We ride this emotional roller coaster, feeling valuable when things are going well and insecure when things are not. We become haunted by the fear of public failure, overwhelmed with insecurity about our every blemish being exposed. We become desperate to succeed in the eyes of others because, literally, our whole being depends on it. *We are looking for love in all the wrong places.*

Some abandon this social rat race only to then replace it with a romantic game of cat and mouse. Hollywood has made us believe that if we just found that one person, then we would finally be loved and complete. In the Twilight series, Bella (Kristen Stewart) says she "can't live in a world" where Edward (Robert Pattinson) doesn't exist, and he responds in kind by later saying, "You are my life now." In *Bridgerton*, Lord Bridgerton tells Lady Sharma, "It is maddening how much you consume my very being." In *Jerry Maguire* (1996), Jerry Maguire (Tom Cruise) literally tells Dorothy Boyd (Renée Zellweger), "You complete me."

Now, don't get me wrong; marriage can be awesome. I love my wife, and I try to do whatever I can to make her feel valued and loved. But I can't be her ultimate source of self-worth, and she can't be mine. I'm not good enough to be her everything. There will be days and seasons that I fail and where I can't be that for her. And one day I will die and won't even be here anymore. Defining yourself in relation to other people will always be a temporary thing. People's opinions change, and people change; loved ones get old, fade, and eventually die.

Making another human our ultimate source of self-worth, value, and love sounds romantic in theory. But in reality, it's not romantic at all. It's obsessive and needy and desperate. It doesn't reveal our inner romantic, only our inner emptiness. The best partners aren't the ones who desperately need someone else in order to be okay with themselves. Rather, the best partners are the ones who have a foundation in something deeper than the other person. Those people are solid enough to actually bring something to the relationship instead of just taking and taking to feel better about themselves. Other people cannot be our ultimate source of value, identity, and self-worth. *We are looking for love in all the wrong places.*

However, in contrast to church, society, or romance, God really can be my everything. God's love for us does not have off days. God's love does not go up and down depending on your social status. It doesn't change or walk out on you. It doesn't fade or get old and die. No, God's love is eternal. All my social connections and clout and relationships will one day fade like the Roman Empire, but God's kingdom of love will never fall.

We may have experienced many fleeting loves on this earth—young love, obsessive love, parental love, platonic love, erotic love. But there is only one who is *love itself*. God's is the heavenly and perfect love of which the imperfect loves of earth are but fleeting reflections in the morning. As the goodness of created beings point back to the one who is goodness and Being itself, so too does all earthly love point back to God, for "God is love" (1 John 4:8). If love is objectively better than hate, then it must be an eternal value grounded in an eternal and unchanging entity who is love itself. It must be grounded in something like the three and one—those eternal lovers—who did not invent love at some later point but who forever *are* love and *in* love.

And that divine love so overflows that it eventually had to drop and kneel to this earth to profess itself. God so loved the world that God came down and died for us. Jesus endured countless lashes of the whip and endless hours of one the most cringing, despicable, and torturous executions ever known. And he went through all of it for us. Every scar from the whip was a tattoo of love, every cry when the nails went in was a love song to you. To him you are valuable; to him you are important, worthy, loved. 1 John 3:16 says, "This is how we know what love is: Jesus Christ laid down his life for us."

If the Creator of the entire universe loves me enough to die for me, then that's it. That's who I am. Everything else should be *second* to that. Whether we succeed or fail in society need no longer define us at our core. Whether our relationships or marriages succeeded or failed in the past need not define our value in the future. What our parents said or failed to say need not haunt our days. What our church gossips about us in the pews need not replay in our head at night. For nothing else could ever possibly compare to the Creator of the entire universe dying for me. That is all we need to know our real value. That is the basis of our self-worth. That is the greatest love we will ever know.

And nothing we do can make God stop loving us this way. Jesus died precisely because we couldn't be good enough on our own. That's why Romans 5:8 says, "God demonstrates his own love for us in this: While we were still sinners, Christ died for us." Jesus loved you, even while you were a sinner—and continues to love you even when you're not awesome or a good person or super holy in your community's eyes. You don't have to work for it, earn it, or succeed to get it. You don't have to earn God's love any more than a toddler must merit its mother's milk. We are God's children, made in God's image. And I'll tell you, when I look at my kids' sleeping faces at night, I know there is nothing they could do to make me stop loving them; they could become serial-killing, pedophilic, unabombing Beliebers, and I would still visit them in prison. And apparently that's how God feels about us all.

Now, God might still be furious about what you're doing and call you to repent. God is not some self-help guru who says, "You're perfect just the way you are," or "Your inner goddess is a flawless snowflake." No, God knows you're sinful. God knows you're messed up. God sees *everything*. God sees what you're afraid to show the rest of the world, sees what impure motives truly drive you. He knows everything about you, everything you've ever done, the good, the bad, and the fugly. Yet God *still* adores you. Which is why, despite everything, the Bible still says, "Neither death nor life, neither angels nor demons, neither the present nor the future, nor any powers, neither height nor depth, nor anything else in all creation, will be able to separate us from the love of God that is in Christ Jesus" (Romans 8:38-39).

God is the right place to look for love.

❰❳❳❭

A few chapters back, we explored how individuals need church and community. And I'm not negating that. What I said was that *we all need community*, not that *community is all we need*. It would be easy to read that previous chapter and swing from absolutizing yourself to the opposite mistake of absolutizing your community, family, relationships, church, country, empire, and society as your whole identity. But the individual is not absolute, nor is the love of the community absolute; only the love of God is absolute. Only the love of God is eternal, unchanging, ever abiding, unconditional, always patient, always kind. When we replace God with our church or society or empire, we ground our identity and value on the fleeting opinions of groups of people who are just as finite and fallen as we are. Other humans cannot be our everything. Yes, we need the love of community, but that love needs to be grounded in something deeper than the community itself. Our spiritual house should be full of people, but its foundations shouldn't be (or else we're getting into a Great Wall of China situation).*

Individuals and their *communities* need each other, but both need the God who grounds all identity, value, and love. The church is called to love

---

*Harsh conditions meant many died working on the Great Wall, with their corpses integrated into the structure itself, where they remain today.

not only horizontally but also vertically—to not only love other humans on earth but to love and be loved by God in heaven above. This is not to flee from human community but to bring the divine love and trinitarian community down into our human relationships, for "if we love one another, God lives in us and his love is made complete in us" (1 John 4:12). We are to take the love that God gives us, pour it out onto others, and then return to the divine source of love itself to replenish and repeat. Unless we are first filled up with this absolute love, then we don't have enough to give others and so can only take, using society, lovers, friends, family, and children to fill the hole in our own heart. When you put others before God, you end up loving neither. But when you put God before others, you can end up loving both.[†]

Which is why the church merging with the Roman Empire was such a mixed bag. When Emperor Constantine converted and believers were no longer dying for the love of God, the temptation became to live for the love of society and social status. When the church became synonymous with empire, politics, economics, or respectable society, it lost its ability to rise above and prophetically critique those social institutions—Christians started living for the applause of people rather than God, maintaining the apple cart instead of flipping it upside down like Jesus did. When the church becomes socially acceptable and even advantageous, it can become just another *wrong place to look for love*. It becomes possible to go to church solely for community or to uphold the status quo or because it's what everyone in town does on Sunday. Yet the church, the whole point of movement five, is nothing if it is not inhabited, indwelled, and vivified by the Spirit of God. Which is why movement five did not begin with a chapter on the church itself but with the Spirit showing up at Pentecost. For the church is just another building if its walls don't echo with flickering tongues of fire.

〈 ✖ ✖ 〉

[†]To clarify a potential misunderstanding: harming others in the name of God is not putting God before others but putting your own will before both.

To close this chapter, here's a brief story that preachers often use to guilt people into going back to church. The tale goes that a man refused to go to church with his wife. One day, the local pastor came by his house and sat down next to the man by a big wood fireplace. He asked why the man refused to come to church, and the man retorted that he could have a vibrant spiritual life all on his own. "I don't need others for that." And so the pastor silently took a fireplace poker and used it to prod one of the logs away from all the others at the center of the fireplace. Alone at the outer edge, it sustained and burned brightly for a bit before quickly flickering and fading out. However, the logs that remained piled together burned brightly on into the night for hours and hours, long after the pastor had left. Intuiting the metaphor, the man apparently was in church the very next Sunday.

I've always enjoyed this emotionally manipulative metaphor, but I think it is incomplete. For if the individual is the log and the community is the pile, then God is the spark needed to ignite them both. A single tree in a lightning storm may burn for an hour, while a forest of trees may blaze together for weeks. Yet both must first be struck and set ablaze from above.

CREATION

Creation Begins

Creation Is Not God

Creation Is Good

FALL

Humanity in God's Image

Humanity Gone Wild

NATION

Abraham Finds Faith · 2000 BC

Moses Meets I Am · 1400–1200ish BC

Goodness Is Commanded

Beauty in the Promised Land

King David and His Boy · 1000ish BC

Justice Exiles the Nation · 586 BC

REDEMPTION

Jesus Is Born · AD 0

Jesus Is Walking Around Saying Stuff · AD 30

Jesus Is Dying to Meet You · AD 33

CHURCH

The Spirit Arrives · AD 33

The Church Begins · AD 33

The Apostle Paul Converts · AD 35ish

The Church Expands · AD 300ish

The Church Today · The Present

END

The End of the World as We Know It

Highway to Hell or Stairway to Heaven?

NINETEEN

The Church Today

IN MOVEMENT FIVE, Jesus left and left us his Spirit. The Spirit helped the church begin and expand, leading to some pushback from the powers that be, including from the murderer Saul. But Saul converted and became Paul, helping the church spread to Gentiles, women, slaves, and minorities across the Mediterranean world. Intermittently oppressed for centuries, the church suddenly became powerful overnight when Emperor Constantine converted in the early 300s. The Roman Empire became Christian, and from there all of Europe eventually followed suit, for better or for worse.

As such, when Europe began conquering the world around the 1400s and beyond, it didn't just export European capitalism, democracy, and industrialism but Christianity as well. Therefore, much of what you may have witnessed of Christianity has likely been filtered through a church that is historically bound up with a culture that is deeply Western, White, imperialistic, and powerful. Yet this was not the case in the beginning; the early church was Middle Eastern, brown, and primarily composed of powerless women, children, and slaves. And it will not be the case in the future either; in fact, Christianity is already declining in the West, yet booming almost everywhere else. The greatest concentration of people in the church today is not in the United States but in Latin America and Africa. There are nearly more Christians in China then the total number of people living in England. Globally, the church is growing, and the trajectories suggest there will be three billion Christians in the world by 2050. Christianity is no longer a Western religion. So when you think of a church, some of you, depending on your context, may have a stereotype of traditional, White

Europeans/Americans. But statistically, the average churchgoer today is actually a Latin American or African woman, perhaps living in a village in Zimbabwe or a favela in Peru.[1]

On a local level, churches can be tainted by local squabbles, systems, homogeneity, assumptions, injustices, prejudices, politics, and power. However, when we step back and see the bigger picture, things begin to look a lot more like Pentecost, with the Spirit speaking every language and tongue and burning outward in every direction. When we step back, we begin to see the church of Paul, where there is "neither Jew nor Gentile, neither slave nor free, nor is there male and female, for you are all one in Christ Jesus" (Galatians 3:28). We begin to see the faint and hopeful outline of a community of divine love that embraces every kind, shape, style, color, and individual person, overcoming the social boundaries and walls of nations and empires. This is the church.

And the church is also me, because we are still only in movement five today in the third millennium. Church is not a completed act in a play that went off Broadway ages ago but an ongoing *movement* that still crests and dips in us today. We have arrived at the part of the story we are living now. This chapter is like a park map with an arrow saying, "You are here." And so this chapter is much shorter than all the others because this chapter is still being written—by me, by you, by us. As Walt Whitman writes, the "powerful play goes on, and you may contribute a verse."[2] The church is ongoing, and we await the coming dawn of movement six, when the story is resolved, the climax reached, and the end nigh.

MOVEMENT VI

End ✳

LAST MONTH I MADE a Lord of the Rings reference in one of my university lectures, and a bunch of the class gave me a blank stare before someone reminded me the films came out before any of them were born. Last week someone casually referred to me as middle-aged, as if this weren't the earth-shattering news flash that it felt like to me. Then earlier this morning I bent down to grab a book and made an old-man gasp. I am approaching that odd middle space where—depending on genetics, stress, and sheer luck—I may or may not have more years behind me than in front of me. On a gut level, I don't think I'd ever fully accepted that death was real, or that my references and jokes and words would eventually be passé, or that my feet would one day look rough and cracked like my father's. It seems like just yesterday that I was a kid creeping onto the roof or a questioning teenager, with all the hopeful time in the world to figure things out. I have no idea when it happened, but somehow the end has become far more frickin' nigh than I ever honestly believed it would.

Things end. In movement six, we explore how they end and where we'll all end up. The rising action of creation, fall, nation, redemption, and church comes together in these concluding scenes, before the screen flashes *The End* and all goes black. And when your eye is on the clock and time is running down, cosmic questions about our eternal destination suddenly become far less abstract. . . .

CREATION

Creation Begins

Creation Is Not God

Creation Is Good

FALL

Humanity in God's Image

Humanity Gone Wild

NATION

Abraham Finds Faith	2000 BC
Moses Meets I Am	1400–1200ish BC
Goodness Is Commanded	
Beauty in the Promised Land	
King David and His Boy	1000ish BC
Justice Exiles the Nation	586 BC

REDEMPTION

Jesus Is Born	AD 0
Jesus Is Walking Around Saying Stuff	AD 30
Jesus Is Dying to Meet You	AD 33

CHURCH

The Spirit Arrives	AD 33
The Church Begins	AD 33
The Apostle Paul Converts	AD 35ish
The Church Expands	AD 300ish
The Church Today	The Present

END

The End of the World as We Know It

Highway to Hell or Stairway to Heaven?

TWENTY

The End of the World as We Know It

AUGUST 6, 1945, 8:15 A.M. The streets of Hiroshima bustle with bikes, buses, trams, and shuffling feet, beneath crisscrossing utility wires and clothes-strewn balconies. Children walk to school to start the day, while fisherman drag in hauls from the night. The sun already rose hours before, yet suddenly seems to rise again, igniting the horizon. A flash blinds every eye and turns every head, followed by a rippling shock wave that levels streets and souls and high rises. A brief pause, as if for effect, then the sound of destruction catches up to the destroyed, harmonizing with a city of shrieks and sobs and snapping wood. Tens of thousands of men, women, and children gone in a flash, in what was by far the deadliest minute of human history. Until three days later, when it was nearly rivaled in Nagasaki. The Japanese surrendered soon after, and World War II was finally over. But the end of one war was just the beginning of another.

By 1949, Russian scientists have figured out how to make an atomic bomb as well. For the first time in history, humanity has the technology to destroy itself—the end of the world is a real possibility. The modern scientific age that was supposed to be full of hope for our future has led to a world where we might not have any future at all. A world where children are shown videos of bomb sites and trained to get under their desk in case of attack. A world with bomb sirens in town and bomb shelters in the backyard. For decades, humanity lives in fear that any moment could be the end, that at any moment a button could be pressed in a room somewhere, and every building you've ever entered, every restaurant you've ever eaten in, every park you've ever played in—all of it could be gone.

You can still see the lingering apocalyptic effect of this in pop culture today: *Terminator, 2012, World War Z, I Am Legend, Mad Max, A Quiet Place, Planet of the Apes, Hunger Games* (postapocalyptic Jennifer Lawrence), *Don't Look Up* (pre-apocalyptic Jennifer Lawrence), *X-Men: Apocalypse* (mid-apocalyptic Jennifer Lawrence). And then, of course, there are the Godzilla movies. The original Godzilla movie was made in Japan in 1954, only nine years after Hiroshima, and was meant to be a metaphor for the atomic bomb. The movie begins with atomic bombs going off and waking up Godzilla from his sleep, and Godzilla himself gets his power from the radiation off atomic bombs. Godzilla was a cathartic way for Japanese culture to articulate their horror at a world where the bomb had been set loose and where no one knew how to stop the monster.

Culture is still processing the anxiety and imminent fear of the bomb. On top of that, things have reheated with Russia. Add the Covid-19 pandemic. Add climate change. Add that science has pretty much confirmed the world will eventually end one way or the other, either through being swallowed up by our expanding sun, or our galaxy crashing into Andromeda, or the universe tearing itself a new one and/or shivering into a heatless death. Add all that together, and it means that even if you're not religious, you nonetheless live in an eschatological age—an age that has become obsessed with how the human story *ends*.

The end is our sixth and final movement in the Christian story. And indeed, Christians have always talked about how the world will end. But even we went a bit overboard in light of everything happening during the twentieth and twenty-first centuries. You might have heard of the Left Behind books. In them, Jesus comes back, and all Christians are taken up into heaven, leaving suddenly driverless buses and planes to crash. There was recently a movie remake of it with Nicolas Cage, which makes it even better. Movies and books like these are part and parcel of a Christian culture that is waiting, almost daily, for the world to end. A culture where a common joke is to leave clothes lying out on a seat to make people think you've been raptured. A culture where everyone is trying to find clues in the Bible about when exactly Jesus is coming back: "Elon Musk is the antichrist! All of this was foretold in the Scriptures!" I was in Chicago a few years ago and a guy came up to me with a Bible in his hand, yelling, "Repent, the end is near!" And then he told me about how aliens are a sign that Jesus is coming back. It was very informative.

A lot of people have been saying a lot of things about the end of the world, and it's all very confusing and hard to distinguish the real from the reactionary and ridiculous. So the rest of this chapter provides an eight-point outline of what the Bible actually says (or at least, what I think it says) about the end of the world:

(1) *The world is going to end.* Yes, the Bible clearly says that. But the Bible also says, (2) *no one knows* when *it will end.* In Mark 13 Jesus is talking about the end of the world, and he says, "About that day or hour no one knows, not even the angels in heaven, nor the Son, but only the Father" (Mark 13:32). Which means that trying to read between the lines to predict the end of the world is completely bogus, according to Scripture itself. Christians who keep trying to find hints about the date of the apocalypse in the Bible aren't taking the Bible too seriously but rather not seriously enough. Because if they were taking it seriously, they would take Jesus at his word when he says, "About that day or hour no one knows."

(3) *No one knows exactly* how *it will end.* Some Christians spend years deciphering not just *when* the world will end but *how* it will all go down. The problem, though, is that the end-of-the-world bits of the Bible—such as the book of Revelation—are some of the most overtly metaphorical and symbolic parts of Scripture. There are sheep with seven eyes, and a beast comes out of the earth that has two horns and a voice like a dragon. To take each book of the Bible seriously means taking its specific style and genre seriously; you wouldn't read a love poem the same way you would read an instructional manual (if you did, being shot with Cupid's arrow would be far less endearing).

Yet that doesn't mean we can't learn anything from the Bible's apocalyptic symbolism. Of course not. We can get a firm sense that the Bible believes the world is going to end, even if we aren't sure about all the literal details of *how* it will end. In the same way, we can discern from a love song that he really does love her, even if we know it's not literally true that *all you need is love*. Paul McCartney and John Lennon also presumably needed oxygen, food, shelter, and to not have a bullet in the head. So instead of wasting our lives figuring out the apocalypse, we should spend them loving God and others while we still can. We should spend our time living like the end is coming, not trying to figure out *when* and *how* it is coming. Live every day like it's about to be dashed.

(4) *It's less the end of the world and more its renewing.* Just as Jesus died but then was resurrected with a renewed physical body, so too the Earth will die but then resurrect anew like a phoenix from the ashes. The Bible says that our resurrected bodies will live forever in the new earth, the new Jerusalem, the new resurrected world (Revelation 21:1). So contrary to what you might have heard, the end of the world is not us ditching earth to float off like ghosts to heaven. No, the end of the world is the earth and every-thing in it dying, then being reborn as heaven—the old being remade new, the imperfect being raised perfect, reality remade.

But if God plops us in the new earth, won't we just screw that one up too? Won't we do exactly what we did to the old earth, with wars, greed, and daylight savings time?

No, we won't. Because (5) *The end of the world is also the end of our sinful flesh.* You see, our sins affect us on a bodily level. The body is not inherently sinful ("and it was good"), but it can become polluted by our sinful choices. Steal a candy bar, then your neural pathways begin to rewire, and next time you'll loot the whole canteen. Kick the dog in anger one day, and muscle memory sets in, and it just gets easier. Push through your anxiety and sweaty palms to sneak out and cheat in a hotel room, and soon your bodily warning signs will stop flashing at all. Sin permeates our bodily brains, muscle memory, and chemical dependencies. Our minds/souls aren't just free rational agents who can make free decisions whenever we want any more than a smoker can quit anytime they want. No one knows this better than the newly religious person who has gotten over the initial high of their conversion experience, only to find that they are still a greedy, horny, glut-tonous, lazy, hormonal wreck. They still have years of bad habits, bodily addictions, and neural pathways to work through. Something may indeed have happened on a spiritual level—a real change has begun within, and that should eventually begin to manifest in their external and bodily life as well. But not all at once, and (probably) not all in this life. I do know someone who came to Jesus and immediately gave up alcoholism once and for all, but I know for a fact that they are still rude to their mother.

We will never be entirely free of our sinful flesh until our body literally dies and that part of us that keeps making a mess of things is allowed to die with it. Then and only then can we be resurrected in a new earth free from the sinful flesh that ruined the old one. (Harry Potter spoiler alert: This is like how part of Voldemort's evil latched onto Harry. In order for his evil to die, Harry had to die as well. But luckily, Harry had the resurrection stone, and so he came back to life, but this time freed from the evil of Voldemort that once lived within him.)

So the new earth won't fall apart like last time. We'll be resurrected anew with pure bodies cleansed of our past habits, addictions, unhealthy coping mechanisms, neural pathways, and whatever other self-help/science-adjacent terms happen to be popular when you're reading this. We will be resurrected people living in a resurrected world with our resurrected Savior, Jesus. This all may sound a tad fantastical (the Harry Potter analogy probably didn't help in that regard). But there's a certain logic to it. The evil within us must die. But we are too tightly bound to it; if it dies, so do we. Yet the opposite is also true: if we die, so does it. And luckily, God knows a thing or two about resurrection.

However, this resurrected state will be different from the Garden of Eden, such that we won't just fall all over again. Adam and Eve were not perfect; rather, they were innocent. Naive. Untainted but also untested. They were essentially what all of us once were—innocent children who had yet to decide what kind of adults we wanted to become. Human autonomy and freedom had not yet been factored into the equation—we had not chosen evil yet, but neither had we chosen good. God had shown and offered humanity the good life, but we had not yet chosen it and made it *ours*. In the end times, that will be rectified. When we resurrect in the end, those in heaven will be pure and good while having actually *chosen* to be so. They will have freely chosen God, chosen to repent, chosen to chase the good life. Heaven and the new earth will not be like the Garden of Eden prior to the fall but like the Garden of Eden had Adam and Eve chosen *correctly*.

The end of the story perfects the one thing God couldn't force from the beginning: us. On earth, governments and families and friends are constantly torn between trying to get people to do what is right while also giving them the freedom to do what is wrong. In heaven this dichotomy will finally be overcome; we will all do what is good but will have freely chosen to do so. Freedom and goodness will finally come together; who we *choose* to be and who we *ought* to be will be united as one. The choices we made in time and space on earth will be eternally locked into their trajectory (which is why, after Adam and Eve sinned, God did not let them eat from the tree of life and live forever, because they would have lived forever in sin). This locking in of our choice will not negate our freedom any more than someone who chose to go on a flight needs to remake that choice all over again every five seconds but can simply lay back and enjoy the movie.

But of course, freedom goes both ways, and many might choose a very different trajectory. Some of us are so attached to our sinful flesh that we'd rather indulge it in hell than be rid of it in heaven. Which brings us to (6) *The end brings judgment.* It's a day when all people—rich or poor, famous or infamous—will stand before their maker, stripped of the glamour and status of this world, and have to give an account for how they lived. Romans 14 says, "We will all stand before God's judgment seat" (Romans 14:10). Of course, Romans also says, "There is no one who does good, not even one" (Romans 3:12). Twist ending. The angry preacher man was right: the sinners will be judged. He just was wrong to think he wasn't one of them. None of us are good enough to deserve heaven. Not me. Not you. Not anyone. Even Martin Luther King Jr. had dozens of affairs. Do you think you're better than MLK? (If so, I want to hear you say it out loud.)

Thankfully, (7) *The end also brings mercy.* We might not deserve heaven, but God has put it on the table anyway. If we are willing to humble ourselves and admit our wrongs, we can be forgiven. If we are willing to let go of our sinful flesh and let it die like Christ died, then we will also be raised to life like he was, ready to live in the new earth. Our past need not define us forever; evil can be unmade and our hearts unhaunted. Things can be good again.

Which sets the stage for (8) *The end is about hope.* People think of the end of the world as this fiery, apocalyptic vision of bombs and wars and terror. But the end is when all that bad stuff *stops*, when all the insanity *ceases*. Sure, there's a climactic moment where the feces hits the fan, but that's just the manure from which hope springs. The end is when happily ever after finally happens after all. I said in the fall chapter that *this was not how things were meant to be.* Well, the end is when things are finally put back the way *they were meant to be.* Whatever good things you have ever hoped for—if they were truly good and not just you being greedy—have been mere signposts hinting toward this moment. This doesn't mean the end is when you finally get the Ferrari you've always wanted. Rather, it's when the hole in your heart you've been trying to fill with dumb stuff like Ferraris is finally filled with the love of God and others (like it was always meant to be).

It is in this sense—this sense of the purified and deeper longings underlying our hopes—that I say the end is about hope. Hope that one day all our sin and secrets and shame will be brought out in the open and haunt us no longer. Hope that one day our depressed, lonely, anxious, insecure brains will let go and be reborn free. One day, unjust earths will die and be reborn without class, walls, or hate. One day, broken hearts and homes shall mend. One day, the children of Hiroshima will rise and run through unbroken streets to parents who perish no more. One day, unknown soldiers will return to lovers who never moved on and to mothers who finally can.

Perhaps that's too cheesy for you, so let's get more philosophical. I've mentioned in previous chapters about there being an eternal and ideal standard of the good. Now, either that is a social construct that doesn't exist outside our heads, and so nothing we do really matters. *Or* an ideal good actually exists. In which case, the end is just when broken reality and this ideal good come together, when heaven comes to earth. The end is when the real dies and resurrects as the ideal it was always meant to be, when what *ought* to have been finally *is*, when every tear is unshed and every drop of blood unspilled. This is not wishful thinking but admitting that if our deepest wishes and moral intuitions are truly good, and if goodness has truly intruded into our thoughts and hopes, then it might one day intrude upon every facet of this earth. If our minds can actually link up with what is good, then perhaps our whole planet can as well. We must either admit that possibility or abandon the notion that morality exists or that life has any objective meaning.

The end is when the ideal is finally real. And while this may be idealism, it is not idealistic. But what *is* idealistic and naive is to think that humans will be able to bring about heaven on earth through our own human means—through the power of the state, or human progress, or technology, or indefinite life extension, or uploading to a virtual reality heaven. In contrast, the religious vision is actually quite gritty, frank, and realistic. It says humans are too fallen to ever bring about paradise on our own. Its hope is *for* humanity, but it is not *from* humanity. Human technological progress doesn't get us paradise; it gets us an atom bomb. Human history doesn't just naturally incline to the better; sure, industrialization brought us a lot of new toys, but it also brought child labor, factory smoke, frantic workaholism, and global warming. Human history will not naturally or inevitably bring about the good; what we need is the *end* of history.

Of course, we should still strive to raise our reality to the ideal, yet we should also recognize we never fully will and that only the ideal coming down and rudely interrupting our reality will get us all the way home.[1] Divine intervention is needed, with God finally interrupting the historical process. The kids will never figure out the rules or play fairly on their own; we need a parent to intervene and restart the game.

CREATION

Creation Begins

Creation Is Not God

Creation Is Good

FALL

Humanity in God's Image

Humanity Gone Wild

NATION

Abraham Finds Faith — 2000 BC

Moses Meets I Aᴍ — 1400–1200ish BC

Goodness Is Commanded

Beauty in the Promised Land

King David and His Boy — 1000ish BC

Justice Exiles the Nation — 586 BC

REDEMPTION

Jesus Is Born — AD 0

Jesus Is Walking Around Saying Stuff — AD 30

Jesus Is Dying to Meet You — AD 33

CHURCH

The Spirit Arrives — AD 33

The Church Begins — AD 33

The Apostle Paul Converts — AD 35ish

The Church Expands — AD 300ish

The Church Today — The Present

END

The End of the World as We Know It

Highway to Hell or Stairway to Heaven?

TWENTY ONE

Highway to Hell or Stairway to Heaven?

DANTE WAS LOST—LOST in the forest and lost in life. He pushed forward, crunching twigs and rustling things below, on through endless thickets illumined only by occasional flickers of moonlight. Suddenly, stumbling, he damned near fell through an opening in the earth, an orifice to the underworld, archway lips wrapped round a jagged staircase throat. The steps led so far down into the belly of the earth that you couldn't even begin to glimpse the bottom. Taking a deep breath, he plunged through the underground archway. If he'd looked closer, he might have seen words carved into the entrance way, reading, "Abandon hope, all you who enter here."* In other words, Dante was going to hell.

Sinking down, the hallway hourglassed out into a vast underground cavern. And then, green fields. This wasn't that bad. Dante had only entered the outermost rim of hell: limbo. Limbo was reserved for people who weren't all that bad yet never asked for Christ's forgiveness. They weren't pure enough for heaven, but not bad enough to be tortured either; they were stuck in limbo. Dante suddenly wondered how low he could go, descending down further into the second ring of hell.

Feeling the pounding of a violent wind, he looked around for protection from the elements and instead saw thousands of stripped mortals being tossed back and forth by an underground storm, their naked bodies flailing

---

*I have this posted on my university office doormat. Students need to step over it if they want to meet with me.

like rag dolls in the rain. Dante learned that this ring was called lust. It was where adulterers, perverts, and those who abused sex went. The erotic wind thrust and blew their bodies all over the place without a night's rest, just as in life their sexual whims sent them flying from person to person trying to fill the hole in their body and heart, chasing the unchaste. As in life, so now in the afterlife, the latter merely the natural continuation of the former. Hell is just getting what our earthly selves mistook for heaven.

Horrified, Dante sprinted down to the next ring, where his eyes beheld thousands more swimming in slop. These were the gluttons, those who greedily hoarded food in times of famine, whose stomachs trumped their heart and head, who hid behind a plate rather than face reality. They were not fat, per se; in fact, many of them were gaunt, skeletal snobs, refusing to eat anything but the finest delicacies. A spoonful of caviar may be far worse for the soul than all-you-can-eat fish and chips. They'd so long used food as a means to some other end—status, comfort, distraction—that they no longer tasted the food itself anymore. Unhinging their jaws, they wade open-mouthed through slop that wades through them, unsure whether they're drowning or feasting.[†]

Vomiting, Dante hunched over and hobbled down to the fourth ring of hell, where a mass war forever raged on an equally undying battlefield. This ring was called greed. The people there are so insatiable that they forever fight over who gets to keep this or that for themselves, even though there's technically enough for all. Greed is its own punishment, making a hell of every heaven and a demon of every dame. One might not even call it a punishment but simply the reward they always thought they wanted. It's just greedy people finding comfort and chaos with like-minded folk, many of whom they already chose to associate with in boardrooms and private islands back on earth.

Perhaps tempted to seize some possessions for himself, Dante was quickly ushered to the fifth ring of hell: wrath. Here people drown in a river of their own rage, sinking down into a sulky furiosity that finds no joy in

---

[†]Okay, maybe not all of this is in Dante. But I couldn't help myself.

God or others. Moving quickly to the sixth level, Dante sees heretics trapped in flaming tombs. Then he comes to the seventh ring, a lake of boiling blood and flames, reserved for people of violence. Here boils Attila the Hun and Alexander the Great in the blood of the innocent they spewed. Oh, and the minotaur is here too.

It's getting hotter and hotter as Dante descends deeper and deeper down into the eighth ring of hell, set aside for liars. Here people bathe in human feces, representing how full of crap their own words were in life. Corrupt politicians boil in a lake of tar, representing their dark and sticky secrets. And instead of the trumpets that once announced their arrival in parades on earth, now demons fart to announce them. Hell has a sense of humor.

Finally, Dante arrives in the final ring of hell. You'd assume it would be the hottest of all. But instead, Dante finds himself walking out onto a frozen lake, devoid of life, blood, warmth, motion, or embrace. Slipping, he slams down onto the ice, finding himself eye to eye with the undying corpses of traitors below, forever frozen in place. Though betrayal is a form of lying, the traitors get their own distinct ring, for they're defined as those who had a personal relationship with their victims, and so do not only deceive but *betray*. Cain is here for turning on his own brother. And at the very center of hell is Satan, the former angel who betrayed God. Satan is a giant with three heads and massive wings. In his left and right cheek, he chews Brutus and Cassius, who betrayed Julius Caesar to death. In the center of his mouth, Satan gnaws forever on the head of Judas Iscariot, Christ's betrayer.

❮❰❱❯

In the 1300s, Dante Alighieri wrote a book of Italian poetry, setting himself as the protagonist stumbling upon the gates of death and hell (in a baller move, he also places many of his personal enemies in hell, as well as all the popes he didn't like). His *Inferno* became one of the classic tales of world literature, its scenes depicted on church walls and preached in many a fire-and-brimstone sermon. Even today, when people think of hell, they don't tend to reference Scripture but instead draw on images from Dante without realizing it.

But is Dante our only option? Is this how the journey of God ends for those who refuse to tag along? Do I have to believe in eternal fire, boiling excrement, and little red men with pitchforks in order to be a Christian? Is it all or nothing? What are my options? Well, the first option, of course, is (1) eternal fiery torment. This is what you're probably already familiar with and is closest to Dante's *Inferno*. There are lots of Bible verses about torment and fire, so it's not like Dante invented that out of nowhere.

Yet throughout history Christians have often held to a different interpretation of these Bible verses, seeing them as (2) metaphors for separation from God. Yes, the Bible describes hell as fire and brimstone, but it also describes hell as complete darkness, utter silence, a dark pit, death, and destruction. So how literally are we to take these images? Can hell literally be fire if it is also literally darkness? Wouldn't the glow of fire bring light and undermine the darkness? Wouldn't the crackling of the fire undermine the utter silence? So, this view says we shouldn't take things so literally. Perhaps what the Bible is really trying to say, is that hell is separation from God (2 Thessalonians 1:9) and that separation from God sucks. Perhaps hell is not so much a literal, active, physical, fiery torture and more just spiritual separation from God.

Of course, this seems easier for us to swallow. *Metaphorical fire doesn't sting.* People today seem a lot more comfortable with hell just being separation from God. But I don't know that we should be. Think about it. We aren't talking about separation from Zeus, the kind of being that could be casually replaced with other friends or activities. No, the God we have been talking about in this book is the author of life, the one who sculpted the mountains, spun the seas, and invented time, music, and emotions. God is Beauty, Truth, Goodness, Being, and Love itself. So to be separated from God is to be separated from all that is beautiful, true, good, loving, and real in this world.

Put this way, the possibility of hell becomes a necessary and inescapable consequence of human freedom. Beauty, truth, goodness, and love exist, and you can choose to be near them and shaped by them. But no one is forcing you. You're always welcome to choose to go where none of those things resound, always welcome to go to hell instead. Now, you may be thinking, "Yeah, right, who would choose hell?" But humans constantly choose what we know is not good for us. Like when you know that guy or girl is toxic for you, but you go for it anyway. Like when you know you need rest but instead stay up past two a.m. sinking into a mindless, meaningless sludge. Like when you know worrying won't change a thing but still spend hours checking your phone. Hell doesn't need little demons torturing us against our will; no, our acts of will are the very thing fueling the fire. Hell doesn't drag people in, it just leaves the gates cracked open—build it and they will come. As Oscar Wilde writes, "We are each our own devil, and we make this world our hell."[1] An afterlife in hell may just be the natural extension of the life many of us are already choosing to live now. Even in Dante, the punishment is often simply getting what you want.

Honestly, I think if people in hell could choose whether to stay there or go to heaven, they might just choose to stay in hell. Heaven is a place where every race, color, nation, and language live in harmony; a racist would be miserable in heaven. They would probably prefer hell. Heaven is a place where money no longer has any meaning, but many of us would rather be rich in hell than poor in heaven. Heaven is a place where every tear will be wiped away, but sometimes we just want to keep on crying, keep on hurting ourselves, keep on repeating the same cycles. Some days I'd rather complain in hell than have nothing to complain about in heaven. Heaven is a place of intimacy, vulnerability, and love—but isn't that something we keep running from all the time? Closing ourselves off to love, building up walls to prevent others from getting too close? Perhaps the walls of hell were not built by God but by the citizens of hell, to keep heaven out. As C. S. Lewis wrote, "The gates of Hell are locked from the inside."[2]

Yet, given enough time in hell, is it possible that people might eventually change their minds and cross the no-man's-land into heaven? Over thousands or even millions of years, might not even the cruelest dictator or murderer eventually repent and choose heavenly goodness, beauty, and love? This thought leads us to the next potential option: (3) universalism. As in, everyone, everywhere, will eventually, *universally*, be saved. Given enough time in hell, might even Hitler's actions eventually come around to the good, and his second-rate art come around to the beautiful? Given enough time, perhaps even Satan himself (herself? Let's give a new meaning to suffrage in hell!) will come back around.

Universalists say their position gives God the glory. God's love and sovereignty will triumph over all, even hell, in the end. God "reconcile[s] to himself all things" (Colossians 1:20). No corner of existence left behind, not even hell. As Philippians 2 says, "At the name of Jesus every knee should bow, in heaven and on earth and under the earth, and every tongue confess that Jesus Christ is Lord" (Philippians 2:10-11). Of course, then the question becomes: Is it still freedom if everyone chooses the same thing in the end? If every knee shall one day bow, did we ever *really* have the choice to rise in defiance?

So the nice thing about universalism is it doesn't involve suffering in hell forever. But some think that makes our free choices less significant, because we all end up in the same place no matter what we choose. Which is why a fourth view tries to chart a middle way between these two pitfalls: (4) annihilationism. Annihilationists believe that God is Being itself, and to be separated from the one who is Being itself is to cease to *be*. Hell is just nonexistence. In this sense, your choices really do matter; you really can choose to ultimately reject the God of love and Being itself. But you also don't have to burn eternally in hell for it; God mercifully allows you to cease to exist. If you choose to be separated from the one who is Being itself, God honors your choice by allowing you to cease to be. Some philosophers have complained that they did not consent to be born, that existence was a gift thrust on them against their will at a surprise party they never wanted.[‡] Yet annihilationists believe that God includes the receipt; if you find the light and beauty and goodness of existence lacking, you can always return it for something else.

❮ ◼ ◼ ❯

[‡] The BBC recently reported on a man who sued his parents for giving birth to him without his consent. Geeta Pandey, "Indian Man to Sue Parents for Giving Birth to Him," BBC, February 7, 2019, www.bbc.com/news/world-asia-india-47154287.

Those are some options for where we all end up. And you might think it is deeply important to figure out which of these options is correct, so we can know exactly where everyone else is going and what it is like there: Where are Dante, John Lennon, and my grumpy uncle? Yet it's when we hyperfocus on the eternal destination of others that hell gets the largest foothold *in us.* For after Jesus forgave Peter three times, Peter then glanced over at the apostle John, pointed, and said to Jesus, "But what about him? What's going to happen to him?" And Jesus replied, "What is that to you? You must follow me" (see John 21:22). So, I don't know for sure where anyone else will end up. That's beyond my pay grade. All I know is that Jesus is calling me from heaven, saying, "Follow me." My faith is not fueled by a fear of hell but by a desire to draw ever closer to the one who is Being, goodness, beauty, and love itself. Sometimes I forget that, and the wrath of hell below distracts and displaces love as the apex of my faith. At these moments I have to give myself the same advice I give my kids when we are too high up and wobbly on a Ferris wheel: "Don't look down—keep your eyes fixed up on the heavens."

❰ ❰ ❱ ❱ ❱

Leaving Satan behind, Dante also leaves behind the perverse curiosity he once had about who was here in this land of death. He resets his mind on higher things, continuing on his journey through the center of the earth. Gravity suddenly shifts as Dante passes through the hellish core of the earth to the other side, rising through the lower and upper mantle. Emerging through the outer crust of the planet, he rises further still up the mountain of purgation, beyond clouds and atmosphere and the earth's pull altogether. Floating now into outer space and the higher heavens, he dances with angels and tastes the ecstasy that transcends all sweetness, the goodness that comes from goodness itself, the light that refracts from beauty itself. Words fail the poet as his will and desires are moved by love, the same love that moves the sun and the other stars.

Conclusion

IN THE BEGINNING, God created the heavens and the earth. And while the creation was not God, it was *good*, made in the image of the one who is goodness itself. Yet part of being made good was being made free. We used that freedom to choose not to be good. Humanity fell, and we've been falling ever since.

The journey of God sets into motion a rescue plan for creation, working through Abraham to build a faithful nation from his descendants, down the line through Moses and David all the way to baby Jesus. Jesus' life gives us a taste of the original goodness of creation, while his death undoes the sinful fall that marred it. Creation is on its way to redemption. But it's not quite there yet. Jesus passes the baton to the Holy Spirit, the church, the apostle Paul, and the rest of us to end the race well.

That's the journey of God in six movements: creation, fall, nation, redemption, church, end. It is a story spanning the ages of history. Yet it is also the story of my own life over the past few decades as I found God and myself. And in an even more immediate sense, it is the story I replay every day. Each morning my eyes flash awake as if for the very first time. I turn and find myself next to my wife's hair; the pillow is cold against my cheek; kids run in and jump on me; nature hums and chirps outside. And it is *good*. Then the phone starts ringing or the kids start making demands, and busyness sets in. I forget my coffee, someone cuts me off on the road or undercuts me in front of a coworker, and suddenly foul words slip from my forked tongue and evil comes slithering out of me. In my worse moments, I sit in that annoyance and let it spiral and grow within me, ruining the whole day. But in my better moments (rare though they may be), I pause, close my eyes, breathe, and then ask for forgiveness and for God to help me start again.

And for a brief but real moment, I recapture a hint of that lost peace from the day's first dawn. Then I get back to reality, trying to still be in community with friends and family and colleagues who I may have just sinned against moments earlier (or who may have just sinned against me). Rage, repent, repeat. On and on it goes, with some real progress and growth but an equally real sense that I'm never going to be totally past the cycle until Jesus returns for good and all things are made right in the cosmos and in me.

That's the story. But is it a good story? Do these six movements fit to-gether well? Is there anything uniquely important or necessary about this tale and how it's been told? Could we have just as well cut some of the movements or replaced them with bits from other stories, philosophies, and religions? Well, let's find out. . . .

❰ ❚ ❚ ❱

If you cut the first movement of creation, a few things tend to follow. When societies do not actively affirm that the material world was created good, they tend to quickly assume it is bad (or at least unimportant). We become world-weary, body-shaming, sex-repellent, anti-environmental haters of the earth. This attitude quickly gets spiritualized (often by Christians who don't understand their own story), with religion jettisoning earth for heaven and the body for the soul. The material universe begins to be seen as gross, empty, meaningless, sinful, or even an illusion. This would be bad enough on its own, but the problem got compounded when the modern West, after devaluing nature and matter, decided it was all that exists. We rejected any *Creator* at all, with science now apparently showing the ma-terial universe is all there is. Nature explains itself without needing to appeal to any higher source or maker. Now combine the belief that matter is meaningless with the belief that it's all there is, and nihilistic despair seems inevitable. If there is no unchanging, spiritual beauty and goodness beyond, and material creation does not reflect those higher qualities, then morality and meaning and human value are an illusion. A heartwarming and enjoyable illusion for as long as you can keep it up, but an illusion nonetheless. And atheists are indeed doing an excellent job of keeping it up while refusing to admit that their moral humanism only makes sense within the first acts of a religious story they claim to have rejected.

Yet while the first movement emphasizes the goodness and glory of creation and its Creator, the second movement brings in a healthy dose of tempering grit and realism. Things may once have been inherently good, but we squandered that inheritance pretty quickly. Humanity fell and pulled creation off the ledge along with us (been to any rainforests lately?) The fall plays an incredibly important role in the Christian story, and any worldview that lacks a fall story or a philosophical equivalent to it tends to slip into naive optimism. We begin to see the world through rose-colored goggles, unaware of what we and others are capable of. We blissfully blind ourselves to the sex-slave industry going on in basements within our own city, or the systemic injustices committed against those outside our insulated demographic. We become content with how things are and the status quo (especially if we are on top), with no sense that things can or should be any different. Inaction is inevitable if you don't think there's anything that needs to be acted on. There's no need for humanity to get back up if it never fell.

Without a fall narrative, we develop an unearned and overabundant confidence in our own smug goodness, epitomized by New Age affirmations that you are perfect just the way you are. We might manipulate, tantrum, trick, lash out, smash, and abuse, then quickly say, "I'm sorry. That's not who I am. That wasn't really me." But it was me. I really am capable of that, and so is everyone else. Humans are capable of pretty much anything, of great and wondrous good or great and woeful evil. Every one of us has the potential for sainthood, yet every saint first recognized they were a sinner. If we only had movement one, we would feel like we are the good, perfect, and divinely imaged pinnacle of creation, and if we only had movement two we would feel like filthy pond scum. But it's the mixture of both movements into one cohesive story that makes it so true and revealing of the complexities of the human condition. We are the image of God, yes, but crooked and falling off the wall.

Moving on to movement three, Christians have often been tempted to ignore the Old Testament tales of the Jewish nation. Many think the Old

Testament is just primitive justice and wrath, while the New Testament is merciful and lovey-dovey. But as a matter of actual history, focusing on the New Testament to the detriment of the Old hasn't always made us more forgiving. For example, the Nazi regime censored the Old Testament, precisely because of a thousands-year-old hatred initially spawned by an unwillingness to *forgive* the Jews for killing Christ. Sadly, antisemitism is never far behind whenever people start to ignore movement three (Jewish nation) and only read the New Testament alone (especially when they conveniently ignore the Jewishness of Jesus).

Plus, the New Testament only makes sense in light of the Old. Jesus' claim "I am" makes sense only in light of God revealing the divine name to Moses. Jesus' sacrifice on the cross could only be understood by a nation that had a long-developed theology of sacrifice and justice. The brilliant tension of the Trinity could only be upheld by a monotheistic Jewish culture that wouldn't dare let it slip into pagan polytheism. So, it's not like Abraham's descendants in movement three are just sperm donors to eventually bring about the birth of Jesus. Rather, it took centuries to till the Jewish cultural, theological, and social soil in which Christ's message could take root and flower. The third movement of nation wasn't just a roundabout way to birth Jesus but to breed a culture that might actually have the language and framework to receive him. Without movement three, there is no movement four, five, or six.

Act four (redemption) is obviously a big one. If a worldview doesn't have a source of redemption from sin and failure, two things tend to result. The first outcome is moralistic legalism. If there is no redemption, then we have to be super careful not to fall, because we won't be getting back up if we do. Perfection becomes compulsory, slavishly observing every moral and social rule in fear of the slightest mishap. Of course, such perfection is well-nigh impossible, and so people still mess up; they just have to hide it when they do. Which leads to shame, self-hatred, repression, superficiality, and hypocrisy.

Yet a second outcome is also possible when you have no redemption in your worldview. Recognizing that everyone is full of it and secretly hiding their sin, you can become a pessimist: *No one changes. No one gets redeemed or forgiven. No one gets better, except perhaps at hiding their misdeeds. People stink and will always let you down.* Along with that cynicism often comes permission to openly and unapologetically serve yourself, because that's what everyone else is secretly doing anyway: *At least I am being open about it. Everyone is in it for themselves, so I'm going to be too* (this seems to be the favorite justification of many on Wall Street).

So, many people believe in something equivalent to a fall without believing in redemption, which makes it very easy to become pessimistic, legalistic, or hypocritical. Yet the opposite can also be true, with many worldviews trumpeting redemption and positivity but without a proper appreciation of our fallenness. These people are overly optimistic, having an annoyingly counterfeit cheeriness that ignores the very much ongoing insanity in themselves and the world. Redemption without a fall is just as imbalanced as a fall without redemption. We need both movement two and movement four, both fall and redemption, sin and salvation, realism and idealism, pessimism and optimism, or else the story doesn't work or ring true.* Any worldview that lacks either of those parts—either a fall or a redemption—is lopsided, and any Christian who overemphasizes one of those movements over the other loses sight of something important. On the one error, they end up preaching about redemption in the main chapel while not taking the proper precautions to prevent the sexual abuse going on in the playroom. On the other error, they preach so much about condemnation and sexual sin and hell that they forget the gospel of love, forgiveness, and hope.

Moving on, if one rejects movement five (church), *individualism* tends to swiftly follow. Humans are spiritual beings and we are social beings, and those two things inevitably overlap. But if we reject communal religion for an entirely personal spirituality, we can soon end up with an individualistic and isolated faith. Of course, individuals don't isolate for no reason; it's often because they've been hurt by the community. Indeed, if you overemphasize

---

*Likewise, if you only watch one part of *Life Is Beautiful* (1998), it's a comedy. If you only watch the other part, it's a tragedy. But it's the mixture of both parts into one cohesive story that makes it work so well and ring so true.

movement four (redemption) and five (church) over movement two (fall), you'll be shocked when you realize the redeemed church is still capable of the same despicable behavior as fallen humans in general. But if you go to the other extreme and overemphasize movement two (fall) over movement five (church), you may just give up on community and humanity altogether. Which doesn't really work in the end either, because you as an individual are also fallen, and so the underlying problem just follows you into your isolation. Indeed, if God cannot work through the messiness and sin and bureaucracy and drama of human social life, then how could God ever possibly work through someone as messed up and messy as me, especially when isolated and left to my own devices without communal accountability or support?

So we need to hold movement five (church) in tension with movement two (fall), having grace and patience with our fallen comrades and spiritual communities, while also recognizing that some communities may milk that grace to death and it may be valid for you to move on at some point. Movement six has not happened yet; none of us are perfect on this side of heaven; no church leadership or human community should have our unconditional trust and allegiance. Save that for God alone.

Movement five is also when things expand beyond a Middle Eastern religion for ethnically and culturally Jewish people to a universal religion for every tribe, tongue, and nation. Paul brings the story of Jesus to the Gentiles. No longer is God a local deity of a local tribe but the universal Spirit who comes with tongues of fire speaking every language and conversing with every culture. No longer does God dwell only in a particular temple in a particular place but now comes to dwell in the hearts of every man, woman, and child, wherever and whoever they are. We cannot skip movement five and go straight to the glory of movement six, for God cannot redeem all *creation* until he is God of *all* creation. Any religion or worldview that claims to be true—not just useful or comforting for me in this time and place, but actually true for everyone in every time and place— must have this kind of *universality* in its worldview and story.

Yet we could not have skipped over movement three (Jewish nation) and gone straight to movement five (church), for God is not only universal and wide but also personal and deep. God does not wash over cultural differences and homogenize them into a bland universal but enters into and meets each time and place and person in their own way. God spent millennia investing in the particularities of the Jewish people, rituals, meals, heritage, language, and land, showing that what is most personal can be most divine. God is wide enough to encompass all the earth and galaxies yet narrow enough to meet me in my bedroom prayers, or in the candlelit laughter of a Jewish Passover, or in the histories and stories and minutiae of one man and his family. I would never have written this book if I thought otherwise, for while God is infinitely broader and bigger than anything I could put into words here, I nonetheless believe God can still meet me in the smallness of these pages and the limitations of the English language and the inadequacy of my prose.

God is bigger than we could imagine, yet smaller than we could have ever dreamed. God meets us in both ecstatic visions of eternity and in the eccentricities of our time. Any worldview or religion that claims to be true—and not just true in an abstract, distant, unknowable sense but actually true *for me*, true in a way that I myself could come to know and enact and relate to—must have this personal dimension to balance out its universality. It is not enough to have only the universality of movement five (church) or the particularity of movement three (Jewish nation) on their own. We need both, held together in tension. And what holds them in tension is movement four, for Christ is the universal made personal, the eternal in time, the absolute made intimate, the omnipresent God incarnate in a specific place and body and culture and language. God expands with the universe yet shrinks to our door.

Finally, we have movement six, which comes after life and history and earth as we know it ends. If you don't have an equivalent *end* in your story, a number of things may follow. First of all, despair, both personal and social. Personal despair in that there is no life after death. Some atheists find a way to overcome that despair and face their extinction admirably, but even they would likely admit it was quite a big pill to swallow. Social despair in that history is cyclical, not linear. There is no beginning, middle, and

final end to things. Time just sort of loops on and on without final reso-
lution, like Bill Murray in *Groundhog Day* (1993) or Sisyphus rolling the
boulder uphill for eternity. Sure, humans might improve things for a while,
but then someone will blow the planet up, and the whole project starts over
again. Sure, a century of injustice may be followed by a century of growth
and trying to move away from the past, but then a new generation comes
along who doesn't remember those hard-earned lessons, and the whole
process starts again. Two steps forward, two steps back. All this has happened before, and all this will happen again. Things will never be made
right once and for all.

Now, in the face of that social despair, some have tried to perfect humanity faster than we can mess things up. Many have tried to force history
into an age of equality and peace and paradise—an age without hierarchy,
class, money, or social injustice. For example, Karl Marx essentially sought
to bring about a nonreligious, secularized heaven on earth here and now.
He longed for a socialist government to take control of human society and
engineer it into a classless, stateless, moneyless, communist utopia. Once
this had been achieved, the government was supposed to release the reins
and slowly fade into oblivion, leaving humanity in its natural state. But
sadly, the revolutionaries that overturn their governments tend to be just
as bad as those they overturn. And even if they had been willing to give up
control after they'd removed the social structures of power and inequality,
ungoverned people don't magically become saints. You can take the people
out of sinful systems and evil economies, but you can't take the sin and evil
out of the people. It's not just power that corrupts people; it's people that
corrupt power. It's not just the powers that be or the government or the
economy or society or the church that's the issue. *It's me.* I'm fallen. I need
redemption. Sure, you can remove the systems that oppress me and oppress
others, leaving humanity in its natural state. The problem is that our natural
state is not all that great.

So you can't fast-forward to movement six without taking into serious
consideration movement two (fall) and the subsequent need for movement
four (redemption). Which is why some have argued that Karl Marx did not

have a strong enough sense of personal sin and the individual human condition. Yet Marx *did* have a strong sense of social and economic and systemic evil (a sense that in many ways he borrowed from Jesus, who strongly subverted the reigning social order). Marx understood how the social world affected everything and believed the problems of the day were due to these broader currents we're all caught up in. You don't need to *personally* have a child laborer in your home to be part of an economy and shopping system that is built on foreign child labor. You don't have to *personally* hate poor people in order to exist within, benefit from, and implicitly support a classist, bourgeoise system that keeps the lower classes down. Marx focused on the things that were broader than the individual, such as the community, class system, economy, and government. And to some extent, he was right. It is not just the individual that is fallen but the community, not just the *personal* but also the *social*.

Yet imagine if we actually succeeded in fixing all of our social problems. Imagine that one day—perhaps not that far from now—humans obtained the technology to overcome poverty, world hunger, disease, racism, sexism, and every social issue at the push of a button. Obviously, that would be fantastic. Yet, I still wouldn't think of that as utopia—it would just be taking the inner emptiness of a privileged boardroom and expanding it to welcome the rest of the world into its emptiness. Utopia cannot just mean everyone having the same food, medicine, opportunities, wealth, and cars as rich White men, because rich White men are some of the most miserable, unfulfilled people I know. Everyone having everything doesn't actually solve the human condition; some of the wealthiest countries in the world have some of the highest suicide rates.[1] Our fallenness is such that even those privileged individuals who have everything can still be dissatisfied. Not being oppressed doesn't make life perfect; it just resets things so you can start from the same existential emptiness as everyone else. If humanity ever actually solved its social problems, there would be a massive existential crisis as it slowly dawned on us that the problem wasn't just communally out there but individually in here. External oppression would merely give way to internal depression. Having filled every nation with every outward delight, we'd still come up empty inside. Society may make communal progress, yet each person starts the struggle with themselves from scratch. Our fallenness is not just the result of social injustice but also its cause, and so even if the symptoms are dealt with, the underlying disease remains. It is not just the community that is fallen but the individual, not just the *social* but the *personal*.

Yet most worldviews tend to pick one of those—social or personal—to focus on while ignoring the other, or even pick and choose depending on what is most convenient for their stance on whatever specific issue is at hand.[†] But part of the beauty of the Christian story is that it tries to do both at once. We are made in the image of the Trinity, of a God who is three and one, both communal and individual. The social is personal and the personal is social; the parts and the whole cannot be fully scalpeled out. So if I am fallen, there is no way for that to affect me as an individual without also affecting my social life as a father, husband, lover, son, brother, friend, worker, consumer, and citizen. In turn, if I exist within and complicitly benefit from social, economic, and political systems that are built atop the backs of others, then there is no way that does not affect the state of my individual soul.

If the fall (movement two) affects us as both social and individual beings, then redemption (movement four) must do so as well. Marx's mistake was not that he tried to heal our social and economic systems but that he thought he could do so without also addressing the spiritual fallenness of the individual before God. Now, for the Christian, redemption is indeed about accepting Jesus as your *personal* Lord and Savior. Yet the personal is always bound up in the communal, and vice versa. The Spirit of God on earth is not only moving to change individual hearts but the broader systems to which they pump blood and funds and power. Which is perhaps one of the reasons movement five (church) is so essential; it's God's attempt

---

[†]For example, in America, a Democrat might focus on individual freedom in terms of sexual ethics and abortion yet focus on communal oversight in terms of gun control, poverty, or health care. In turn, Republicans might focus on communal oversight for sexual ethics and abortion yet insist on individual responsibility in terms of health care, poverty, or gun control.

to redeem whole spiritual *communities*. The ethnic, social, and economic divide between Jews *and* Gentiles is overcome so they can now live and worship together in one church.

This new vision of church was merely the natural continuation of the radical social restructuring Jesus began in movement four. Jesus came to save rich people and poor people, and to subvert the economic relations between them (Luke 16:19-31). Jesus came for the disabled (Luke 13:10-13), the unclean (Mark 5:25-34), and for both social and literal lepers (Mark 1:40-42), welcoming them all back into society. Jesus came to redeem Pharisees and Sadducees and tax collectors and centurions and governors and bring them all together in one church, so that the divisions of the polis might be overcome in the pulpit. Jesus came to redeem Romans and Samaritans (John 4:5-30) and Africans (Acts 8:26-40) and Canaanites (Matthew 15:21-28) and Russians and Americans and the Chinese and Koreans and Jews and Palestinians, and to wed them all under one steeple. To save a human is to save a social being; you cannot fully redeem individuals without redeeming the relations they exist within. The kingdom of heaven is only a kingdom if it brings its diverse citizens under one banner, and only heavenly if they get along.

However, that kingdom of heaven is not yet fully here. We are still on earth (and not the new one). As of my writing this, humanity is only in movement five—the end has not yet come. Redemption sprouted in movement four with Jesus but will not be fully grown until movement six. Which means that movement five is stuck in an awkward transition stage— no longer a boy but not yet a man. And like an awkward teen, there are two extremes we tend to veer to: clinging to the immaturity of childhood or trying to grow up too fast (which is childish in its own way). To speak plainly, the church sometimes focuses so hard on the future heaven that is to come that it loses sight of the earth that is now. *We're trying to grow up and leave the earthly nest too fast.* We become so focused on setting the stage for movement six that we forget we still have lines left and a part to play in movement five. As Leslie Knope says on the show *Parks and Recreation*, "Turns out that when you think the world is ending you don't aim so carefully in the port-a-potties." We stop caring about the earth here and now.

However, we can often make the exact opposite mistake. We can collapse our future heaven so much into present-day earth that we confuse earthly kingdoms such as America, Rome, or the British Empire with God's kingdom. *God is on our side.* We can become so comfortable here and now on earth that we become materialists, clinging to our earthly toys. We forget that we can't take any of it with us, amassing wealth and status and stuff, building personal empires that will inevitably crumble. And when that crumbling begins—when the stock market tanks, or we lose our job, or we get sick, or a family member dies—then we curse God and despair, for we got so comfortable down here that we forgot this was the deal all along. Movement five was always meant to be temporary. The building blocks and toy castles we've so carefully arranged were always going to be swept up and put away in the end, in preparation for the coming day.

So, the goal is to not lean too far either way. The sweet spot is in the tension between movements five and six, with one eye on what is *now* and one eye on what is *not yet.* Like great performers, we have to simultaneously say the lines in the current scene while preparing the prop in our back pocket for the next. We need to look forward to the day when all struggling, pain, and perseverance cease, yet not cease persevering in the meantime. We should look forward to our heavenly union with goodness, truth, love, and beauty itself, yet not forget to manifest those qualities on earth here and now. We must let the stars above help us navigate the seas below, not distract us from them. We must try our best to grow and improve in movement five yet have patience with ourselves and others in the knowledge that none of us will be fully perfect until movement six. We must strive to make earth more like heaven yet recognize that fallen human attempts to do so often make it more like hell. The church must seek to redeem the social and economic systems of the world, yet not lay its hands on the wheels of history to violently force what can only come about fully in movement six. We must strive all day to make the world a better place, then rest at night in the knowledge that we've done all we can and it's ultimately in God's hands to bring about a new heaven and a new earth. It's God journey—we just get to decide whether we want to tag along.

〈 ▨ ▨ 〉

That's the six movements of the Christian story and what happens when any of them are missing. I happen to think it's a good story, one that fits together rather well. Yet you could say that about many stories, so why believe this one is unique or more worthy of our time and religious devotion than any other? I mean, the three parts of the Lord of the Rings may fit together nicely, but I still don't worship Galadriel (at least not anymore). There are many other great and cohesive stories with many great things worth hearing and retelling. We can learn about love from Rumi or Shakespeare or Jane Austen, about suffering from Buddha or Elie Wiesel. Even fairy tales and myths are worth retelling, for their untruths point to higher truths. Whether or not Notre Dame ever really had a live-in hunchback, his story still teaches us about real beauty. Jean Valjean may never have stolen a loaf of bread, and yet he stole our hearts and filled them with real redemption. To the chagrin of many a young heart, Mr. Darcy is not real, and yet we can still learn about the nature of pride and prejudice from him. Whether or not Odysseus truly set sail, we still learn much about perseverance from his odyssey. All the greatest stories, even the fictional ones, point to higher truths.

The difference, though, between the Christian story and most other stories is that they claim to point to higher truths, while Jesus claims to be the truth. Jesus did not say, "I am going to help guide you on the way," but rather, "I am the way." Even Muhammad came only as a prophet pointing toward heaven, not as heaven itself. Jesus is not claiming to be another sign or story pointing to being, truth, goodness, beauty, and love, but to be the Being, truth, goodness, beauty, and love that all the other stories were pointing to all along. This does not mean every other story is totally false—in fact, just the opposite. Those other stories can only be beautiful and true and good, if there is one who is beauty, truth, and goodness itself. They can only be valid signposts if there's actually something there to point *to*—road maps only work if there's a real destination at the end. All the happy endings in all the fairy tales were not false but fair, for they pointed not to a present state in history that was factually incorrect but rather to a future time when history itself would be overcome by the one who is love. Jesus did not come to abolish every other religion, movie, myth, poem, opera, orgasm, song, dance, dirge, or fireside fairy tale. He came to fulfill them. Not everything in life and history points to Jesus, but everything that is good, beautiful, true, and lovely in all our experiences and in all the stories has been gesturing to him all along.

Or maybe not. Your call.

Endnotes

1 CREATION BEGINS

[1]Mario Canseco, "Most B.C. Residents Believe in God, but Few Attend Church Regularly," Vancouver Is Awesome, April 19, 2019, www.vancouverisawesome.com/local-news/bc-residents-believe-god-church-1943321.

[1]Put its foot in what exactly, you ask? I will merely note that the original Hebrew word for "In the beginning" is *bereshit* and allow you to draw your own conclusions.

[2]Though God could sustain the world without creating it. Additionally, some scholars contend Genesis 1 is God molding preexistent matter rather than "out of nothing."

[3]See Martin Rees, *Just Six Numbers* (New York: Basic Books, 2001).

[4]Martin Heidegger, *Introduction to Metaphysics* (New Haven, CT: Yale University Press, 1959).

[5]I am unable to track down the translation of Heidegger, *Logic: The Question of Truth* that put it quite this way.

[6]Mary Beckman, "Farting Fish Keep in Touch," *Science*, November 7, 2023, www.science.org/content/article/farting-fish-keep-touch.

2 CREATION IS NOT GOD

[1]Quoted in David Niose, "Why Oprah's Anti-atheist Bias Hurts So Much," Psychology Today, October 15, 2013, www.psychologytoday.com/intl/blog/our-humanity-naturally/201310/why-oprahs-anti-atheist-bias-hurts-so-much.

[2]Lee Bladon, *Awakening to Wholeness* (N.p.: Lulu.com, 2012), 203.

[3]Neale Donald Walsch, "There is no separation between me and God, nor is their [*sic*] any difference, except as to proportion. Put simply, God and I are one," Twitter, November 20, 2019, 9:00 a.m., https://x.com/realNDWalsch/status/1197167718002233345.

[4]Quoted in Charisse Glenn, "The Wisdom of John Lennon," *The Let Go* (blog), June 3, 2023, www.theletgo.com/the-wisdom-of-john-lennon/.

[5]These may be closer to panentheism or panvitalism than to pantheism. But the popular imagination isn't nuanced like that, so this all feeds into a broader pantheistic zeitgeist.

[6]Adyashanti, *The Direct Way: Thirty Practices to Evoke Awakening* (Boulder, CO: Sounds True, 2021), Chapter 19.

[7]Thich Nhat Hanh, *The Miracle of Mindfulness: An Introduction to the Practice of Meditation* (Boston: Beacon Press, 1996), 94.

[8]Quoted from Dorothy Soelle, *The Silent Cry: Mysticism and Resistance* (Minneapolis: Fortress, 2001), 16.

[9]E.g., the I AM Activity Movement founded by Guy Ballard, which has had a trickle-down effect into numerous contemporary movements.

[10]This is a more extreme proposal than the moderate, potentially even persuasive view defended by Rupert Sheldrake.

[11]Paul Selig, *I Am the Word* (New York: TarcherPerigee, 2010).

[12]Shakti Gawain, *Creative Visualization* (Novato, CA: New World Library, 2010), 171.

[13]Dr. Suess, *Happy Birthday to You!* (New York: Random House, 1959).

3 Creation Is Good

[1]While a helpful distinction, ancient Greek is sometimes more nuanced than that. E.g., even Jesus has *sarx* in 1 Timothy 3:16.

[2]*How I Met Your Mother*, "The Best Burger in New York," directed by Pamela Fryman, aired September 29, 2008, CBS.

[3]I say "thought to have said," for while this quote is sometimes attributed to Harrison, it is only based on an apparent letter he wrote a fan, which I can find only one fairly dubious source for online: https://harrisonarchive.tumblr.com/post/96921495629/in-the-last-year -or-so-of-his-life-harrison-was. I think it is likely an alteration of a similar quote from Teilhard de Chardin.

[4]E.g., Michael B. Foster, "The Christian Doctrine of Creation and the Rise of Modern Natural Science," *Mind* 43, no. 172 (October 1934): 446-68; Thomas F. Torrance, *Theological Science* (Oxford: Oxford University Press, 1969); Torrance, *The Ground and Grammar of Theology* (Edinburgh: T&T Clark, 1980).

[5]Why "allegedly"? Well, having used, and heard respected scholars use, this quote for decades, I have tried to track down the source myself, only to discover many of the references to this trace back to just one online encyclopedia article (https://www.newworldencyclopedia .org/entry/Johannes_Kepler) which does not itself disclose the source. I also found one older source connecting it to Sir John Herschell: https://www.google.com/books/edition/The _Reformed_Quarterly_Review/vnsQAAAAIAAJ?hl=en&gbpv=1&dq=%22thinking+god %27s+thoughts+after+him%22&pg=PA52&printsec=frontcover.

[6]Quoted in Becka A. Alper, "How Religion Intersects with Americans' Views on the Environment," Pew Research Center, November 17, 2022, www.pewresearch.org/religion /2022/11/17/how-religion-intersects-with-americans-views-on-the-environment/.

4 Humanity in God's Image

[1]Martin Luther King Jr., speech at Illinois Wesleyan University, 1966, www.iwu.edu/mlk /page-2.html, emphasis added.

5 HUMANITY GONE WILD

[1]Francis Spufford, *Unapologetic: Why, Despite Everything, Christianity Can Still Make Surprising Emotional Sense* (London: Faber & Faber, 2012), asterisks added.

[2]Marija Lazic, "Saddening Children of Divorce Statistics for 2022," Legal Jobs, May 20, 2023, https://legaljobs.io/blog/children-of-divorce-statistics.

[3]"Scope of the Problem: Statistics", Rainn, https://rainn.org/statistics/scope-problem

[4]David Leonhardt, "The Black-White Wage Gap Is as Big as It Was in 1950," *New York Times*, June 25, 2020, https://www.nytimes.com/2020/06/25/opinion/sunday/race-wage-gap .html; see also Andre M. Perry, Hannah Stephens, and Manann Donoghoe, "Black Wealth is Increasing, but So Is the Racial Wealth Gap," https://www.brookings.edu/articles /black-wealth-is-increasing-but-so-is-the-racial-wealth-gap/.

[5]Briana Sullivan, Donald Hays, and Neil Bennett, "Wealth by Race of Householder," United States Census Bureau, April 23, 2024, https://www.census.gov/library/stories/2024/04 /wealth-by-race.html.

[6]See Glenn Kessler, "The Stale Statistic That One in Three Black Males 'Born Today' Will End Up in Jail," *Washington Post*, June 16, 2015, www.washingtonpost.com/news/fact -checker/wp/2015/06/16/the-stale-statistic-that-one-in-three-black-males-has-a-chance -of-ending-up-in-jail/.

[7]"2017 Demographic Differences in Federal Sentencing," The United States Sentencing Commission, Nov 4, 2017, https://www.ussc.gov/research/research-reports/2017-demographic -differences-federal-sentencing#:~:text=Black%20male%20offenders%20received%20 sentences%20on%20average%2020.4%20percent%20longer,which%20such%20data%20 is%20available.

[8]Rashawn Ray, Jane Fran Morgan, Lydia Wileden, Samantha Elizondo, and Destiny Wiley-Yancy, "Examining and Addressing COVID-19 Racial Disparities in Detroit," Brookings .edu, March 2, 2021, www.brookings.edu/articles/examining-and-addressing-covid-19 -racial-disparities-in-detroit/.

[9]J. R. R. Tolkien, *The Letters of J. R. R. Tolkien* (Boston: Houghton Mifflin Harcourt, 2014).

6 ABRAHAM FINDS FAITH

[1]Alvin Plantinga, "Is Belief in God Properly Basic?," *Noûs*, 15, no. 1, A. P. A. Western Division Meetings (Mar., 1981), 41-51.

8 GOODNESS IS COMMANDED

[1]Exodus 20:2-4, 7-8, 12-17, my paraphrase.

[2]Francis Schaeffer, *How Should We Then Live?* (Wheaton, IL: Crossway, 2005), 135.

[3]C. S. Lewis, "A Christmas Sermon for Pagans," *Strand* 112 (December 1946): 32.

[4]This is commonly attributed to Russell but may actually be a paraphrase of the nearly identical sentiments found in his letter to Moorhead, dated January 10, 1952, and his 1960 reply to Father Lundmark. See Barry Feinberg and Ronald Kasrils, *Dear Bertrand Russell* (Boston: Houghton Mifflin, 1969), 95.

9 Beauty in the Promised Land

[1]See 2 Samuel 6:14-15, when they brought the ark into Jerusalem and eventually the temple.

[2]Emily Dickinson, "Beauty be not caused—It is," in *The Poems of Emily Dickinson*, ed. R. W. Franklin (Cambridge, MA: Belknap, 1999), 292, emphasis added.

[3]John Muir, *John of the Mountains: The Unpublished Journals of John Muir* (Madison: University of Wisconsin Press, 1938), 208.

[4]While some of this might seem more in the vein of Greek philosophy rather than Jewish biblical theology, I believe it is a natural and logical extension of the Jewish rejection of idolatry and of mistaking any creaturely beauty/goodness/truth for the absolute and divine Creator of all such things.

[5]John Clare, quoted in Jonathan Williams, "Symphony No. 3, in D Minor," The Poetry Foundation, 2005, www.poetryfoundation.org/poems/54573/symphony-no3-in-d-minor.

[6]This is an intentional retort/play off William Blake's quote: "The tree which moves some to tears of joy is in the eyes of others only a green thing which stands in the way. . . . As a man is, so he sees." Quoted in Maria Popova, "William Blake's Most Beautiful Letter: A Timeless Defense of the Imagination and the Creative Spirit," The Marginalian, July 7, 2014, www.themarginalian.org/2016/07/14/william-blake-john-trusler-letter/.

[7]I've not been able to track down the original source. Some say it's actually Charles Kingsley.

[8]Mary Oliver, though not from one of her poems but a public lecture she gave. See Lindsey Mead, "Thoughts on a Sunset, and Mary Oliver," *A Design So Vast* (blog), October 21, 2010, https://adesignsovast.com/2010/10/thoughts-on-sunset-and-mary-oliver/.

10 King David and His Boy

[1]Note that there has been some vigorous debate about whether the issue was kingship itself or rather a specific type of king.

[2]I've extrapolated the language of this New Testament passage back onto the Old Testament, as the underlying concept (that God alone fully lives up to the paternal leadership role) is undeniable throughout both Testaments.

[3]Note that marriage in the ancient world was not exclusively nor even always primarily about intimacy but often about shoring up alliances. However, even so, such alliances still fit within the broader narrative here about Solomon's insecure need to supersize himself and his empire.

[4]"How Many American Children Have Cut Contact with Their Parents?," *The Economist*, May 20, 2021, www.economist.com/united-states/2021/05/20/how-many-american-children-have-cut-contact-with-their-parents. The studies listed in this paragraph are, of course, localized and context specific (as all studies are and should implicitly be assumed to be).

[5]B. Rose Huber-Princeton, "Nearly 40% of US Children Lack Strong Emotional Bonds with Their Parents," The Chronicle, accessed September 6, 2024, www.evidencebasedmentoring.org/nearly-40-of-us-children-lack-strong-emotional-bonds-with-parents/.

[6]US Census Bureau, "Living Arrangements of Children Under 18," July 1, 2012, tables CH-2, CH-3, CH-4.

[7]I first quoted this decades ago but lost the original source and haven't been able to find it online.

[8]Bruce J. Ellis, John E. Bates, Kenneth A. Dodge, David M. Fergusson, L. John Horwood, Gregory S. Pettit, and Lianne Woodward, "Does Father Absence Place Daughters at Special Risk for Early Sexual Activity and Teenage Pregnancy?," *Child Development* 74, no. 3 (May–June 2003): 801-21, www.ncbi.nlm.nih.gov/pmc/articles/PMC2764264.

[9]I think this may originally have been a paraphrase of something, but I've never been able to remember what, and searching for it online brings up nothing.

11 JUSTICE EXILES THE NATION

[1]*Gladiator*, directed by Ridley Scott (Universal City, CA: DreamWorks, 2000).

[2]"Remaining Awake Through a Great Revolution," speech delivered given at the National Cathedral, March 31, 1968, quoted in Pangambam S, *The Singju Post*, August 31, 2022, https://singjupost.com/transcript-the-last-sunday-sermon-of-mlk-march-31-1968/?singlepage=1.

[3]Quoted in David Segal, "The Dark Art of 'Breaking Bad,'" *New York Times*, July 6, 2011, www.nytimes.com/2011/07/10/magazine/the-dark-art-of-breaking-bad.html.

12 JESUS IS BORN

[1]There's a whole bunch of literature nowadays about whether it was a barn or the first floor of a house where the animals were stored. The introductory nature of this book has allowed me to justify avoiding those kinds of discussions, for the nitpicky details have been intentionally kept secondary to the overarching story, ideas, and drama.

[2]Brené Brown, "Brené Brown on Empathy," RSA, December 10, 2013, video, 2:53, www.youtube.com/watch?v=1Evwgu369Jw. My next few paragraphs are mostly quoted and/or paraphrased directly from her video.

[3]Again, these paragraphs are all quoting and/or paraphrasing Dr. Brown's video. You really should watch it.

13 JESUS IS WALKING AROUND SAYING STUFF

[1]We can admit that Second Temple Judaism was more complex than just rule following while still holding that Jesus was dealing with a subsection of that group for whom moral legalism was a real struggle and tendency.

[2]There are multiple claimed sources for this evolving phrase, including Lao Tzu and Margaret Thatcher.

[3]Alright, maybe a couple of days later. But I'm trying to tell a story here.

[4]See James Cone, *The Cross and the Lynching Tree* (Maryknoll, NY: Orbis Books, 2013).

[5]This doesn't negate the *ultimate* triumph that ends the Psalm (22) he's quoting. Strategically taking a loss in battle can be genuinely traumatic, while still helping better position one for ultimate victory.

⁶This crawling into ground-level tombs is not meant to be a scholarly claim about first-century Jewish burials but is merely a theatrical device meant to help us re-see and reimagine his death and resurrection afresh. We've seen this scene so many times and need something to help jog us awake and feel its weight again.

⁷The way John 21 phenomenologically unfolds, it feels as if this is Jesus' first appearance and forgiveness of Peter, and I've leaned into that in order to better capture the emotional register of John's telling. However, for more historical/literal concerns, this chronology should be held in tension with Luke 24:34 and 1 Corinthians 15:5 (and potentially even with John 21:14, though that's less specific to Peter).

14 Jesus Is Dying to Meet You

¹Graham Stanton, *The Gospels and Jesus* (Oxford: Oxford University Press, 2002), 145.
²Bart Ehrman, *Did Jesus Exist? The Historical Argument for Jesus of Nazareth* (San Francisco: HarperOne, 2013), 12. Combined with his appearance on the Infidel Guy, "Bart Ehrman vs. Reginald (The Infidel Guy) Finley on Existence of Historical Jesus," Ken Ammi, September 20, 2016, video, 7:33, www.youtube.com/watch?v=yPq64vncKQQ.
³John Lennon, "Imagine," from the album *Imagine*, 1971.

15 The Spirit Arrives

¹G. K. Chesterton, *Orthodoxy* (Peabody, MA: Hendrickson, 2006), 19.

16 The Church Begins

¹John Lennon, "God," track 10 on *John Lennon/Plastic Ono Band*, Apple Records, 1970.
²Jean-Paul Sartre, *No Exit* (New York: Vintage International, 1989).
³While commonly attributed to Dr Seuss, the origin of this quote is disputed. See "Those who mind don't matter, and those who matter don't mind," Quote Investigator, December 4, 2012, https://quoteinvestigator.com/2012/12/04/those-who-mind.
⁴Deepak Chopra, "Religion is belief in someone else's experience. Spirituality is having your own experience," Twitter, January 17, 2014, 6:36 p.m., https://x.com/DeepakChopra/status/424339573783539712#; Chopra, "Spirituality Means More Than Ever Now," February 15, 2021, www.deepakchopra.com/articles/spirituality-means-more-than-ever-now/.
⁵Quoted in David Gerken, "Ram Dass's Quote About the Spiritual Path," Medium, April 29, 2022, https://medium.com/illumination/ram-dasss-quote-about-the-spiritual-path-be-the-captain-of-your-ship-d323dd2868ea.
⁶Eckhart Tolle, *The Power of Now* (Novato, CA: New World Library, 2004), introduction.
⁷Mario Canseco, "Most B.C. Residents Believe in God, but Few Attend Church Regularly," Vancouver Is Awesome, April 19, 2019, www.vancouverisawesome.com/local-news/bc-residents-believe-god-church-1943321.
⁸Kathryn Schulz, "The Moral Judgments of Henry David Thoreau," *New Yorker*, October 12, 2015, www.newyorker.com/magazine/2015/10/19/pond-scum. For a retort, see Jedediah

Britton-Purdy, "In Defense of Thoreau," *Atlantic*, October 20, 2015, www.theatlantic.com
/science/archive/2015/10/in-defense-of-thoreau/411457/.

[9]Sean Pean, *Into the Wild* (Paramount Vantage, 2007).

[10]Sarah Johnson, "WHO Declares Loneliness a 'Global Public Health Concern,'" *Guardian*,
November 16, 2023, www.theguardian.com/global-development/2023/nov/16/who
-declares-loneliness-a-global-public-health-concern.

[11]"Loneliness Minister: 'It's More Important Than Ever to Take Action,'" Gov.UK, June 17,
2021, www.gov.uk/government/news/loneliness-minister-its-more-important-than-ever
-to-take-action.

[12]Colby Itkowitz, "For 79 years, This Groundbreaking Harvard Study Has Searched for the
Key to Happiness. Should It Keep Going?," *Washington Post*, April 17, 2017, www
.washingtonpost.com/news/inspired-life/wp/2017/04/17/this-harvard-study-found-the
-one-thing-we-need-for-happier-healthier-lives-but-researchers-say-theres-more-to-learn/.

[13]Isaac Newton to Robert Hooke, February 5, 1675, https://digitallibrary.hsp.org/index.php
/Detail/objects/9792.

[14]Zach Everson, "Here's How Much 2024 Presidential Candidate Marianne Williamson Is
Worth," Forbes, October 1, 2023, www.forbes.com/sites/zacheverson/2023/10/01/heres
-how-much-2024-presidential-candidate-marianne-williamson-is-worth/.

[15]What a broke loser! Just kidding—he's now godfather to my children. Though he still *loses*
to me every week when we play Risk Online.

17 The Apostle Paul Converts

[1]Babylonian Talmud, Menachot 43b-44a.

[2]This is another "commonly attributed" quote, for which I have had some difficulty actually
tracking down the original source. It is regularly attributed to Corrie Ten Boom, yet multiple authors seem to have posted versions of it as if it were their own (e.g., Tim Keller, Max
Lucado), while a search through of Ten Boom's *The Hiding Place* did not yield the expected
quote. For an example of an article that claims it is from Ten Boom, see Toni Rypkema,
"Time to Ponder: Corrie Ten Boom," *God Time with Kids,* March 8 2019, https://www
.tonirypkema.com/2019/03/08/increased-faith-from-a-bit-of-corrie-ten-boon/.

[3]Some people argue that Junia was actually a man's name, but it was always interpreted as
female until a much later period in history.

[4]See Rodney Stark, *The Rise of Christianity* (San Francisco: HarperSanFrancisco, 1996).

18 The Church Expands

[1]See Tertullian, *Prescription Against Heretics* 36.

19 The Church Today

[1]Doug Priest, "Life for the Average Christian," Christian Standard, January 4, 2009, https://
christianstandard.com/2009/01/cs_article-1084/.

[2]Walt Whitman, "O Me! O Life!," in *Leaves of Grass* (1855).

20 The End of the World as We Know It

[1]This need not exclude postmillennialists, as humans could never bring about a millennium of progress on their own without God's involvement.

21 Highway to Hell or Stairway to Heaven?

[1]Oscar Wilde, *The Duchess of Padua* (Germany: Outlook Verlag, 2018), 105.

[2]C. S. Lewis, *The Problem of Pain* (London: Centenary, 1940).

Conclusion

[1]"Suicide Rate by Country 2024," World Health Organization, accessed September 6, 2024, https://worldpopulationreview.com/country-rankings/suicide-rate-by-country.

Scripture Index